HIGH STAKES

This is a true story, although sometimes I
can't believe it really happened.

When you instituted the human reliability
tests you assured me there was no possibility
of such a thing ever occurring.
Dr Strangelove, 1963

HIGH STAKES

How I Blew £14 Million

NIGEL GOLDMAN

MAINSTREAM
PUBLISHING
EDINBURGH AND LONDON

First published in Great Britain in 2004 by
MAINSTREAM PUBLISHING COMPANY (EDINBURGH) LTD
7 Albany Street
Edinburgh EH1 3UG

ISBN 1 84018 853 7

Most of the names of persons appearing in this book have been
changed to protect their identities. Where pseudonyms have been
used, they have been identified in the first instance by the use of
inverted commas

A catalogue record for this book is available from the British Library

Typeset in Galliard and Meta
Printed and bound in Great Britain by
Creative Print Design, Wales

Acknowledgements

I would like to thank the following, who have made this book possible: London Metal Exchange; the Commodity Exchange in New York; The Jockey Club; Moët and Chandon; Ferrari, Lamborghini and Porsche; Rolls-Royce Motor Cars Limited; the London Stock Exchange; Carmel College, Oxon; my parents; Missoni; the Education Department, HMP The Mount; Wensley Clarkson; Susan Brady; and my girlfriend, Caroline Brown.

And all the bars, clubs and brokers' offices I have crashed into all over the world.

Contents

Author's Note

I've done the lot, you know. Funny how that can mean a couple of things. What are you thinking? The gambler who tosses his last chip over the green baize in some smart casino in the early hours? The mug at the bookies? Or the winner? The winner – beautiful girls, tailored suits, handmade shoes, expensive restaurants, fast cars, chilled vintage champagne, sunny afternoons at the races, a heavy investment in the stock exchange, maybe in futures.

Ever traded in futures? The spivs call them derivatives now. I have. I suffer from compulsive futures-trading disorder – big time. I've traded gold in New York, currencies in Chicago, the Nikkei in Tokyo, metals in London. I've traded them all. I've won big, lost big. I've paid, been paid. I've knocked, been knocked. It's funny how my outlook alters when I'm trading. Especially when I'm trading for real. Mind you, the spivs don't trade with their own money, you know. Those itinerant vagrants trade for banks and brokerage houses on a salary. There's no fun in that – I trade with my own money. Well, I did at first.

You see, I've been under the influence of this obsession for the past 20 years. It's a devil on my shoulder, urging me to do one more trade, as I cunningly calculate winnings and how to spend them. One might say it's a thrill-seeking addiction, I just call it my tiger. As time goes by, it's becoming impossible to pull myself away from it. I've had to learn to juggle streams of numbers on the back of this beast. I've become an expert at juggling. I've had a lot of practice. I've tried to escape it, but it follows me. It's travelled first class all round the world, my tiger.

Along the way, I've come to know a fair bit about numbers. I've polished my act to include buying and selling, wheeling and dealing, bidding and offering, backing and laying, punting and gambling. You know, City biz. Roulette, cards, horse racing and the like. No wonder the digits wander around my head at night, especially when I'm in the middle of a heavy trade. Sell at forty, buy at thirty. April at seven, six bid. Thirty-one and the neighbours. Six to one the field. They haunt me, these numbers. Credits, debits, overdrafts, uncleared effects, Tote returns, losses. Sometimes I have a drink or three to get rid of them, but they always come back. I think they're in cahoots with my tiger.

I may have had the choice, once, a long time ago. 'Fancy an adventure, Mr Goldman?' the beast may have whispered. I don't remember now. But I've ended up knocking, that's for sure. Tax, VAT, my mortgage, landlords, hotels, car companies, card companies, banks, The Jockey Club, casinos, lawyers, the list goes on.

Funny how your outlook alters when you're knocking big time. I think I've blown my credit.

Sometimes I wonder where all the money's gone. Slightly over £14 million at the last count. Apparently I've been living beyond my means.

Apparently I've done the lot.

Nigel Goldman
Spain, 2004

PROLOGUE

Beyond the Reach of the Law

The Lamborghini swung into Richmond Hill Road. Expensive properties with long drives and chimney stacks lined the street. Mature trees rustled in the summer evening breeze. As I accelerated, I was satisfied with the growling resonance of the exhaust and the rich tang of Connolly hide, gently cooled by the air conditioning.

The sun glinted off the red bonnet, momentarily blinding me as the Sundym glass adapted to the brightness, but within a fraction of a second I was into third gear and cruising up the hill at seventy, four Blaupunkt speakers delivering a crystal-clear graphic-equalised rendition of *The Marriage of Figaro*.

During the summer of 1985, I lived at Petersham Place, a small cluster of luxury apartments at the top of Richmond Hill Road in Birmingham. Although I didn't realise it at the time, in many respects this period in my life was going to be cemented onto my memory as one of the most memorable. As I approached my home, I felt content. I should have, too. The car had just cost me £65,000, almost as much as my flat, and it was the very first one to be delivered into the country. I was no stranger to fast cars, of course, having gone through a selection of Porsches and Ferraris in my early 20s. But the Lambo was something special and had turned plenty of heads already, notably outside Liberty's

11

nightclub the previous evening. Especially the head of the tall, pouting blonde whom I couldn't resist chatting up and treating to rivers of champagne. I took her out to dinner the following evening.

The Lambo actually hadn't cost *me* £65,000 at all – it was my clients' money. But I wasn't going to let that small detail worry me. I was out to enjoy myself. After all, I had been making plenty of money with a bullion deal I'd fallen into and there were more in the pipeline. I initially had my suspicions, secreted in the back of my mind, about the source of the bullion I was buying. You know, that feeling in your stomach when stories don't quite add up? But I needed the money. I had a lifestyle to finance. Anyway, I had the right paperwork. I had paid my VAT (more of that later). Plus, I had a large position in the gold futures market in New York and a healthy splattering of silver and platinum for good measure. I was fully leveraged, that was for sure. All I needed was a modicum of good luck or, more to the point, a bull market. That was what was needed – a bull market. Then I would have been out of it. Out of it completely. I was getting sick of the pressure, the juggling and the lies, and longed to be free of it to concentrate on the profitable side of my business. But let's face it, everybody is at it at one time or another, aren't they? Everybody has heard about the corporate managers, directors and accountants dipping temporarily into the client account for their own purposes, only to replace everything in the nick of time before the annual audit. With a healthy profit to boot, of course. Jesus, I was dealing with brokers every day who wouldn't wipe their ass without skimming 10 per cent off the loo paper first.

As I swung the car into my driveway, had I turned my neck just ever so slightly I would have noticed an unoccupied dark-blue Jaguar parked opposite my home. I would later find out, through surveillance images and court exhibits, that although the Jag was empty, when the aerial rose silently to its full height, the tiny pin-prick camera lens could rapidly photograph me going about my daily routine. It would seem the normal-looking car was being used, on and off, by undercover officers from Customs and Excise, who were involved in a multi-million-pound investigation codenamed Operation Grandslam, with me at its centre.

Except that I didn't notice either of these things because my mind was cluttered with other, more pressing matters. Like my huge precious metal position on Comex, the Commodities Exchange in New York. And my pouting blonde.

I made a mental note to keep an eye on the booze. I was driving that spaceship of a car all hours of the day, well over the limit, at all sorts of speed, with all sorts of female company. I was extremely lucky not to get a pull.

If only I had known that the powers that be, resting in the high echelons of Customs and VAT investigations, far beyond the reach of the Old Bill, had given very strict instructions to the operators of the secret camera to let me, Nigel Goldman, chairman and managing director of the International Gold Bullion Exchange, go about my business totally unhindered, no matter what (more about that at the trial).

PART ONE

Foundations for Fraud

1977–87

The VAT Man Visits

1

How do I look? I've just spent ten minutes picking off the label from the sleeve of my new dark-blue, silk double-breasted jacket. Why on earth do designers have to label the outside of their clothes?

I'm just going down to the hotel bar for a couple of squirts before I go next door to the casino. It's opening night. Don't worry, I've given the obligatory 48 hours' notice to play. After I've had a drink or two, I think I might try my hand at some roulette. I've just discovered silk ties that cost sixty-five quid each. They're made by an Italian company called Missoni. Buy shares in Missoni, if you can. Sixty-five quid is outrageous for a tie. My father would kill me. I'm only 20, you know. Mind you, I've done quite well, so I can afford the extravagance. You see, I have this little office just out of town where I buy and sell coins. I know quite a lot about coins, especially gold ones. Sovereigns, krugerrands, rarities. I spent years studying them when I should have been concentrating on my A levels, before going to university and becoming a barrister or something. Get something behind you, my parents would say. Get something behind you to fall back on.

High Stakes

I've just installed a Reuters ticker in my office to keep me up to date with the markets. It ticks away all day and all night, little lengths of paper trickling to the floor. Gold fixes, currencies, stocks, news. One night, on my way out, I'm going to forget to switch the bloody thing off and will come in to an office full of ticker paper the next morning. Very *Wall Street*, very *Capital City*. Except this is Birmingham, in 1977. Still, I'm making a good living. I'm dressing well. I'm drinking well. I'm screwing well. I live in the Stratford Suite at the Grand Hotel. I drive a metallic ice-green Porsche Turbo 911. That mischievous tiger's preparing to storm into the picture, along with the yuppies. My mum's just died. My dad's just signed the lease guarantee for my Porsche. I've got money in the bank and cash in my pocket. I'm going to the casino. I might go to a club later. I might get laid. Gold might go up tomorrow, then I'll be able to pay for all the coins I've bought. You see, I haven't got that much money in the bank. The tiger's just dying to storm in. I'm having to hold myself back. Maybe a win in the casino will stall his arrival.

The casino has that smell of virginity about it: new, unused, recently applied beige suede covering the walls. The lighting is soft, but bright light bathes the gaming tables. The carpet is dark and the gaming tables are neatly spaced, inviting, enticing, attended by smart, uniformed croupiers. The bar is at the far end of the club, up a small flight of stairs; away from the gaming area and just off the bar, tables are laid up for diners.

Soft, soothing music is piping through the invisible speakers making the whole atmosphere calming, intoxicating and intimate. Plastic gaming chips click as bored croupiers, waiting like vultures for punters to appear at their table, deftly finger their chips into neat stacks. The gaming floor is still quiet. There is only an Indian gentleman, already over 300 down, at the roulette table and a small game of blackjack is in progress.

I head for the bar; just a couple more squirts to keep me buzzing. The alcohol is already starting to piss on my brain, but I need a little top-up before I play. Not Dutch courage, you understand, I just have to feel in the right frame of mind before I start my little adventure with the wheel. Just one more and I'll play. I promise.

At last. I'm ready. I've been to the loo (no sense in getting caught out in the middle of play, is there?). I saunter over to the roulette table; the same Indian still cursing the outcome of every spin of the wheel.

'Bloody 33,' he splutters. 'I've been on it all evening and as soon as I leave it, it bloody well comes in.'

He reaches into his pocket and pulls out another bundle of greasy, sweaty, tax-evaded notes. 'Change this!' he yells at the croupier. She is in her early 20s, quite tall and has a beautiful face. Her name is Melanie. She wears a little badge giving that secret away.

Then I place the first bet of my life in a casino. A bet that I will never forget, and a bet I will repeat, on and off, in various gambling establishments all around the world, over the next 20 years. 'Thirty-one, black, ten quid, straight up.'

Melanie spun the wheel. The Indian was perspiring heavily and was mesmerised. I looked on with interest as the little white ball spun round and round, before slowly finding its home in one of the numbered canoes. I could afford about 20 of these bets with the cash I had on me, but I had already made up my mind that if I lost this first bet, I would have a much bigger bet the next spin. I wasn't in the mood to let my money dissipate slowly over the whole evening; I wanted sudden, quick action. The ball stopped. Number eight, black. The croupier swiftly gathered together and removed all the losing chips, then stacked them up neatly by the wheel.

The second spin. I chose 31 again. This time £10, straight up on the number, £10 on each of the splits, plus £50 on high and black, just for good measure. I would have enough left over for a curry, if this bet went down. She spun again. The ball hovered around the right section and seemed to change direction a couple of times before making up its mind where to land, finally resting in a canoe close to number 31. Except that I couldn't see exactly where it had landed because the wheel had already spun around again, out of sight. For a long second, the wheel took its time to come back into view. It seemed to have a mind of its own.

'Thirty-one, black,' Melanie called. The Indian threw up his arms in defeat, and Melanie leant over the table, displaying ample breasts as she placed the little dolly on the chips which covered the winning number. My chips.

She paid out the side bets first, and black, at even money. It didn't take me long to realise that I had won about £1,000. The croupier gathered together stacks of brightly coloured high-value chips and pushed them across the table, as she had been trained, with one hand and not a chip out of place.

Again? Why not. Why not, indeed.

The ball was already spinning as I pressed my bet. This time £50 on the number and the same on all splits. This would come to over four grand if it hit. Now, let me tell you that the odds of a number coming up twice in a row in a casino are exactly the same as it coming up once. No casino will offer a fraction over the odds for the repetition. That's the theory of it, anyway. In practice, it doesn't often happen, especially after a sizeable win. The croupiers seem to have this amazing knack of being able to spin a long, long way away from the last number. Call it beginner's luck, or whatever, but my darling Melanie spun it again for me. And again. Three in a row. She wasn't that far off the fourth time, either, but that would be the stuff of fairy tales. I bet you're dying to know how much I won, aren't you? I expect you imagine that after the second winning spin I pressed the bet a third time. It was their money, after all. High towers of brightly coloured chips reaching skywards to the chandeliers? Aiming for the jackpot? 'Our casino, now *your* casino.' I'm afraid not. The truth of the matter is that I was already halfway up the stairs to the cash desk after the second win to cash in my chips and boldly left the same bet on the table. I didn't know whether to laugh or cry when she spun it the third time. I know I should have pressed it up, but there we are. I had just won nearly ten grand and it was only 9.45 p.m.

I put most of the cash in the hotel safe, out of harm's way until the morning. I had various options: I could go to the wine bar and grab a meal, hit a club or two and pull a nice horny one, or stay in my suite and get drunk. In the end, I stayed in and got drunk. The trouble was, I did the other two first.

2

Maybe my early days of enforced boredom, Judaism and discipline at Carmel College boarding school in Oxon laid the foundations for my extravagance, late nights, risk-taking, whoring and boozing. Sadly, I never knew what a happy home was. I had endured an isolated and loveless childhood and was crippled with a desperate need to be looked after. I sought to buy affection and friendship by recklessly showering gifts on almost anyone. I would while away entire evenings in smart bars with the comfort of a few drinks and the company of a barman who remembered my name, courtesy of a generous gratuity. This emptiness reared its head at the time in my rather sophisticated drinking habits. I wasn't your usual piss artist – I liked to lament with expensive friends. Over the years, I acquired a taste for the better, pricier wines and champagnes. Malt whiskies, brandy, kümmel (try it, it's good, especially after dinner).

I had already begun to stop mixing my drinks, though, after a string of monumental hangovers, day after day. One morning, there was a particularly bad one. God, that one was an absolute motherfucker. I have to confess to running to the loo in my office to throw up while Wilson was on the phone to me from the bank. The unappetising combination of booze (I'd not long since finished a large brandy in some Greek restaurant on Digbeth) and him screaming down the phone for funds was just too much for my system. Not just any funds, mind you, he was demanding cleared funds. Cash, telegraphic transfers (TT), wire. The real McCoy. By three o'clock, sharp, or he'd start bouncing my cheques.

I promise not to mention them again, but boarding schools bore the socks off you. Remember that when you're a parent paying the exorbitant bill from the bursar for your kids. They're worse than the nick. I've done time in both, so I know. Of course, there are the similarities: the petty rules, the drugs, the crooked card and backgammon games, the bullying, the loneliness, waiting every day for letters and visitors that don't show. But boarding school is far worse really, because there is a choice. I am astonished how hard my father worked to pay the fees for my unhappiness – late into the evenings in his dental surgery, peering into mouths, my mother at his side assisting. I made up my mind at a very early age (I think it was ten), during lonely summer holidays and continuous parental arguing, that I wanted some excitement in my life, some thrills, some happiness. I itched to rid myself of my unhappy memories, dispose of my enforced misery, remove it like a snake sheds its old skin. Forever.

Urge me to invest my ten grand wisely. Tell me to use it to build solid foundations. To build it up. Slowly. Into some institution. To create something. The assistant manager at my local bank, 'Paul Wilson', kept reminding me about solid foundations. From little acorns . . . The manager had given up on me months ago and handed my account over to his subordinate. He was a raving loony, that man. The branch I used was about a mile down the road from my office. It was tiny, the last building in a row of shops next to a new(ish) housing estate that used to be the old dog track. I've never told anyone this before, but when I was a kid, about eight years old, I used to cycle up to the dog track to watch the action through the fence, like a voyeur. Pretty girls in white coats paraded the six dogs, each dog assigned a coloured coat to denote its trap number, the number one dog sporting a bright red coat, while number six wore black and white stripes. While the dogs were paraded, the bookmakers in the ring, brilliant mathematicians the lot of them, started chalking up the odds on offer. Then, as the dogs approached the traps, ready for loading in a frenzy of activity; as punters desperately thrust money at the bookies, shouting their bets; as the bookies, repeating their wagers, chucked their money into their large leather satchels, came the bell, the hare running, the action. 'Go on three, my beauty. Go on, my son.' Maybe that was the start.

A hardware store, dry cleaners, hairdressers, used-car lot (stock constantly changing, generous part-exchange allowance, low mileage example), newsagent and florist completed this line-up. Hardly high-rolling territory, is it? 'How are you this afternoon, Mrs Kleinfelt? Your hair's looking lovely . . . Yes that's the right book for your deposit account. Just take a seat over there, the manager will see you in a moment.'

Nothing prepared them for me, not in this branch. Certainly not the poor old manager. He was due to retire in less than a year (he told me, in confidence, in his little office, in hushed tones). He couldn't risk his pension on what he called *speculative* activities. 'Working from too small a capital base,' he would mutter. I was buying massive quantities of gold sovereigns and krugerrands, and gambling on them going up in price. I would then dump them in the City and get the money wired directly to my bank in time to cover the cheques I had issued for them originally.

That was how I ended up with the madman Wilson. For a start, he was always yelling at me down the phone. Especially when I was hungover. It was high-turnover stuff that bullion dealing. It wouldn't surprise me if I had turned over more than any other customer in the branch. Sometimes a million or so a month. High turnover disguised those gut-wrenching transactions, of course. Like the invoice for the Porsche.

High Stakes

Performance-car service bays are the ultimate accessory for your investment. Gleaming hydraulic ramps and state-of-the-art computers kit out the station, like some private health care clinic for vehicles. My little beauty deserved the best, after all. Vehicle BUPA. Shame the staff weren't quite so upmarket. 'You need four new tyres, mate. Been overdoing it with the turbo? They're worn flat out, guv.' Three hundred quid. Each. Has the whole world gone fucking barmy?

Anyway, he had his good points, Wilson. He'd got me credit at that fine, upstanding institution in the City, NM Rothschild & Sons. They'd take my cheques for gold coins. Good move. Wilson would say I was playing the clearing system – issuing cheques with no funds in my account, having until the third business day to find sufficient money to cover them when they were presented for payment. I was never sure if that was better than working from too small a capital base or not. Sometimes, I had cheques stacking up against me for thousands, sorry, tens of thousands of pounds. But I sure had fun with the credit while it lasted. See how the numbers are starting to play their little haunting game? With access to this money, for a few days at a time at least, I added another game to my portfolio. Futures.

Commodity or financial futures were the latest concept in the world of high finance. Contracts on paper in all sorts of markets – precious metals, base metals, oil, coffee, cocoa and sugar – were traded all over the world on official exchanges. The attraction to the private speculator was that these markets were very volatile and a punter could make or lose a fortune in a matter of minutes. Leverage was the powerful overriding feature of these markets. What this meant was that for as little as a 5 per cent deposit of the total contract value, one could get on the markets moving up or down. A 5 per cent movement in either direction could double your investment or wipe you out, depending on whether you called the market correctly.

Meanwhile, I had until three o'clock to get hold of some cleared funds. But I had an ace up my sleeve. Silver.

The VAT Man Visits

That day, in New York, just before nine o'clock, most of the floor traders were in the bathroom, attired in their gaudy, brightly coloured trading jackets. Pencils sharpened, badges straight, flip cards at the ready. Just having a quick squirt, line, draw, fix or puke before the bell. Gold was called 3–4 higher, silver up a dime. There was a rumour on the exchange that an oil billionaire in Dallas was amassing a huge position in silver.

Trading in futures is the most exciting, dangerous and volatile last bastion of free trade left in the world. On the exchange floor, at least. Off exchange, the odds are against you. The spread – the difference between buying and selling – will kill you. Plus, the ability for the floor to cleverly cross orders, stop you out, mug rally or dip the market, almost at will, will exterminate you. And the pros know who's got what and have a fair idea of which way the market's heading. In Vegas, they'd call it playing with a stacked deck. No wonder seats were trading at half a million bucks, just for precious metal pits.

Moi? I could beat the market, me thought.

I had been running a big position in silver through my London brokers, 'England Futures Limited'. He was a lovely man, that 'Douglas Hilton', and had looked after my investments with the company well. That day was my chance to cop some big bucks. I was long 20 contracts of silver on the London Metal Exchange, 10,000 ounces each. Each and every penny silver went up, I made £2,000. We had already gone up 7p that morning. Fourteen grand, so far that day. And I hadn't even had a drink. A few more pence and I would be able to call my broker to wire some money to the bank. Just a few more pence. Please, I prayed. Pretty please. Don't let me down. Don't let me down, silver, my little baby.

Then at nine o'clock in New York they were off and running. Arms outstretched, shouting their orders, the boys on Comex start their day. Up we go. Bid, bid, bid. Five thirty bid for twenty, May! Thirty-two bid! Thirty-three bid! Thirty-five bid! (Fifty for

July!) A brave local tried to stem the tide, taking a deep breath and yelling his offer to sell. May at thirty-six! A herd of colours rushed at him, eager, desperate to mop up contracts at almost any price. Yes! Bought! Mine! Buyer! Pushing, shoving, yelling. Everyone in the pit tried to buy from him at once. The local quickly re-bought his mistake, five ticks higher, and retreated wounded to the bathroom. The phones were ringing off the hook in the booths around the pit, as brokerage-house clerks received endless buy orders from all over the world. Underpaid runners handed time-stamped order tickets to their traders in the pit. As sure as night follows day, London would follow suit.

The pit was becoming frantic, flooding with buy paper. By 2.30, UK time, London was up 20p and New York could have still gone up the daily permissible limit of 50 cents an ounce. The bears were starting to dig their own graves. My tiger was booking in for hibernation. The rally was holding. The bulls had control. They were dancing in the streets, their heads bobbing under the New York skyline, the damp air pulsating on their greedy heads like a strobe. Up, up, up we went. The bell rang on my ticker. New York had gone limit up. I reached for the phone and requested the wire. It was 3.25. I was in funds, cleared funds. I had saved the day and my credibility. I'd paid my dues. The wire had just hit.

In Dallas, oilman Nelson Bunker Hunt had also had a good day. He calculated that he had made just over $100 million on the back of silver's surge. As I see it, he would have climbed into his Chevy pick-up, collected his brother and gone for a burger, just as they had done every afternoon for the past ten years.

It was getting dark. It had been raining, and the water gleamed off the tarmac in the early evening dusk, glossed by daggers of light from the street lamps. The Porsche ate up the miles into town, hugging the road happily courtesy of my new rubber investment. Whizzing, gliding, turbo-ing. King's Heath,

Moseley, Edgbaston, Digbeth, the city. Neon, bars, heading for refreshment and relaxation after a long, eventful day. A deserved escape. And rest.

Silver was still limit up in New York.

3

My lovely, leggy secretary Sue put the call on hold and buzzed through. 'Customs and Excise for you,' she said.

Now, either one of my mates was playing a sick one, or they had the wrong number.

I took the call and, to my surprise, it *was* the bleeding VAT man. What the hell could they want with me? I pictured the Scottish civil servant's office while he droned on. Pre-printed files, dossiers, paper clips, target posters, squash leagues, regulation paperwork, filing cabinets, coded memoranda, noticeboards, steel desks, cheap chairs, poor lighting. A bit like the police, really. Establishment, don't you just hate it?

This VAT man was a definite Scot. Long on 'oos', short on humour. 'A routine visit to have a wee look at your books,' he said. I tried, I tried hard, I promise you. I bought a week. I booked him in for the following Wednesday morning. Ten o'clock. I pencilled him into my diary.

I suppose I had been trading for a couple of years by then. My first year was fairly uninspiring, turning over about a mill, showing a small profit. I had an income tax liability of just over five grand. I ought to have got round to paying them, but they didn't seem to be in too much of a hurry to collect, despite threatening distraint warrants and bailiffs and other such rude things. How dare they?

My accountant managed to get books together for the first

year, after a lot of persuasion from me, mainly with money, booze, the odd dinner and the promise of a fat fee. I didn't bribe him. As such. But the second year was not quite so easy. I had been doing quite a lot of business, you see. Gold coins, rare coins, futures, options. And I haven't even got round to mentioning stocks and shares yet. I'd found a nice little angle on the stock market and just carried on, in cavalier fashion, regardless. Dealing, trading, buying, selling, paying in, drawing out, spending, wiring, wining, dining, kiting. No proper records, no proper books. No nothing.

What the hell was I supposed to show this geezer when he showed up on Wednesday? Picture it. 'Can I have a wee look at your sales files, purchase files, creditors, debtors, stock book and day book?' And those are just the things I knew I was supposed to have – and didn't. What about all the other beauties he would come up with? Bank reconciliations, ledgers, VAT returns and calculations, management accounts, cash flows? I'd been keeping a note of what I was owed jotted on the back of a business card with my readies in my pocket. One evening at the casino it got wedged in by mistake with some notes I was changing up. The croupier handed it back over the baize, after the cash had been counted out. He held it like some exhibit in a court case with a puzzled look on his face, my little note daring to trespass on the sacred domain of plastic and baize. When he handed it back to me, he had a look on his face that suggested he ought to be wearing disposable surgical gloves. Those scribblings were precious to me. What did he know, anyway?

God, those VAT guys had some powers hadn't they? I had heard through the grapevine that they could turn your office upside down during these innocent-sounding visits. And your house. They could take you in, seize your stock, fine you, jail you. Maybe my mind was working overtime. Fear of the unknown and all that. He couldn't know anything, could he?

I sent Sue out with a shopping list. She was looking more like Purdy from *The Avengers* every day. One or two of my customers actually called her that when they came in to see me. She was very good to me when my dear mum died; loving, caring, supporting. I suppose I was a bit in love with her, really. We'd travelled all over the place together, to shows and exhibitions. I got a real kick out of having her working for me during the day, all professional and that, and then sharing my bedroom in the evening. Every boss's fantasy come true. She seemed happy with the arrangement, although I had noticed that she seemed very keen to go and look for a flat with me. I'd been doing a fair bit of house-hunting at that time. Not that there was anything wrong with the suite, of course. Apart from the bills every fortnight. It was just that I thought it was time for me to have my own place. The suite did have its advantages: booze on call 24 hours a day, snacks, meals, and, of course, it was cleaned to perfection daily. And there were no bills for lighting or heating or rates. Maybe I'd stick it out for a few more weeks. It was no hardship, really. Sue would have liked me to have my own place, for sure. She was always talking about curtains and carpets and colour schemes and plants – all those things ladies like to do to a bachelor's gaff. I think she was pretty keen, really. I had noticed one day, though, that my friend Richard Williams had been eyeing her up, when he popped into the office to sell me some gold coins. Richard was a cautious coin dealer; accurate, methodical, precise. His price labels were the neatest in the industry, and he had built himself a good reputation, dealing in all types of material. I estimated him to be worth about a quarter of a mill at the time. He would, like me, enjoy a roller-coaster ride in the industry in the years to come.

Sue's shopping list included some ledgers, VAT accounting books, ring files, purchase and sales files and a day book. I told her to keep the receipt, for VAT purposes, you understand. Got to start somewhere. Then I directed her to the filing cabinet in the corner of my office, and she got down on her knees and started sorting out the mountain of paperwork that had been festering in its hideout – untouched, unfiled, unindexed – for the past 12 months.

High Stakes

When the VAT man turned up, he seemed to have a very large chip on his broad Scottish shoulders. Maybe he had his suspicions that this visit was going to end up in one of those special pink investigation files on Colin Peters' desk.

4

I had bumped into the girl Melanie from the casino by chance. When I first met her that evening in 1977, it was impossible to ask her out, casino rules forbidding a client–employee relationship and all, but now we were free to start what she called a 'clandestine relationship'. She used to pop up to see me in my suite after work at about five in the morning, after she'd finished helping to count the take. That was like five in the afternoon, her time. George, the night doorman, opened the door for her and she tiptoed down the corridor and gently tapped on my door. I'd got used to getting up at that ungodly hour to let her in. We sat around and nattered, opened a few bottles from the minibar, and then had explosive, hungry, demanding sex, before she crashed out in bed. Then I ran a nice bath, complete with loads of bubbles. (Another perk of the suite I forgot to mention was the non-stop complimentary toiletries.) As I soaked in my bath, I started to plan my day ahead. Futures, stocks, gold coins, maybe some lunch. One thing was for sure though – I'd end up in some bar, somewhere in town, early evening. I'd become a townie – a familiar face at all the better watering holes around the city centre. Melanie liked that. She liked it when we were acknowledged by bar staff, waiters and bouncers on our little jaunts. When I took Sue out for a few cocktails, she was taken aback, I must admit, at how well known I seemed to be. 'Who else do you bring here?' she asked playfully.

Once out of my bath, I put on a fluffy dressing gown, ordered some breakfast and started on the morning papers. Very civilised. Then I would make some calls to my brokers, get dressed and set off for the office. If I was lucky, Melanie would stir while I was mooching through my Missonis, and if I was very lucky, I'd end up in bed for seconds. I was happy with the arrangement. Even some of the brokers I dealt with were getting used to their early morning phone calls. I had worked out that if I made do with two hours less sleep a night and lived to the average age of three score and ten, I would spend an extra 12 years awake! I'd acquired a reputation for being an early riser. Not so bad; the early bird catches the worm and all that. What was more impressive, though, was my staying power at night. No problem with the late nights, or the booze. Thank God.

She was pushing all the right buttons, Melanie. Stockings, lacy suspenders, heels, red lipstick, nail polish. I loved it when she called at lunchtime after she'd just woken up and summoned me back to the suite. It was becoming a regular little feature of my day, those lunchtime call-ups. I couldn't complain! I had to keep Sue sweet, though, as well. Christ, things were starting to get complicated. One of them only had to say no! I was taking Melanie to Henley Royal Regatta that weekend. I had got hold of a couple of tickets for the Stewards' Enclosure at well over the odds.

My little coup on silver had kept things ticking over quite nicely for the previous few weeks. England Futures had been sending more transfers to the bank as silver continued to climb, and it had kept me very nicely in the way to which I had become accustomed. When you are sitting on a winning position in the futures market, you generate, on paper, positive equity on your account, which is above the original margin money required to maintain your position. The surplus money is available on demand from your broker, or can be used to finance further contracts. In the same manner, the customers who are holding the opposite losing trades are required to wire money immediately to their brokers to top up their accounts.

High Stakes

I was up to date with all my bills at the office, I'd paid off the Porsche, had a nice stock of coins in the office safe and some money in the bank. I'd even paid the Revenue. It broke my heart to part with that five-odd grand. I ripped the cheque up three times before mailing the fourth one, almost in tears, second-class post. I bet the bulk of the Revenue's cheques arrive second-class. Serves them bloody well right. The only fly in the ointment was the forthcoming visit from my friends from Customs and Excise on Wednesday. A couple of days down at Henley would take my mind off it and give Sue the time to get to work on the books. She was doing her best, but deep down I knew it wasn't enough. Not enough to satisfy the lust of the VAT man. A pretty lawyer's clerk I had been chatting up the previous evening had summed it up nicely. Not that I mentioned anything about my forthcoming VAT visit, of course, we were just happily chatting away. What was it she said? Something like the law always catches up with you. It always gets its sweet revenge in the end.

Now, there were a dozen or so firms of stockbrokers in Birmingham. Mainly branch offices of the larger London firms. I had opened accounts with them all. One or two of them even put a little gold-coin business my way. My favourite firm was 'Hudson, Eyres & Simpson'. They let me trade as much as I wanted.

The beauty of trading stocks and equities is that you don't have to pay for them. Whoever designed the stock market account system deserves a gold medal – I'd even pay for it. It's a haven for those who insist on working from too small a capital base and works like this. You buy stocks at the beginning of the account, usually a two-week period and, in exceptional circumstances, three weeks, and there is a settlement date just after the expiry of the account period. If the stock goes up, you sell, and those nice broker people send you a cheque. If the stock goes down, you also sell, but you immediately re-buy for the next account. It's a little-known trade secret called 'sell and renew', designed originally under the old pals act, to assist traders who were in temporary financial difficulties. Rumour has it that it was put to use when, following a huge loss at the baccarat table the evening before, a well-known city broker couldn't pay for his stock one account. As long as the stocks you have chosen eventually climb, you are in constant receipt of cheques from the brokers. Nice one, huh? Of course, in the circles I was moving in, it wasn't difficult to obtain the odd bit of help, if you know what I mean. What I was waiting for was the big one. Proper insider stuff. The takeover coup, or something like that. With all the account facilities I had with the brokers, I would be able to play big. Very big. Maybe I could have even let Douglas Hilton, that nice man from England Futures Limited, in on the next deal? He had just put me into a little trade in coffee. I was in and out in two days. Made a couple of grand, but I only played small. I owed him one.

I wasn't particular about trading things I didn't understand. Mind you, what the hell did I understand about silver, for Christ's sake? I think I was just lucky – in the right place at the right time or, more to the point, the right market at the right time. A bit like the Hunt brothers in Dallas, really. There was an article about them in one of those American monthly magazines at the time. Apparently, they started playing in silver because their broker suggested it.

The Hunt brothers were no strangers to controversy. The US government had fined them heavily earlier in the decade for cornering the soya bean market. They decided to invest in silver futures to test their theory that the market was based on paper, not actual product. The Hunts decided to take delivery of the silver when their contracts matured, causing upset in a market which survived on investors selling out their contracts, not acquiring the commodity.

5

Douglas Hilton's beloved company was on the verge of bankruptcy by the summer of the previous year. The markets had been moving viciously against England Futures Limited. As its finances continued to deteriorate, the company learned (after receiving some preferential information) that coffee futures were about to tumble. In a final attempt to wipe out its clients' equity balances, England Futures advised its customers to do the opposite – buy instead of sell. The plan was to run the positions 'in-house' – in other words, profit from their customers' misfortune when the market fell, as they had been tipped.

However, newspapers – the *Financial Times*, the *Daily Telegraph* and the *Daily Mail* to be accurate – had suddenly started writing headlines like 'SHOCK FROST WIPES OUT BULK OF BRAZIL COFFEE CROP – MARKET RALLIES STRONGLY IN FINAL MINUTES OF NEW YORK TRADING'. As a result, England Futures was pushed to its financial limits because of its losing coffee in-house trading, and the company was acutely aware of the difficulties it was facing in paying out their winning clients. In the midst of the panic, my account details were flagged. I had over 100 contracts of silver on the London Metal Exchange. If silver crept up again that day, England Futures would be in serious difficulty. I assume I had the largest position of any of the company's clients by far, gambling massively now for nearly a year on silver's rise, already having taken a huge amount of money out of the market, and my current position amounted to almost a free bet.

England Futures took a monumental decision that would make or break them. They decided to pray that the coffee market would turn itself around and took a gamble on silver's run being over. They started selling silver short. Whatever impact England Futures' short-selling had on London (the company had noted that their movements had been chipping away at the price single-handedly), it would pale into insignificance once the US markets opened after lunch.

That same week, Nelson Bunker Hunt and his brother bought enormous quantities of silver. They had instructed their broker at Drexel Burnham Lambert to mop up silver in both New York and Chicago at almost any price. They must have had a strong suspicion that the exchanges were going to have difficulty delivering all the silver they had amassed. They were going to call the market's bluff and ask for delivery of their silver when their contracts expired, instead of selling the contracts back into the market. They were going to squeeze silver till it hurt. And, if they had calculated correctly, the ensuing price surge, resulting from traders realising what they were up to, would enable them to buy even more contracts with the paper profits they had under their belts. They were in good company, too. A couple of other investors had agreed to team up with them to form a silver pool, just to help the market along. Bringing in this outside help was a very clever strategy for the Hunts. With virtually unlimited funds, these new investors were a powerful addition to the Hunts' game plan. A corner was forming. Woe betide anyone who dared to bet against them! And so by three o'clock that day, the Hunts had started to take control of the world silver market.

Although these upward price movements were minuscule in comparison to what we were about to see, they were sufficient, nevertheless, for Douglas Hilton to receive the dreaded phone call from his own firm's brokers. Margin call – those two words would have been enough to make his lunch churn in his stomach. The transfers due shortly, and immediately, to his soft-commodities clients would be ten times the one he had just made himself for silver.

6

It was the spring of 1979 as the VAT man made his weary, early-morning way to my office premises. He whiled away a couple of hours purporting to complete his examination and writing up notes, then he called me in to have a chat.

He explained in helpful terms how he would like to see my books written up and offered some helpful hints for the future. At no time did I suspect that from that moment onwards I would be under a full HM Customs and Excise investigation, but I also couldn't believe that this would be my first and last run-in with Customs. The VAT man then put his files away, clicked his briefcase shut, put his cap on and made his way slowly back to headquarters via the bookies – either to work on their books or for a little flutter. And if it was the latter, then good luck to him.

7

Later that year, my office was beginning to look like a high-tech dealing room – Mission Control. I had bought an expensive Italian desk from my antique-dealer friend called 'Giles Hampton'. He and his girlfriend Stacey lived in a large country estate and had retail premises in town. They were a lovely, eccentric couple and we quickly became friends. This desk he had sold me had a built-in TV, a bank of phones, a safe, an air-conditioning unit and a loudspeaker system to summon in waiting clients or members of staff. I now had two secretaries on the payroll and a full-time bookkeeper.

The VAT Man Visits

I leant back in my expensive Italian chair, lit a cigar and extracted the cutting from my pocket. I dialled the number. Then I called Wilson at the bank, ordered a banker's draft for thirty grand, payable to Cooper Cars, and waited for the latest Porsche Turbo model to arrive. I had new wheels.

Some people maintain that when you splash out on expensive toys, your luck changes for the worse. What a load of bollocks! Then again, within a fortnight of taking delivery of the Porsche, misfortune came my way. England Futures Limited formally went into liquidation, owing me £300,000. Worse, silver was starting to climb aggressively and the potential profit on my positions would have come to millions. We were looking at 10p in the pound, if we were lucky. I was also windmilling huge gold-coin positions through my credit accounts with Rothschild and other members of the London Gold Market. One evening, I was keeping a close eye on the gold price, and I was running the equivalent of a 5,000-ounce position in gold coins I hadn't paid for yet. At 5.15, the price of gold hadn't moved for an hour and a half. By 5.25, it dropped $2. At 5.35, it fell another $5. I stayed glued to Reuters. The London market had closed, but, if I had wanted to, I could have watched prices move all night. New York, five hours behind London, was in full swing. When New York closed, Chicago would still be open, then Hong Kong, and when that closed it would be morning in England and London would be open again.

I didn't stay the night, but by the time I got up from my desk at 7.30 the price of gold had dropped by $18.

I eased the Porsche out of its parking space and switched on the stereo. An early '70s Elton John track was playing, and the music took me back to my rowing days at college. And my first girlfriend – there had been countless ones since then – and I started to feel a little sad. Memories of my mother came flooding back to me, and I felt a little nostalgic, as I always did when I thought of her. She had struggled against the terrible handicap of chronic asthma and an unhappy marriage. To remain alive she needed daily doses of powerful drugs. My father, working around the clock, never seemed to be able to comfort her.

I started driving towards Stratford with no particular destination in mind, just a change of scenery. I got the Porsche up to over 100mph on the open road, and I started to think about my gold position again. Maybe the market would rally later that day in New York.

It didn't.

You lose some, you lose some. One door closes, another one slams shut. I part-exchanged the Porsche for a powder-blue Rolls-Royce Corniche, to change my run of bad luck.

When Lady Luck goes into reverse thrust, there is no better antidote than to go out to a pub or wine bar and get more out of life. I was about to say this to myself, when I remembered that I went to a bar almost every night, no matter which way Lady Luck was spinning.

Twilight was setting in when I arrived at the Old Contemptibles, an upmarket bar in central Birmingham. A few expensive cars were already outside. I carefully parked up, went in and climbed the stairs. Past the function suite on the left, past the sign that said 'Private Bar', past the couple chatting at the top of the stairs and into the bar on the top floor. This was where many of Birmingham's legal nobs hung out. A colourful, local solicitor called 'Peter Kinsley' held court most evenings. As a partner in the pub, there was a rumour going round that he could sign for his drinks and get the tab sent to his chambers at the end of the month. I liked Peter immediately. He was a playboy. He lived in a flash house, had loads of lady friends, he liked a drink and owned a couple of Ferraris. He had a sharp legal brain, as well. The OCs was also regularly frequented by townies, businessmen, con men in blazers and the hoi polloi.

A few other customers were already in. A man who ran his finger along the next day's racing form, a group of solicitors, some junior accountants from Peats, a couple of barristers and now a smartly dressed young man who drank huge gin and tonics with some haste.

A pretty, dark-haired girl slid up to me. 'Another, Nige?'

'Yes, please, and how about you, Carol?'

'Same again, thanks.'

Same again, thanks. Slame agin. Sime aglain, shame again.

'Nigel, we'd better go,' Carol slurred. 'You're gulping your gin and tonic.' We left.

Unbeknown to me, the VAT man was folding up his newspaper and likewise preparing to leave his table in the corner.

8

The raid took me by complete surprise. It was a Friday morning, the preferred time for the authorities to pounce on their victims ahead of the weekend, when most good defence lawyers are packing their bags for mini-breaks away in the country. I hadn't long been in the office when four plain-clothes Customs officers burst in, led by 'Colin Peters'. Peters was the only one to speak. 'Nigel Goldman, I'm arresting you on suspicion of evading VAT.' I had been busted.

The officers searched my premises thoroughly, bagging up into exhibit sacks every single item of paperwork. They took an inventory of my gold stock in the safe, looking out for evidence of illegal imports, and told my staff not to expect me back in a hurry.

A while later, I gained information about an investigation Customs were carrying out involving me. I employed a local security firm to do a sweep of my home and office and they found a bug that I assume had been planted during this search.

The officers escorted me to their offices for an interview. HM Customs and Excise Investigation Department occupied offices in St James's House, bang opposite Giles Hampton's antique showroom. They led me in. Pre-printed files, dossiers, steel desks, poor lighting – just how I had imagined it. The stage was set for something. The stage was set for disaster.

They sat me down. 'Pass me Judges Rules, would you?' Peters asked his colleague. Then he read me my rights, just like they do in the movies.

'We're not happy about the way you have been trading. We believe a large amount of VAT has been misappropriated by you. That's why we arrested you and uplifted your paperwork. This paperwork will be thoroughly examined to determine the extent of the suspected evasion. You may be interested to know that we have had you under surveillance for quite some time. Casinos, nightclubs, wine bars, pubs. Quite an appetite. Quite extravagant, too, it would appear.' He turned to my VAT man and smiled. 'The new drum isn't going to look too good in court, is it? And your Roller? How much was the Corniche? Thirty, forty grand? Phew! Meanwhile, I have a few questions I want to ask you. I'll remind you that you are still under caution.'

'There must be some mistake, did you check with . . .?'

'Mr Goldman,' Peters said, 'can we please cut the crap.'

They interrogated me for hours. I answered their questions as best as I could, always in the back of my mind attempting to portray myself as an honest trader. They seemed to have extensive knowledge of all my activities and all the people I had dealings with, but I didn't want to give anything away. A lot of what they were saying was pure conjecture or suspicion. They led me up this path and down that path, always trying to trip me up. I felt I was doing well, but then who knows? At the conclusion of proceedings, they said they would examine my uplifted paperwork thoroughly, calculate my liability and would then be in touch with an assessment. They indicated that they had the power to compound the VAT with a penalty, but that it was more likely their superiors would want the case to go to court, just to set an example. After this first chat with the officers, it struck me how very well informed Customs were.

The VAT Man Visits

My interview continued and I was plied with black coffee until I had answered all their questions. They released me without charge at 8.48 p.m. I was absolutely exhausted. I headed straight to the OCs. Back through the doors, up the stairs, past the sign saying 'Private Bar' to the top of the stairs and into the bar. 'Evening, Nigel, how are you?'

Bliss.

Now, I needed a good lawyer. A local associate of mine recommended 'Rupert Casewell', of 'Casewell, Boyce, Metcalfe & Wren'. I just hoped Customs wasn't going to be too much for him to bite off and chew. I made an appointment to see him and took a gentleman called 'Barry Lewis', one of my financial advisers at the time, with me. Lewis had been introduced to me by my mortgage broker, and he had hurriedly prepared suitable accounts for me to get my mortgage for my new house. From there on, I had employed him to sort out the company's books. He used to treat his trips to see me in Birmingham as working holidays, arriving scruffily dressed, his well-preserved wallet containing a fiver. I'll never forget the first time he assisted me in getting facilities from the bank back in 1979, the day we were going to ask the manager for an overdraft. At the bank, he took off his raincoat, folded it on his lap and clicked open his briefcase. It was one of those old-fashioned brown-leather cases with the handle on the top and the leather strap that folds over into a choice of three slots, depending on the volume of paperwork inside. He took out the accounts that he had prepared and swivelled them round on the bank manager's desk so that they faced him.

'These accounts are prepared under the historical cost convention,' he announced sincerely. I could hardly keep a straight face. The manager immediately homed in on the profit-and-loss account and the balance sheet, his trained eye zooming in like a hawk's for confirmation of the correct multiples and figures to keep the bank within its limits. Lewis was one step ahead of him and had ensured the balance sheet would meet his lending criteria. My facility was approved on the spot. I had just acquired my first overdraft by deception.

These days, Lewis and I had a far more difficult task at hand, namely dealing with Rupert Casewell. He was a 50-year-old Hush-Puppy-wearing senior partner in the law firm and occupied the best office suite in a corner of the company's premises, which overlooked the car park where I had just deposited the Rolls.

On his desk, he had a copy of the statement I had made to Customs a couple of weeks earlier. He lifted it up and announced, 'This is a hanging statement.' He allowed the sheets of paper to fall to his desk as if to emphasise the fact. 'I have spoken to Peters,' he continued, 'he's a very good investigator. Very thorough.' Whose side was this guy on? He paused for effect. 'The good news is that Customs are prepared to compound your liability to them in the form of a financial settlement.' A huge wave of relief swept over me. I'd beaten the system. I wasn't going to court. I wasn't going to prison.

'The bad news is that they won't budge from the £15,000 they assess you have evaded.' Fifteen grand! This was too good to be true. What a great lawyer! My hand reached for my inside jacket pocket. I'd write a cheque out straight away.

'Not so fast,' Casewell continued. 'That's just the tax – there are penalties on top for the evasion.' He opened up a legal book on tax rulings, before continuing, 'They have the power to impose penalties of one, two or three times the tax they assess to have been evaded. They are looking for a maximum penalty, I'm afraid.' He did the calculation on a piece of paper, but I had worked it out in an instant. He cleared his throat. 'So that's £15,000 for the tax and £45,000 for the penalty, making a total of £60,000. And, of course,' he said gravely, 'there will be the question of my fees, which will not be inconsiderable.'

'How long have we got?' I asked, hoping for some time to get my thoughts together and discuss all of this with Lewis, who had gone white at the mention of £60,000.

'They've given us two weeks. I want you gentlemen to go away and think about this, have some discussions, and come back to me next week with some proposals. I think I may be able to persuade them to accept the money in instalments. As I said, go away and discuss it. Have a board meeting, if you like, and come and see me again in a week. My secretary will book you an appointment.' He rose to let us out.

Lewis didn't say much as we drove home. Sixty grand! Is this tough, or what? Tough wasn't the word for it. Back home, in my lounge, Lewis still didn't say much. He sat quietly, watching me drink voluminous quantities of gin, probably wondering to himself where on earth his next audit fee cheque was coming from.

I paced up and down, crystal glass in hand, all sorts of thoughts passing through my mind. I decided to have a serious trade. A good trade always made things better. I picked up the phone, dialled New York and purchased 4,000 ounces of nearby gold futures, concluding the transaction in nearly cogent syntax. Lewis might just have been thinking, what excellent gin.

9

Despite the £60,000 VAT fine hanging over my head, the last dregs of the '70s were fun times for me. Carol, my friend from the OCs, introduced me to the most beautiful girl I had ever seen. She was called 'Martina Kent'. A model, with a string of titles to her bow, she was dating a car dealer called 'Richard Evans'. I could tell that her toes were asleep, needed twitching. I asked her out and soon we were dating. One weekend I took her and Carol to Peter Kinsley's house for cocktails and to watch the Grand Prix. The house was full of legal eagles and business types, and the booze was flowing in rivers. Peter's brother was there, too. He drank like a fish. I had never met people with such capacity. Curiously, many years later, both Carol and Martina would feature in both the Kinsley brothers' lives.

Richard Evans had threatened to have my legs broken if I didn't stop seeing Martina, or Marti as she preferred to be called, but by then it was too late. I was besotted with the girl, head over heels in love. We got engaged. We were the talk of the town; the whole of Birmingham couldn't believe my luck. They would have given their right arms to go out with her. I was a local superstar; the luckiest guy around. To use her words, I had captured the elusive butterfly. Some weekends, we would take the ferry over to the Isle of Wight to visit her mother, who lived in a huge house in Ventnor. A high-flying financier who lived next door had designs on my Marti; he couldn't keep his eyes off her. Just before we met, she had come across Peter Scott, the notorious cat burglar, and had encouraged him to take up tennis. Marti and I became friends with Scott's third wife, Fay, and we would all dine at Knightsbridge Sporting Club, where she seemed determined to squander her share of her ex-husband's ill-gotten gains at the blackjack tables.

Martina's parents were separated and her father Peter, a surgeon, lived in Salisbury. We immediately got on well, often going out together to smart restaurants, where he would always check the temperature of the champagne and white wine with the back of his hand the minute it was brought to the table. This was a habit I picked up on and have copied to this day.

Nevertheless, I gave up on Martina pretty rapidly. She was always flying away to do modelling assignments and photo shoots and I just got bored waiting around for her. I did it one evening over dinner in Giovannis, a restaurant we frequented in Stratford-upon-Avon. To cushion the bad news, I told her that she was the most supernaturally beautiful girl I had ever met and, later in the evening, in a moment of sheer madness, I told her that we would never forget our beautiful times together. That was bad enough, but then I kissed her hand and said, 'Goodbye, Jenny.'

Life was to unfold in a mysterious way as far as Martina was concerned. She was to pop up again twice in my life, in the most unusual circumstances: first when she married a friend of mine, and second when she featured in Peter Scott's book. Richard Evans forgave me for stealing Martina from him and later we became friends when I moved into a new house just along the road from him. My new pad had a snooker room and heated pool, and was always an open house. Most weekends there were parties.

Richard would always introduce me to people as 'Mr Wall Street', telling them that I was an over-enthusiastic financial genius and would either be a multimillionaire or in prison by the time I was 30. He was to be proved right on both counts. As I was now footloose and fancy free from Marti's clutches, Richard introduced me to a very pretty Irish girl called Marie, and we started dating.

Businesswise, I was trading in ever-increasing quantities of precious metals, and having a great run. I always had plenty of cash to spend. Christ knows how much I was getting through each week in those days, but I bet it was three or four grand – an absolute fortune at that time.

The good times rolled. Gold kept going up on the back of a lack of confidence in President Carter, trouble in Afghanistan and the 1979 Iranian hostage situation. I couldn't get out of my mind the fact that if England Futures hadn't gone belly up on me, I would have been a millionaire many times over.

I started investing in stocks and shares. Sarah Smith was a sales rep for the *Birmingham Evening Mail* who called in to see me every week for my advertising. She had recommended a few investments which had come up trumps, so when she suggested buying shares in First National Finance Corporation (FNFC) at half a penny each, I decided to go with it. They had just been rescued by the Bank of England 'lifeboat'. She was confident they would one day reach £1 each, so I bought three million shares.

I took on a full-time chauffeur. I had a couple of radio phones installed in the Rolls (pioneer technology in those days) and travelled all over the place making phone calls. Soon I would chop out the Roller and go back to a Porsche, leaving a Mercedes 6.9 for the chauffeur. I bought a personalised number plate, NG2, and thought nothing of affixing it to both of my cars at the same time, in flagrant breach of the regulations. I never got a pull for it.

I did have one incident though, just before I disposed of the Rolls. I had been for lunch in town with Giles Hampton and Stacey and had parked the car illegally. When I returned to the car, it was surrounded by police. They were looking very suspiciously at it (possibly because it didn't have a valid tax disc on display) and because of my apparent youth, they were also very suspicious of me and refused to believe that I was the owner. They promptly arrested me and took me down to the police station. An *Evening Mail* photographer happened to be nearby and took photos of me being carted off. At the police station, an officer made me strip naked and accused me of starting a fight with him. Fortunately for me, a sergeant appeared on the scene, gathered my clothes together, told me to get dressed and gave the officer concerned a severe ticking off. I was released without charge, but it always made me remember that there was a dark side to the police; that they were capable of anything. Mind you, in all my run-ins with the law since, this was the only time I experienced such disgraceful treatment. The *Evening Mail* ran a good article and Casewell got a written apology for me from the chief constable.

Meanwhile, Customs and Excise had agreed to an out-of-court settlement of £1,000 per week. They had insisted on 60 post-dated cheques, which I grudgingly handed over to my solicitor. He would have to wait 18 months for his not inconsiderable fee.

Soon it would be 1980. I took Marie to the Canaries for Christmas. As we jetted off, some of the most remarkable events in the financial history of the gold market were about to unfold.

10

While most of the world was recovering from a seasonal hangover, traders in precious metals were enjoying volatility and price swings which even the most ardent bull hadn't dared imagine in his wildest dreams. On 4 January 1980, gold was moving up $5–10 an ounce, an hour. Silver was in a class of its own, often soaring a dollar an ounce in a single session. The Hunt brothers were achieving their self-fulfilling prophecy of cornering the entire world silver market. The bears were getting financially crucified. On the futures exchanges, the deposits required to trade had increased tenfold. The spread between buying and selling had widened enormously, as well, discouraging the private trader. At the peak of the market, the spread between buying and selling on a 10,000-ounce contract of silver in London reached £1 per ounce. A pound an ounce! It was unreal! A punter would face a £10,000 spread locked in against him the moment he traded. You would have got very long odds indeed that silver, which traded in excess of $50 an ounce in January 1980, would trade at less than $5 an ounce the following decade.

All this activity was being relayed to me via the British media while I bathed in Christmas sunshine. I decided to fly back early, to capitalise on the boom. I phoned the *Birmingham Evening Mail* and spoke to Sarah Smith. She took down the details of a huge display buying-in advert to coincide with my arrival back at the office. Pleased with my unexpected budget, she also promised me extensive editorial coverage, for which I was very grateful.

I couldn't believe the speed of the response to the advertising. I was definitely in the right place at the right time. The queues of sellers at my office were enormous. Heavily laden with valuables, the queues extended at one stage right around the corner of my building into the next street; people were waiting to see me for over two hours, paying to jump the queue; fights broke out and spivs tried to buy directly from those in line. Pensioners, housewives, businessmen, knocker boys, villains and thieves all queued up to weigh in their precious metals, scrap gold, silverware, coins, anything. I employed a couple of corps of commissionaires on the door. Some of the local townies, who I knew from nightclubs, were given special treatment and went straight to the front of the queue. I even furnished one or two of them with cash loans, so they could go away and buy in town on my behalf. A chap called Micky Fletcher made a fortune plying his trade on the other queues that were forming outside the jewellers and bullion dealers in town, hustling for the precious metal before it reached the door. He would then come round to me, weigh in his haul, get paid and start again. Years later, our paths would cross again at the races, when he became a rails bookmaker. I was inundated. I was buying in and scrapping Georgian silver, sets of cutlery, soup tureens, gold jewellery, platinum, coin collections, krugerrands and sovereigns like they were going out of fashion. I emptied over three company-sized chequebooks – 240 cheques per book! Miraculously, they all cleared. Every evening I would sort out and carefully weigh the day's purchases, then send my man to the bullion dealers in London early the following morning to cash in my wares. By the following day, the price had moved up again, so instead of making ten grand on my scrap, I'd made fifteen. By the end of January 1980, I'd made over £300,000. Cash. I bought an extremely rare 1933 penny from Richard Williams as a publicity stunt for £25,000 (plus VAT) and went on television with it. That coin was to come back and haunt me 16 years later, when Williams took the stand for the prosecution during a later court case. Lewis was in full-time, writing up the books. Wilson was at full stretch at the bank and kept a special ledger working out the cleared position on my account each day.

The VAT Man Visits

Customs paid in their cheques for a grand every week and they were absorbed unnoticed. I took Marie out most evenings for fine dinners and we hit the clubs. Champagne flowed. I was on a fabulous roll. I say always make the most of a roll because it never lasts. Gravity is very heavy. Within a year I would be living in exile, hiding from my creditors.

The astronomic level that precious metals had reached was about to crumble. Soon, the massive price swings up would become massive price swings down. My physical bullion wasn't affected too much; I had such a comfortable margin built into what I was buying from the public that even when prices fell sharply overnight, I still made a profit, just a smaller one. Of course, on some days there would be a technical rally – the declining market would have a correction, or an up day, and I would have a bonanza once more.

My undoing, again, was to be futures. Still smarting from my experience at the hands of England Futures, where I still felt I was robbed of my multi-million-pound profit, I was keeping an ever-watchful eye on the silver futures market in London.

I formed a company called Leander Commodities and poached an experienced trader called Ronnie Davis from Saville Gordon Group, a publicly quoted property and metals company. We hardly did any business for clients, but opened accounts with reputable City brokers, who were ring-dealing members of the London Metal Exchange and had seats on the American exchanges. Flush from success in my physical dealings, and with glowing bank references, they were eager to offer us excellent dealing commissions and extensive credit terms. Every day, I would listen in on the phone to the hectic trading on the exchange floor, dying to trade.

When silver reached £14 an ounce, I couldn't resist any more. I bought 5 contracts of 10,000 ounces each. (Just so you don't need to work it out for yourself, this amounted to £700,000 worth of silver, with only a fraction of the purchase price paid as a down payment.) And I bought again at £13 an ounce, and again at £12. What the hell was going on? I was now holding, on paper, a quarter of a million ounces of .999 fine silver, for delivery in about three months' time from the London Metal Exchange. If the price fell any further I was in deep shit. My cash reserve was all but extinct, my credit at the brokers was exhausted, and I was right up to my limit at the bank. How the hell did I get so involved? But I couldn't help myself.

The price continued to tumble. In the silver market, it was time for the bears to smell blood, just as the bulls had done months earlier. The Chicago Board of Trade had changed the rules of deliveries to stop the Hunts cornering the market. They began to prohibit the purchase of any further silver contracts – allowing only sell or liquidation orders to be made. Everyone, including some of the directors at the Chicago market, were going short – betting on the price going down, creating an obvious conflict of interests. I was in serious trouble. Down it went like a leaden weight, through support at £10, £9.50, £8.50, £8. Maybe I should have bought more to average down? The trouble was, I'd run out of credit. Maybe I should have sold the lot and gone short?

No way, I believed in silver.

You see, when you have a system, you have to stick with it all the way otherwise you'd be leaving everything to chance, which would never, never do.

I drove home, parked the car, went into the house and poured a large drink. I put a wet towel over my head and sat down to work out my exact financial position.

11

I've done my bollocks.

12

That might sound like an unusual way of putting things, but it's a parlance us traders use. We would never say, 'I've blown thirty grand' or 'I've copped fifty large'; 'I've done my bollocks' or maybe 'I've had a touch' (or won a round of drinks) would be enough. What I am setting out here is the worst ever single loss I have ever handled. The worst loss for me, that is. When you're a trader, 'worst' is a flexible concept – the rules are pushed out every day – but for me, this was the worst loss. On a really bad day, we would just say, 'I've done my bollocks.'

So, 'I'd done my bollocks.' I was salvaging what I could from the wreckage and leaving the country.

Exit to America

13

I didn't sleep that night. I started my adventure by packing a couple of suitcases with my favourite clothes and shoes. HM Customs and Excise did not search my home, luckily for me. On top of the wardrobe in the spare bedroom was hidden an expensive Louis Vuitton briefcase, inside which were secured the share certificates for my holding in FNFC.

I drove to my office. It was 5.20 a.m. I ransacked the safes of gold coins, rare coins, cash, foreign currency and a couple of gold bullion bars. I managed to just fit them in the briefcase. Then I phoned British Airways and booked a one-way first-class flight to Los Angeles using my corporate Visa card. I chose LA for a couple of reasons. Marie had gone there a few weeks earlier and had decided not to come back. Maybe I was hopeful of rekindling the relationship. Who knows? (It turned out she had decided to go it alone.) Another reason was that America's an English-speaking country and quite civilised. Simple as that. My biggest worry at the time was whether I could live with the shame of being labelled a fraud.

Ever the perfect gentleman, I wrote a note to my secretaries explaining I was going away and wouldn't be back. I left them some cash to cover what they were owed in lieu of wages and told them to help themselves to whatever they wanted from the office before the bailiffs got their oar in. I locked up for the last time and headed for the car park with my case of valuables. It was just starting to get light.

There was only one really awkward thing left to do. I drove into town and waited for my father to arrive at his dental surgery. It was only 7.30, so I went into the Albany Hotel for some breakfast. I knew a few people there, having their breakfast and business meetings, just as they would on any normal day. I was on remote control. I remember a greedy pension salesman I knew came over to sell me a financial investment proposition. I promised him I would take out a huge policy, and his eyes lit up at the prospect of a fat commission. I handed him my card. He would no doubt get more and more frustrated trying to get in touch with me over the coming months. Priceless.

At nine o'clock, I went to see my father. I told him that I had to leave the country for a while, and hugged him. He was quite taken aback by my sudden decision, but I promised to keep in touch.

My account was just over eighteen grand in credit, but there was over twelve grand's worth of cheques in the clearing against me, including one of the cheques to Customs. I stopped the lot and arranged to have the eighteen grand available for me to collect at a branch in the City.

Then I drove to New Street Station, parked the car in the short-stay car park, where it would remain unattended for weeks, and took the train to London.

At Euston, I deposited my suitcases at left luggage and took a cab to Richard Williams' shop in the West End. There, I knocked out all the bulky coins from my case for about ten grand, which left me a few better pieces in my stock for a rainy day. The clock was ticking, but so far everything was going well.

I then made my way to the bank to collect the eighteen grand.

A pretty cashier asked how I would like the money. 'All at once, please,' I said. I couldn't help myself.

I went to the foreign exchange desk and bought a further $10,000 in cash using my Visa card again. It cleared. I had just one more call to make in the City. I took a cab to St Swithins Lane, which is a tiny road between buildings in the heart of the City, near to the Bank of England, to attend the premises of NM Rothschild & Sons. I issued them a cheque for over £25,000, which I knew wouldn't clear, and took delivery of 100 krugerrands, each one an ounce of fine gold, which I added to my stash. Then, after collecting my suitcases, I took a cab to Heathrow.

I checked in all my cases at the desk and headed straight to the first-class lounge for a drink. I felt as though I had done a week's work in one morning. I noticed a few chinless wonders and a famous actress already settled in, all helping themselves to the freebies. I helped myself to a glass of champagne, sat down in a comfortable armchair and glanced at the *FT*. It was only 45 minutes to check-in. I saw that FNFC had moved up strongly again the previous day and thought to myself that maybe I should have fronted it out, after all.

My heart missed a couple of beats as two uniformed police officers hovered around the entrance to the lounge, but they were soon diverted on their walkie-talkies to another area of the airport. They called the flight. First class boarded straight away. I was off to America.

On board, I found myself sitting next to Joan Collins. She was reading one of those Wall Street books on how best to make your money grow. I introduced myself as an investment banker. We chatted away about the markets, LA, clubs to go to, restaurants to be seen in, lonely actresses. Within three hours, I knew all there was to know about LA. We drank chilled champagne and ate fine food. Stretching out in my seat, I tried to add up in my mind what the stash in the hold came to, but for some reason I had a mental block and couldn't arrive at a figure. It was enough to keep me in LA style for a couple of years, that was for sure, but I had already decided that I would set up an operation there, as soon as possible, to generate more money.

The financial quagmire I had left behind in England was disappearing from my mind almost as quickly as the plane was crossing the Atlantic.

From the air, Los Angeles, the City of Angels, resembles what I imagine would be a Lego dreamland for a town planner; it's a blank board upon which a young child has neatly planted rows of Monopoly houses, like carefully manicured shrubs. All the streets are parallel. It's order and discipline. And crime and plastic materialistic inhabitants, perverts and smog.

We landed gently. I collected my luggage from the carousel and my stash, and I made it through Customs without a hitch. Joan Collins said farewell and recommended I stay at the Beverly Hills Hotel. 'All the stars use the Polo Lounge, dear – maybe I'll see you there for cocktails – I could introduce you to a few friends.' She smiled and waved goodbye. I jumped into a waiting cab, settled on the back seat and instructed the cabbie to take me to the Beverly Hills Hotel. As we pulled out of LAX, I saw Joan Collins step into a long stretch limousine and speed off.

My driver was a chubby, balding, sweaty 50-year-old Yank. He chewed gum and drove with one hand on the wheel, his hirsute free arm resting on the back of the passenger seat. Kim Carnes' 'Bette Davis Eyes' was playing on the stereo.

'Here for a long stay? Business or pleasure? Nice hotel the Beverly, you'll like the Polo Lounge, all the stars use it. You have to queue for ages at the weekends to get in, but you'll be all right, it's an Englishman who runs the door, you know? Did you know that they stock over 50 different kinds of Scotch there? Fifty, Goddamn it!

'Pricey, mind you. Which part of England did you say you were from? London? Do you know Herman Moxton? He's my sister's cousin. Went to London in the '60s, he's in films, sort of. My wife wants me to get into movies, this is only temporary, this driving. Mind you, I've been doing it since 1963. Air all right? I can turn it up a bit if you like.'

Ignoring him, I stared out of the window. I was amazed at the bright, towering hoardings which lined both sides of the road, advertising gum, toothpaste, shampoo, cars – quite a contrast to the leafy suburbia I had left back in England. Had I made one massive mistake coming here? We headed out onto the freeway. The driver didn't let up. 'What's your line of work? Don't tell me, you're into movies. Did I tell you my wife's cousin is . . . '

I feigned sleep, and at last he shut up. Out of the corner of my eye, I saw that we were starting to reach civilisation. The big hoardings were sporadic; we were now arriving in Los Angeles 'proper'. And then Beverly Hills itself.

Palm trees lined the roads. We drove past some very exclusive stores and shops. There were expensive cars everywhere. Everyone was tanned, fit and very well dressed. Even the old-age pensioners sported designer clothes. Finally, we pulled into the driveway of the Beverly Hills Hotel. The pink palace beckoned. A young bellboy took my bags, and I followed him to reception. I was offered a bungalow in the grounds next to the pool at $1,500 a night, but made do with a double at a mere $350 a night. I paid a month in advance on my trusty card and, miraculously, it cleared again.

The room was very comfortable, but slightly over the top. I ran a bath, had a good soak, unpacked and hung up all of my clothes, which had survived the journey remarkably well. Not feeling the slightest bit tired, I changed into a light-blue single-breasted suit, a beige shirt and some loafers. I peeled off $1,000 in cash and locked the rest of the stash in the room safe. I headed for the Polo Lounge. It was a quiet evening, no queue. The door was run by a middle-aged English gentleman who would have looked more at home playing butler deep in the English countryside than here. There was a rumour that he had run the door for years and kept a shoebox full of $100 notes locked in his desk; his post-gratuities from eager queue jumpers. I introduced myself and we started chatting. He told me that the weekends were impossible; that the queue was always full of celebrities waiting for the 'A' tables. I was to appreciate quite quickly that Americans who, in my opinion, are bereft of class, use table positions to determine their status – the 'A' tables at the front of restaurants and bars being used solely by the cognoscenti. Presumably, so they can be recognised by the minions, who have to make do with rear seating. He told me he could look after me; that I was now a regular. I hadn't even been in yet and already I was a regular. I slipped him a century and walked inside. I noticed only a few of the front tables were occupied and that the bar was very long, highly polished and, more importantly, incredibly well-stocked. I sat down at a table, ordered a gin and tonic, and was presented with some dips. I didn't recognise anyone in there, but quite a few young men and women were having themselves paged with annoying frequency, I imagine as a way to get themselves noticed by some famous producer or director and get discovered in Tinsel Town. After a couple of drinks, I decided to go and explore the LA nightlife. I paid my bar bill, which was absolutely extortionate (it included $15 for the dips, which I had hardly touched) and went off in search of some action. The doorman politely acknowledged me as I left, touched his cap and remembered my name. The $100 investment was already paying off.

I had asked the concierge at the hotel to recommend a good bar in town and he said that Carlos 'n' Charlie's was the trendiest place on Hollywood Boulevard, so that's where I decided to venture. The heat of the West Coast summer evening hit me as I stepped from the taxi. I hadn't noticed the hotel's subtle air conditioning until then.

I wandered along the strip. There were bars and restaurants everywhere. High-heeled hookers plied their trade on street corners. Black pimps, who looked as though they spent all morning pumping iron and all afternoon at the orthodontist's investing in 14-carat caps, hustled doorways. Tiny envelopes changed hands for greenbacks. A shiny black BMW convertible, very long on kit, occupied by three Rastas, cruised around, blaring ghetto music. Somehow, it passed me four times.

Carlos 'n' Charlie's, the nightclub. Well, it still takes my breath away. The pink and pale-green colour theme, like Abdullah's racing silks. A pastel green, in fact, but certainly heavier on the pink. The interior designer got the place together on LSD or mushrooms, probably. There are a great many signed photographs on the walls – models, film stars, producers, statesmen.

The place killed me. There were black dudes, mostly with white girlfriends. You didn't see so many white guys with black girlfriends. There were white guys with white girls, though. And, praise the Lord, there were lots of pretty girls by themselves.

The barman called himself Zoro. He shook and poured unpronounceable, exotic and colourful cocktails for the dudes, who stood around, pecked to the nines, sipping through straws and chatting to their Californian blonde babes. I settled on a comfortable bar stool with Abdullah cushion and began on a bottle of champagne. I started drinking slowly from the chilled, frosted glass. One of the black dudes, who I later knew as Victor, was staring at me. Staring, cold bloodshot eyes. He was a dealer: Temazepam, Quaalude, speed, LSD, hash, cut and re-cut coke. He came over, his gold bracelets and chains rattling as he approached the bar. He wore shiny alligator-skin shoes, pale-blue flares and a silky, heavily patterned shirt. He had gold and diamond rings on almost every one of his big fingers. Victor smiled, a mouth like Fort Knox. He got straight to the point. 'Want a hit?'

I looked away, disinterested. 'No, thank you.' He downed his bourbon, deposited his glass on the bar, hitched up his flares and went off to join his friends to talk about semi-violent crime. I was doing really well in this joint. I was only on my second glass and had already been offered an entire pharmacy.

I held my frosted glass up to the light, the drink sparkling and bubbling in its tank. A beautiful, tanned blonde in a short white dress and high heels walked in and sat next to me at the bar. A 60-odd-year-old gay man, with long, shiny grey hair in a ponytail, went straight up to the bar, crowding the space between us. He was dressed like a teenager and ordered a margarita. 'I love this place,' he said. 'I really love it. It's so fucking pink.' He sailed off. I poured my blonde a glass and introduced myself. I even stood up as she sat down. I charmed. We drank, we danced. We moved, with our drinks, over to a comfortable couch at the back of the club. Victor looked over with his metallic smile. I pulled. My dreams of easy sex in the Californian sunshine were materialising. I had one of those flashes that easy money was to follow, too. Just as the hooker finds her trick, the surgeon his patient, the teacher his pupil, I would find my client. Or he would find me. The cheat was not yet a swindler, but the client was already the greedy and ambitious victim. Out there. Out there, somewhere, just waiting to be cultivated, developed and mugged.

14

In Beverly Hills, I played the part of an English gent with great ease. I'd been going out and about quite a lot. Of course, for the first few weeks I didn't have business or skulduggery on my mind. I visited the sights (a little) and wined and dined (a lot). I shopped on Rodeo, frequented clubs and bars, and pulled the most gorgeous chicks imaginable. Most nights I would hold court in the Polo Lounge before venturing out. This was the holiday of a lifetime. But soon business was to beckon.

One of the extraordinary things about the United States is that just about everyone trades in futures contracts. And I mean everyone. School teachers, bus drivers, dry cleaners – all of them regularly have positions in the commodities market. It's a way of life out there. On every street corner there are big brokerage houses where you can open accounts with great ease and trade bonds, stocks, futures and options on easy terms and with massive leverage. Gold, pork bellies, grains and softs (tropical commodities, such as coffee, sugar and cocoa). They trade the lot. On television, there are entire channels devoted to charting movements in the market; radio programmes provide minute-by-minute updates for those stuck in traffic; on the subway commuters read the *Wall Street Journal,* expertly folded into eighths, held above their head. Most offices and banks have Quottrone machines, relaying up-to-the-minute exchange prices. In Vegas, I was to discover, the brokerage houses had installed courtesy telephones in hotel foyers to generate business. Trading is big bucks. They are light years ahead of us, financially. The only drawback about trading on the West Coast is the time difference between LA and New York. When Wall Street opens at nine o'clock, it's six in the morning in Beverly Hills. You see brokers in LA roller-skating to work in their shirt sleeves at five in the morning! Once business beckoned, my propensity to rise early would be severely tested.

One night in May 1980 I found myself back in Carlos 'n' Charlie's. It was my fourteenth visit. I needed the company. I'd grown fond of Victor, with his flared trousers, gold teeth and mobile pharmacy. Even Zoro had grown on me. He popped open a bottle of Veuve Clicquot as soon as I walked in. Still no sign of Mr Client, though, but I was certain he would appear on the scene soon. I was getting hit hard with the bills at the hotel. My stash would be lucky to see the year out at the rate I was going. Of course, I'm never concerned about my spending. Necessity is the mother of invention.

I left Carlos 'n' Charlie's around midnight. The strip was in full swing. Peak-trading period. Discarded fast-food wrappers and newspapers blew along the gutters in the light breeze that cut through the late-night heat. I headed back to the hotel, paying off the taxi at the end of the long drive. I walked up the tree-lined incline, deeply inhaling the fresh night air. And then I found him, right there on my doorstep, sitting at the bar in the Polo Lounge. This was going to be so easy, almost a shame to take his money. Well, not quite.

'I'm suing them for non-compliance and unauthorised trading,' he was telling the barman. I sipped on my gin and tonic. I knew all about unauthorised trading. I used it a lot, that technique. I'd hit form at just the right time. As long as I maintained my composure, and feared no one, this was going to be just so easy.

'Good evening, Mr Goldman, and how are you this splendid evening?' It was my trusty English doorman. 'Mr Goldman is an investment banker from London and conducts business on behalf of the Bank of England, among others. He might be able to help you with your little problem. Mr Goldman, meet 'Henry Bloomberg'.' I smiled, stood up and shook hands with Henry. His hand was damp, clammy and limp. We moved to a quiet table, away from the bar.

'Mr Goldman,' Henry began.

'It's all right,' I assured him, 'please call me Nigel.'

He cleared his throat, a small bead of perspiration appearing high on his forehead. 'Nigel, may I join you for a drink and start from the beginning?'

He talked, non-stop, for three hours. It's amazing, isn't it, how, given the green light, people will go into overdrive, remote control? I'm a good listener, always have been. Don't ask me why, but maybe I enjoy listening. Anyway, I had an ulterior motive to listening to this story. Henry opened his heart up to me, went through all his trading in detail. His silver trading reminded me of the positions I had left behind in England, although mine were small fish compared to the volumes Henry had been trading in. All in all, he had blown $10.2 million betting on gold and silver, the problem being that it wasn't all his own money. Now, don't get me wrong, he wasn't skint or completely tapped out, he had plenty of financial muscle left in him. But he didn't feel good about losing that sort of money and would have dearly loved to get it back. Except that he didn't quite know how. He needed his hand held and some steering in the right direction.

Could I convince him that, given sufficient capital, I could recoup his losses for him in the markets? Could I persuade him to trust me, a man he had just met, to speculate with his further millions? It wasn't going to be too difficult in the end because Henry had very much liked what he had heard from me. In fact, he had already made up his mind. Rapacity had got the better of him. I had met Mr Client.

The very next day the phone rang.

'Good morning, Nigel,' said Henry Bloomberg.

Good morning, mug, I thought.

'Meet me for lunch at L'Orangerie in Rodeo Drive – I have a proposition I would like to put to you,' he said.

'Would 12.30 be an appropriate time?' I enquired politely.

It was happening.

15

Three or four amazing things happened during lunch that May day. First, I bumped into Joan Collins again. She looked stunning in an off-the-shoulder dress. I introduced her to Henry. He seemed so utterly impressed. Second, I ate a fabulous lunch. A lobster cocktail served on a bed of crushed ice and lettuce in a silver bowl, poached salmon, a very good Chablis and coffee with petit fours to finish. Third, Henry paid the bill. It came to over $600.

Oh yes, there was a fourth thing. While I was starting on my salmon, Henry promised me a cheque for $2 million to trade with. Of course, I played the whole thing down, not wishing to give away my extreme excitement and joy at the prospect of handling such a vast investment in the market for someone I had only just met. So, remembering that you can never ask for too much, and bearing in mind what my dear old mother used to say to me – 'you can always go down, you can't go up' – I told Henry that I would let him know. I made out that the sort of sums I was used to handling on behalf of my major clients and the Bank of England were in the tens of millions; I would need a very good incentive to sacrifice my time and expertise on one man. After that, Henry was even more determined to secure my services as his sole trader and investment adviser, and proposed that he would rebate me 25 per cent of any profits I made in the market as a commission. I promised to think it over and give him my decision within the week.

I had to find myself some wheels as the cab fares were killing me. I had to sort out an apartment because the hotel bills were killing me. I had to start renting some office space, otherwise Henry wouldn't come out to play.

First, I decided to knock out what was left of my stash. I found a coin dealer to dispose of my bullion, krugerrands and numismatic items. I got a good price, a healthy profit on cost. Funny that. I still had the instinct to be aware of what they had cost on paper, even though I hadn't paid for them. Next, I attended the premises of Drexel Burnham Lambert, the stock and futures brokers, and disposed of my holding in FNFC. They had rallied strongly since my arrival in the States. I felt sad having to dispose of them. I really believed that they were going to do something astonishing. Later, I would sickeningly realise that my gut feeling about FNFC had been spot on. Drexel were very helpful and their president, no less, unaware of my background, recommended a bank to me, so I could open an account with their cheque. I persuaded him to telephone ahead, so that I had a contact to meet when I arrived there. I also promised them some brokerage business once I got myself set up in business.

High Stakes

I decided to go and open an office. I had seen a penthouse suite advertised for rent in Century City, one of LA's most prestigious business communities. The office was on a sun-kissed boulevard and occupied the top floor of a bank building. The suites were divided into various sizes, and I chose one with a picturesque view of LA Country Club, with an adjoining boardroom and secretarial suite. The reception, which was reached by special express elevator, was sumptuous, and I felt convinced that the office would impress Henry and any other clients that came my way. The rent was frighteningly expensive, but I didn't expect to be there for too long.

Next call, the bank. I opened my account with ease, and its president, impressed with what he had heard from the unsuspecting and well-intentioned Drexel, promised me a gold MasterCard and agreed to mail a chequebook to my new office. I had also organised for business cards to be hastily run off at a local printer's.

I was back in the game.

Tomorrow, I would find some wheels, rent an apartment, furnish my office, find some stooges to fill up the desk space, employ an attractive secretary, and sit down and work out exactly how to deal with Henry Bloomberg.

I had my eye on a smart car showroom that I had passed a few times on my travels. It was stocked with Porsches, Ferraris, Mercs and Rollers. I walked in and browsed around. Within ten minutes, I had agreed to purchase a 1980 Rolls Silver Shadow II, complete with phone and extra-thick US-style rubber bumpers, for $35,000. I promised to get a bank draft and pick up the car within a few days.

My next job was to find an apartment. I was absolutely spoilt for choice! I viewed a few and settled, rather hurriedly, on a top-floor flat in an old building in Beverly Hills. It was beautifully furnished and had a magnificent roof garden; it overlooked Hollywood and I could see the famous white sign in its full glory.

I had settled into my new home and office, found my 'staff'

and was ready to phone Henry. It seemed to me the adventure of a lifetime was about to start.

Sitting at my office desk, which I had moved ever so slightly towards the full length of the window, I managed to spy on Henry Bloomberg as he played his round of golf at the country club, 30 floors beneath me, across the street. He was at the fifth tee, dressed like Rupert Bear, whisking the air with violent practice swings. I could hardly bring myself to look. One of his golfing partners joined him. Henry stopped swinging, instead pointing the polished head of the driver at his hapless victim. Some sort of argument seemed to be brewing. I scanned my binoculars slowly across the greens, quietly wondering what possessed people to pay half a million bucks to join such exclusivity, and then to get up at half five in the morning to play golf. I noticed a group of Japanese at the eighth, and a couple of overweight players taxiing towards the eighteenth in an upmarket electric buggy.

I kitted my office out with the help of 'Robert Jones', who was in office equipment, sort of. Over large cocktails, I let him know what was required for the illusion and he obliged, frighteningly cheaply. The office had the feel of a bank's dealing room – rows of price screens and monitors (a large percentage of which didn't work), banks of telephones (a large percentage of which weren't connected) and half a dozen newly employed youths in $50 suits, sitting around waiting for the cue call. On my desk, I had placed the enormous corporate chequebook which had kindly been mailed over. We had practised it a few times by that stage, the cue call.

As soon as Henry stepped out of the elevator into reception, the receptionist was to buzz us through the signal – three bleeps on one of the phones that was actually connected, and my 'dealing room' was to spring to life. My guys would start yelling down the phones, tapping at their price-screen keyboards, gesticulating wildly at each other, and pretending to be speaking and placing orders to buy and sell with New York, Chicago, London and Paris. We were to give Henry a taste of all of this for a couple of minutes, then I would slide him into the boardroom and relieve him of his funds. I was expecting it to happen that day. He had promised to call in after golf.

I picked up my binoculars again and refocused on Henry. He was on the eighth tee and had just hit a great shot, the ball climbing high into the air and landing well down the fairway for a possible three. I wondered if he had the cashier's cheque in his golfing trouser pocket.

I didn't have to wait long to find out. Just before ten o'clock, we got the three bleep signal. We sprang into action. The boys were at full crescendo, yelling and trading with their silent partners as our visitor was escorted in. I looked up from my desk straight into the eyes of my old solicitor Rupert Casewell.

'Thought I'd pop by and relieve you of the fees cheque you owe me, old boy.' His eyes were fixated on the oversized chequebook. I didn't have time to work out or ask how he had found me, or what he was doing in the United States; I couldn't afford to let him spoil the preparations I had gone to so much trouble over for Mr Client. I tore out a cheque and virtually dragged him out of the office into the boardroom.

'How long are you planning to stay in LA for, Rupert?' I enquired, eager to get rid of him, almost at any cost.

'There's a legal conference out here, I'm representing our Bar association. Did you know they were thinking of extraditing you? But they gave up in the end, there was no value in it, according to the Director of Public Prosecutions. It comes to $8,800, by the way. My fee, $8,800. Looks as though you can well afford it by the amount of business you seem to be conducting.'

I paid him, he left and I went back to my post in the office, which had quietened down again after the false alarm. Then, at last, came the three bleeps we had been waiting for, and in he walked, still attired in his golfing trousers. My $2 million, my client, my future. We bowled him over, I must admit. They were very good, the boys. I took Henry into the boardroom and sat him down. He went into his trouser pocket and produced the money. A cashier's cheque for two million bucks, made out to me. There was very little left to say; the whole thing felt like a bit of an anticlimax. Almost. We arranged to speak at the end of each day's trading, just to monitor how things were going, and agreed to meet for lunch every Friday to review the week. He gave me one of his damp, limp handshakes. As he left, I almost felt sad for Henry – no one in the world but queues of rogues waiting to relieve him of his precious millions. Still, as they say: when you find one, go straight to the front of the queue, for as sure as eggs are eggs, there will be a long queue waiting behind you if you don't.

I started trading with my big-bucks cheque right away. Well, after showing Henry the way out; down he went, 30 floors in the express elevator, with not even the slightest frown on his brow.

I was going to be playing big time, the stakes had risen substantially. I put a million bucks into my trading account for margin. I got a direct phone link to a broker on the floor, who would execute my order for a pittance. I sometimes wonder how they make it pay. He was quick, the floor broker, and his order-taking phone clerk was just by the precious metals pit. I could hear the yelling and screaming from the pit as I traded over the phone. Some days, I'd stay on the phone all morning, with my open line, trading.

Waking early, before the West Coast sun rose slowly over the Pacific, I would drag myself from my bed and into the Rolls, then drive regally to the office to be seated at my screen by 6 a.m. Some mornings, I would drag myself out of Carlos 'n' Charlie's car park at 4 a.m. Theodore, the owner of the joint, reserved me a nice pitch, and I would drive myself, half-drunk, up to the underground office car park. I'd suffer the most unbelievable pangs of nausea and vertigo as I took the express lift to the penthouse floor of the building.

Futures trading dominated my life. I was trading the way some people were doing heroin. But cheating wasn't uppermost in my mind. Not then, anyway. It haunted me, at the back of my mind, as some form of security back-up for a rainy day. It might come in handy one day, that was all. But come on, admit it, what would you have done in that position? Fly straight home with all the money (it had crossed my mind, on more than one occasion) or play with it? I wanted, needed, to play. To participate in the world's most exciting game. All Henry had done was to bankroll me for the game. It was a bet to nothing. I had been told – by various schoolteachers, headmasters, magistrates and many girlfriends – that I sailed close to the wind. I took this, of course, as a compliment.

Like the addict progressing from a joint to Class A drugs, I was soon going to go into overdrive on my trading – not satisfied with just the early morning sessions, I would start to follow the world markets throughout the night, as well. I was even discovering little-known markets, to keep my hand in at the weekends. Kuala Lumpur tin futures or some such nonsense. It's a shame Betfair hadn't been established then. I would have to have a position in something, all the time, just to keep my adrenalin going. I was buying and selling, winning and losing, copping and blowing. Good days turned into excellent days and bad days into good days as far as Mr Client was concerned. I'd keep him happy at our weekly meetings with voluminous computerised printouts of trading positions. He would lift them up with his clammy hands, fold them into A5 sections and place each one in his leather case. I wondered where on earth he was storing all the information? I imagined he had a cupboard stuffed full of bankers boxes at home.

Anyway, I was planning a trip to New York at this time, as a guest of my brokers, to observe the exchange floor at first hand. The exchange. I could hardly wait. First, Richard Evans was flying in to pay me a social visit. I'd promised to entertain him for a couple of weeks as my guest and had planned a trip to Vegas. I was aware that he'd probably relate how I was doing in the land of opportunity to the people back home, so I was keen to impress. Roll out the red carpet for Richard.

16

In September 1981 as I was on my way to LAX to pick up Richard, I noticed an office on Santa Monica Boulevard which promoted Caesars Palace in Las Vegas. Parking the Roller outside, so that they couldn't help but notice it, I strolled in, puffing on a Cohiba cigar. Seated behind the desk was a well-tanned, middle-aged man with more lines on his face than British Rail had across the UK, who looked as though he had seen plenty of action in his life. Tapped out over the years, his job was to suss out the credit worthiness of mug punters who wanted to go to Las Vegas to get entertained, and fleeced. Unlike the British, Americans are able and keen to offer extensive credit terms to gamblers frequenting their casinos and will spend lavishly on them for their stay in Vegas, even going to the trouble of flying in their precious high-rollers on private jets. A couple of unbelievably gorgeous girls hung around the office, not doing too much. At least if you did your cobblers in this joint, you did it in style. I came straight to the point.

'I'm booked into Caesars Palace for a long weekend and I have a guest with me from England. I thought it appropriate to come in and enquire whether it would be possible to obtain a line of credit from your good selves. Here are my bank details, I'm sure that you will have no problem with them.'

'And what sort of figure did you have in mind, sir?'

'One hundred thousand dollars,' I answered nonchalantly.

He promised to phone when his enquiries were completed, within 24 hours, and hinted that if the line was extended to me I could look forward to VIP treatment and a suite upgrade at the hotel for myself and my guest. Naturally, all food and drink would be complimentary. Casinos love to entertain punters who they think they can fleece, or those who have won (so that they get their money back). As I hadn't traded with them before, they thought I fell into the mug category. I eagerly awaited his reply.

Richard's flight touched down softly in LAX, right on time, and I was there at the gate to meet him. He looked fresh after the long flight, not in the least tired, so after carefully storing his luggage in the trunk of the Rolls, I suggested a drink or three. We pulled into the long, now familiar drive of the Beverly Hills Hotel. Richard was gobsmacked with the environment, but the best was yet to come. There was one hell of a long queue at the entrance to the Polo Lounge and I promise I'm not making this up when I tell you that Michael Caine, Dudley Moore and Jack Nicholson all stood patiently waiting in the queue for their precious 'A' tables. And can you believe what my trusty doorman did? He raised his arms above his head like a tick-tack man at the races (he even had his tick-tack white gloves on), pronounced my name at the top of his voice, ushered Richard and me straight into the lounge, and sat us at a 'reserved' table. It was priceless. I was completely blown over. Richard couldn't believe it; we were being treated like royalty. I ordered a bottle of champagne. After a couple of glasses, Richard had regained his composure and couldn't help but glance over his shoulder, through the large, plate-glass windows, to the stars still lining up outside, thoughts of shrinks, analysts and plastic surgeons possibly playing on their minds.

We spent a couple of days in LA before setting off for Vegas. Caesars had phoned, confirming my line of credit – 100K. We were each promised lavish suites, as much food and drink as we could consume and the company of showgirls, who would naturally feature on our list of priorities.

If anyone ever suggests that you drive from Los Angeles to Las

Vegas, don't do it. Don't even think about it. Put the idea completely to one side. Go and lie on a beach somewhere until the urge goes away. Don't attempt this drive even in a luxury car, not even a Rolls-Royce. I'm well qualified to impress upon anyone the sheer stupidity of attempting such a trip. I did it, or rather we did it. Richard and I. I can tell you that my gleaming Roller depreciated by 75 per cent on the trip. The problem isn't the roads (they're fine), or the distance (it's not really that far), it's the heat (and it's scorching and unmerciful). The journey passes through what is known as Death Valley, a particular stretch of desert so named because of its extreme environment. We made it through – just. Coughing, spluttering and overheating, like some old tug's engine whining to a standstill. The poor car just made it to the entrance of Caesars. My gleaming, shining investment looked like a pile of shit.

Still, Caesars Palace. What a joint. Keen to relieve me of my hundred grand credit line, they went to great trouble and expense to make sure we were very well looked after, indeed. We were each allocated suites on the top floor. In mine, there was a lounge the size of a baseball pitch (well almost). A sofa which would seat 20 was surrounded by tables full of fruit and flowers. There was an enormous television set, with 50 channels at least, a sound system, a bar, a bedroom with a huge circular bed and mirrors on the ceiling. The bathroom had a tub which would cleanse a rugby team after a muddy game. All the curtains to the long windows were operated with the flick of a switch, and there was the most magnificent view of Vegas. Over the top, or what? Richard decided to have a rest, so I ventured downstairs to the gaming floor to get a feel for the place.

As soon as you walked into the timeless surroundings of the foyer, you were greeted with action. On the reception desk, there were banks of phones for booking shows, hiring limos, organising flights and getting general tourist information. All the major brokerage houses and stockbrokers had courtesy telephones through which punters could book their trades. Account opening forms were available from plastic dispensers. There were hundreds of slots everywhere. Greedy, overweight tourists pumping them with their plastic cups of quarters and dollars in a feeding frenzy. The casino proper was situated just behind the reception area, and what a casino! The sheer scale of everything was hard to take in. Unlike gaming establishments in the UK, which might have ten or so tables, this place stretched for miles. There were rows and rows of roulette tables, blackjack tables, punto banco and craps. Most tables were in serious action. Smart croupiers, very experienced, dealt the games. Pit bosses supervised the action and nodded to the croupiers when punters requested more chips. Like magic, a debit chit would be produced for signature to confirm their transaction, while stacks of bright cash chips would change hands. I looked closer, as chips with '100' marked on them, running through the pillars like a stick of rock, were pushed towards punters. A senior member of staff looked on unimpressed, arms folded. On a nearby roulette table, a pretty croupier bulldozed through a mountain of losing chips, discarding them into the automatic chip-sorting machine. Managers kept an eye on the pit bosses and the 'eye in the sky', the discreetly placed overhead cameras, kept an eye on the managers. Beautiful girls, 'shills', sat at most of the high-value tables, enticing gamblers to play. These girls were employed by the house to keep the games in action, and they played with house chips, provided for them by the casino. I noticed one of them eye up a punter who was winning heavily, and the thought did cross my mind that the shills may provide other services as well. I wandered over to a baccarat table, where a group of extremely wealthy-looking Middle Eastern gentlemen were involved in a high-stakes game. They were all incredibly well dressed, and wore expensive jewellery and watches. A balding croupier flicked the cards over with a flat wooden palette.

'Bank draws, eight to the bank, the bank wins.'

About a million dollars' worth of plaques changed hands, in the casino's favour. The players placed their bets for the next hand, all of them backing the 'punto' again. This time the punto drew a natural nine, the highest hand, and the money went back to the gamblers again. I took a seat and asked for $100,000 worth of chips. I relished accumulating bets, letting my winnings ride, so that they soared to ever-greater heights. Or not, of course. A few glossy, high-value plaques were pushed over to me, and the white chit appeared for signature. I had a plan. I made up my mind that these well-oiled players were about to lose their shirts, so I decided to play against them – in other words take the side of the bank, or, in this case, the casino. This is known as 'ghosting' and works quite easily. It goes like this. Imagine you are watching someone play in a casino; he's perspiring heavily, he's drunk, he's diving into his inside jacket pocket for some more money after every spin of the wheel or turn of the card. He's chasing. He's under pressure. This is the man who is going to do his proverbial bollocks, isn't it? You'd love to be the casino, wouldn't you, sending him home absolutely skint, not even his bus fare left in his pocket. Well, ghosting puts you in the casino's position, almost. You play the opposite to the unlucky punter – he bets red, you play black; he goes for the punto, you play banco; he plays 'don't win' on the craps table, you play the 'win' line. And so on. Of course, it's not quite as secure as having your own casino because of the little bit of tax involved in baccarat, but it's as good as you're going to get. In Vegas. So, I decided to ghost these high-rollers.

God knows how long I played for. It seemed to be all over in an instant, but it must have been for hours. The fortunes of the team fluctuated wildly for most of the session, until the casino finally started to grind them down. This was the window of opportunity I had been waiting for. I increased my stakes to $5,000, and then $10,000 a hand, as they hit the final run of bad luck which would wipe them out. On their very last hand, when their chips were all but exhausted, I had my biggest bet of the night against them – $35,000. It won. I had won just over $500,000. I tipped the crew the odd change, some $8,500! It was time to go up to the suite, have a shower and change, and go in search of some fun. But as I got up from the table, all of a sudden I felt completely drained. I had no idea at all what time it was. The one thing about casinos, especially in Vegas, is that they are purposely kept at the same temperature and brightness 24 hours a day. You wouldn't know if it was day or night. There are no clocks. It transpired, from the diamond encrusted Rolex on a fellow player's wrist, that it was five in the morning. I had been playing for nine hours, solid.

I retired to the suite for some well-earned rest. As any punter will tell you, waking up the day after a large win is one of the most pleasant experiences imaginable. As you slowly adjust to daylight, the memories of the previous evening's play gradually flow back into your mind, until you wake fully to the lovely, warming, comforting feeling of the big win. This happened to me at around noon, when the phone by my bed gently purred, and Richard announced that he had discovered a couple of beautiful, fun girls he was bringing round for lunch. I had half an hour to get ready.

I kept my win quiet. For the first hour or two, anyway. After I had attended to my second glass of champagne, I loosened up a little. Richard had found two beauties the night before – while I was beavering away at the tables – and they were lapping up the attention, as we told them stories of leafy England, Beverly Hills and us. I got the impression that I was in for a good night. Richard had a self-satisfied look on his face, like he had been spoilt by these two women over the past few hours. Still, I wasn't going to grumble, these two were absolutely stunning. Although it was only lunchtime, in the cotton-wool environment of the time warp we were cocooned in, they didn't look out of place in revealing evening dresses. In Vegas, anything goes. You can have lunch at dinner time or breakfast at 3 a.m. Waiters are quite used to providing any choice at any time of the day or night. Alcohol flows freely (at the tables, as well) and no one raises an eyebrow if you drink champagne in the morning or a bloody Mary for tea.

Exit to America

Now, let's get one thing absolutely clear, crystal. Caesars Palace was not, and I repeat not, getting back my half of a million dollars, and that's final. You see, I really did enjoy winning much, much more than I hated losing. Forget all that nonsense you've heard about people wanting to lose; I was going to return to Los Angeles with their cheque in my grubbies; they weren't going to get it back from me. No way, instead we'd stay a few more days, enjoy the girls, see the shows and buy lots of goodies. Gambling was now off the menu – for the time being, anyway. We'd see how far Caesars would go to try and get their money back.

We didn't have long to wait. Upon returning to the suite, there was the most enormous bouquet of flowers (with the casino manager's compliments), a magnum of champagne (with the bar manager's compliments) and a tin of caviar (with the restaurant manager's compliments), all prominently displayed. There was a also a note from the hotel manager to say that the hotel's limo was available to take us to any shows we wanted to see and that tickets could be booked for us (with the entertainment manager's compliments) at the end of the phone. We took full advantage of their generosity, I can assure you, and Richard had done me proud with his choice of girls. As we left the hotel to go and see Sinatra perform, I noticed that the same crew of baccarat players were back in action at the table, this time elbowed in by a gang of excited Chinese punters. We had a memorable time, seeing Sinatra and some other excellent shows, and wined, dined and screwed like royalty. As we flew back to LA, my cheque for $500,000 still in my wallet, I realised just how small my win was in real terms. Stories buzzed round the plane of high-rollers who had dropped millions on the strip, my not inconsiderable win melting into insignificance as we approached LA.

Talking of Rollers, I dumped mine with a dealer in Vegas for a third of what I paid for it. That's the price of vanity, I'm afraid.

17

A private detective who had been working for Henry and whom I happened to become acquainted with later in my life told me that, after Henry had blown his lump on precious metal futures, he'd taken a strict stance and disciplined himself. He had started reading Chinese books on mind, strength and investment strategy. By combining the various pieces of information that he gleaned from these publications, he had come up with a unique investment plan and formula, namely only to invest in companies (or people) with seven letters in their names. Hence, his portfolio at the time included names like Amstrad, Fortune, Pepsi Co., Textron, Entergy – and, of course, Goldman.

My detective friend told me he had taken to standing on his head for over 20 minutes each day, trying to keep his mind clear of everything except business. Henry could be seen through the window, trying to make some sense of the voluminous computerised printouts I had presented him with at our weekly luncheons.

It would later be revealed that Henry had a secret, though, which haunted him, like some ghostly persona, waiting to grow and spring into life like a cancer. He seemed to be anxious, like he had continuous butterflies in his stomach.

He had been involved in a $30 million bond scam some nine months earlier and, at the time, was in a position that most people can only dream of – except that for him, his dream was turning into a nightmare as the queue of people investigating the bond fraud grew daily: the IRS, the SEC, the Feds, to name a few. When the case was taken up by the media, it was revealed that since his path had crossed with that of a man called 'Irving

Simpson', his life had changed dramatically. Irving had stolen some bonds from a major financial institution some years earlier. Bonds are IOUs issued by companies and governments to raise money. The interest rate is fixed in advance, and on maturity – in anything from 15 to 30 years – the issuer also agrees to repay the bond's full face value. However, bonds can also be traded and ownership can change. When that happens, the bond's transfer agent, in this case a major national bank where Irving Simpson worked, is supposed to issue a new certificate and tear up the old one, something that didn't happen in this case. Instead, the bank allowed the bonds to pile up in its storerooms, which Irving Simpson was in charge of tidying up and keeping clean.

Irving helped himself to the first couple of bonds as souvenirs for his kid's bedroom wall, but when he went to his old school chum's art store to get them framed, the full potential of the hoard was realised. Quite soon after that, Irving was helping himself to handfuls of the bonds, posting them to himself at home from the bank's mailroom in large brown envelopes, thus avoiding discovery in the routine searches on the way out at night.

In theory, the bonds should not have been any use to anyone, but the national bank had made a disastrous mistake: it had neglected to mark the bond certificates with the word 'Cancelled' in big, bold letters. Instead it had perforated the lower corner of the bonds with the bank's initials to indicate that they were worthless. However, when the bonds began to resurface, many institutions mistook these marks as endorsements. Some certificates, Irving found to his delight, bore no marks at all. Irving was well connected enough to get some bonds fenced through contacts, who in turn passed them through their supposedly struck-off attorney friend, Henry Bloomberg (I later found out he had fluffed his Bar exams and used the 'struck-off attorney' label to gain himself some street cred). Henry got himself busy trading the bonds through criminal contacts, based all over the world, whom he had built up through his years as a defence attorney. As a result of Henry's enthusiasm and new-found entrepreneurial flair, the bonds began to surface everywhere – from Britain to France, Germany to Russia. However, wherever investigators looked, the trail always seemed to lead back to Los Angeles, and Henry Bloomberg.

My detective friend told me how Henry had wished he hadn't got so involved, that he had been troubled with the ease in which he was getting through his millions – futures speculation, a few stocks that had gone wrong, the racetrack. Easy come, easy go, they say, but deep down it seemed he longed to get away from it all – to retire in luxury.

He had become suspicious and was convinced he was under surveillance. Probably the usual: the same few people and cars around him on too many occasions, the clicks on the phone. It was about that time I imagine he sat down at his bureau, pulled out some sheets of his pale-blue notepaper and started writing.

18

When I returned to Los Angeles from Las Vegas, I found a note from Henry Bloomberg on the mat. Hand-delivered, in a pale-blue envelope. I ripped it open. Its contents didn't surprise me in the slightest. He wrote that he had had enough, he wanted his positions closed and his investment liquidated. I was amazed, really, that he had lasted so long. Neatly written at the bottom of the letter were the account details of the bankers he wanted his dollar balance wired to. I noted that they were in the Cayman Islands. It always strikes me how the gullible freely volunteer where to send their money – as though they know that you aren't going to be able to fulfil your obligation, but 'just in case you win the lottery, here is where I bank'.

To tell you the truth, I was about $350,000 light – to fulfil my obligations to Henry, that is. That figure included the windfall from Vegas, so I was really well over half a million light.

No worries, though, as I was off on the red-eye that night to New York, to the exchange floor, and I was intending to do some serious trading when I got there. I'd soak up the atmosphere of the place and either make up the shortfall or end up in the hole. Shit or bust. I landed at JFK just after seven o'clock, my eyes gritty from the time lag and the night flight. I took a taxi directly to the Plaza, booked myself in and took a quick shower to freshen up. Then I dressed in a dark-blue Savile Row suit, silk tie and Lobb handmade shoes, and after a quick check in the mirror, downed a black coffee and cabbed it to Comex. I looked the perfect British businessman.

Comex actually stands for Commodity Exchange Incorporated. At the time, it was based at 4, World Trade Center, New York, New York. That's all changed now, of course. I'll always remember the huge surge of adrenalin I felt as I stepped out of the cab that autumn morning and made my way to the exchange floor. I was a guest of the brokers with whom I had conducted my business for the past year or so. They must have thought I was some big player, the amount of action I had got through. For some reason, I had a feeling that that day was going to be rather exceptional. I breathed the cool New York air deep into my lungs and headed for the entrance. Scores of businessmen, brokers, secretaries, runners and clerks rushed past me, eager to get to work and join the action. Some were already dressed in their brightly coloured trading jackets, others arrived in sober suits. 'Locals' – wealthy traders who play on the exchange floor with their own money – turned up to work in limos, not knowing whether their daily gamble would end up with further fortunes, or massive losses.

I headed for the elevator and up to the exchange. As the lift doors opened, I could already hear the brouhaha from the floor. Straight ahead of me was a trophy cabinet containing a large number of silver mementos – for some reason, I thought it a strange thing to have at an exchange entrance. That image of Comex would stay in my mind and in my dreams of the exchange over the coming years.

I had a rough idea of what to expect, but nothing prepared me for the sheer enormity of the exchange. As soon as I was signed in and badged up by my broker's runner, I headed into the trading floor proper. It was the size of two football pitches, with a massive electronic price-monitor board covering the back wall. On this board, the last traded price of gold, silver, copper, cotton, oil and orange juice was displayed. The markets themselves were divided into pits – huge amphitheatre-style affairs with two steps up and six steps down. Traders huddled in the pits, elbowing their way to advantageous vantage points, waving their arms at their opposite numbers and yelling their orders to buy or sell. Buy and sell orders were quickly scribbled onto flip cards, pencil in one hand, cards in the other, while runners handed order tickets into the pit, and clerks hand-signalled the last traded price, and bid and offer to the traders on the phones. To the casual observer, it was amazing that anyone actually knew what was going on, never mind comprehended the millions of dollars that were changing hands at a nod and a wink. Banks of black exchange phones covered both sides of the pits, taking orders from brokerage houses all over the world, while exchange-employed clerks tapped the latest price information into keyboards, for display on the exchange big board, then onward transmission to Reuters, Quottrone and all the real-time world-price services. The whole place reeked of money, lots of it. I was led to the gold pit, where my hosts were situated under miles of phone wires stretched to their limit from the booths to the pit's edge; young, aspiring traders repeating the current market's state to their offices and clients on the other end of the lines. 'Five bid now for December, five to a half, locals buying, five bid again, five trading, five and a half bid now, at six, at six, six bid, six – seven.' Phone clerks yelled to their floor traders, rushing them the order tickets to get in the market quick. Some whistled, others screamed to be heard above the crescendo. I glanced up at the giant price display boards – gold was a couple of dollars better, silver a dime up. I had one of those flashes that the market wouldn't hold today and was looking for a clue to confirm my thoughts, then I would start selling short. I was in my element, convinced I was going to have a day to remember. I often reacted to gut feelings like this when I was trading, but that day, for some reason, the feeling was stronger than ever. It is often said that your first day on the exchange gives you your best day's trading opportunities, and I was absolutely determined to make the best of it.

When we arrived at the gold booth, I was hurriedly introduced to the team, all of them looking haggard, drawn and paranoid, and as though there weren't enough hours in the day. I quickly put faces to names. Jake, the director, was handing his suit jacket to one of his minions, while he donned his blue trading jacket complete with initialled and numbered trading badge. He was glancing through a printout of his previous day's trading statements (I noticed, by peering over his shoulder, that he kept over a million dollars in T-bills in his account). I cleared my throat. 'How do you see the market today, Jake?'

'Lower, sharply lower. Unless we make new highs in the next 20 minutes or so, we're going lower. There's a lot of sell paper out there and stops just below where we are at the moment.'

I wandered over to the silver pit, my temporary trader badge giving me freedom to roam the entire exchange floor. Girls with books of graph paper surrounded the silver pit, plotting every market move with noughts and crosses. This analysis was later used to produce charts for price history information and movement predictions. I discovered there is a huge industry in analytical services.

I quickly introduced myself to my silver broker. He was about 30, had close-cropped hair and chewed gum. He was standing right at the edge of the pit, by the rail, bidding $9.25 for a couple of contracts of December silver. 'We're just about holding here,

Nigel. I think a little selling will push us over the cliff.' This was the clue that I was looking for, and I noticed that he was holding quite a lot of sell paper, just below the market. He had a ticket to sell 100 contracts (on stop) at $9.12 and a further hundred at $9. I whispered in his ear 'sell 100 at market'. He held both his hands up in the air and yelled, 'December at 24.' He sold 20 right away, and then a couple of locals, immediately smelling blood in the pit, joined in the selling. 'December at 23, December at 20,' he yelled, and we got the rest of the contracts away. Now, everyone was joining in the selling frenzy, and the market started to look vulnerable, the mini-avalanche starting to develop into free fall. I noticed that we were approaching the stops in the market, a sure sign that we were going even lower still. A small aggressive trader, who looked to be in his early 20s, positioned just at the back of the pit by his firm's phone booth, now started selling heavily, gesticulating wildly with his arms, his voice hoarse from yelling. I shorted the market again, in size, around $9.15, just above the stops, which I was convinced would be hit any second now. Sure enough, moments later, the stops were hit, and I pressed my action to the tune of a further couple of hundred contracts at all levels down to around $9, convinced that the market would break. I had lost count of how many lots I had sold short, so I grabbed my man's flip cards and did some quick calculations. I was in for 840 contracts, or 4.2 million ounces! Every ten cents in my favour made me $420,000. As soon as I had worked this out, I glanced over my shoulder to notice that the market was coming back, a little. The locals were eager to lock in their profits and were slowly covering their positions. $9.04, $9.05, $9.06, $9.07. I could hardly bear to watch, but the roar of the action and trading left me in no doubt that we were rallying and my hard-fought gains were slowly eroding. I suddenly felt sweat on my palms and my mouth was as dry as flock wallpaper, but somehow I didn't panic. I felt certain we would go lower again and test the all-important $9 level. In a far corner, behind the silver pit, there was a small section cordoned off behind a screen where traders go to have a smoke. A couple of locals were puffing on large cigars. I ventured over to catch my breath and have a rest. I was hyperventilating, the enormity of my position starting to sink in. I was now at the point of highest risk. Everyone was looking for the market to go lower again, but we were running out of time with only 20 minutes to go until the close. At this point, the market was only open in the morning, but still the strange effect gambling had on my sense of time was apparent: just like I had unwittingly gambled my way through the whole night in a Vegas casino, that morning had vanished in a flash. I looked back into the pit. The bidding was much more sporadic now, and far weaker, everyone eyeing each other cautiously, treading carefully, anxious not to make a mighty blunder with their next move. Then, all of a sudden, the market hesitated at $9.07 and the locals smelt blood again. The respite was over, it was time to test the lows once more. Very quickly, the market got offered down to $9.02 again, the young trader, still by the phones, got his signal. 'December at 0,' he yelled. The pit traded briefly at $9 even, then my man went into the market to dump his 100 contracts on stop (God help his client) and, within a second, we broke $9. The big board changed $9 to $8 and we were in new territory, trading at $8.98, $8.96, $8.95. Price display screens displayed the new levels all over the world as the scramble to unload began. This was, without doubt, turning out to be the trade of a lifetime: $8.93, $8.92, $8.90. The selling didn't lighten up, either. I looked up at the big board again. The weakness in the silver pit was now spilling over into the other precious metals, and gold and platinum started to crumble. I looked around and saw Jake sell gold heavily at $430 and quickly re-buy at $426, in what seemed like an instant. I knew I had milked my luck for all it was worth and, with less than ten minutes to go until close, I decided to cover my positions and take my profit. The market spewed yet again, all the way down to $8.72, as the last of the punters gave up. I cautiously gave the instruction. My man did a great job in the pit, crossing orders, bidding for 20 or so contracts, and then immediately withdrawing, waiting for selling to come in again. It was a bit of a roller-coaster ride down there, but we got out, of the whole lot, between $8.74 and $8.82, great fills. I had made some serious bucks – it turned out to be over $1 million dollars – in total.

That night I partied like a millionaire, even though I didn't know I was one then. I lived and partied like a millionaire anyway, always had done. It was Pablo Picasso who once said, 'I would like to live like a poor man, with lots of money.' I had spent the past few years (though it felt like a lifetime) living like a rich man but with no money – now that takes courage (and considerable skill).

We started the evening with Louis Roederer Cristal champagne at the Plaza. Jake joined us briefly, but soon left when the mood became riotous. I then took the floor traders to a Mexican nosh up, followed by New York's 'in' club Studio 21. We drank and danced into the early morning.

I became a legitimate millionaire at precisely 8.20 a.m. Eastern Standard Time. That relates to 5.20 in the morning on the West Coast, about the same time that the asset forfeiture and seizure squad of the Los Angeles Police Department, in the company of the Securities and Exchange Commission (SEC), and officers from the IRS and FBI were surrounding the Bel Air mansion of Henry Bloomberg. It was reported that their raid went like clockwork. After stunning Max, Henry's Rottweiler, with a dart gun, the officers smashed their way into the house through the plate-glass window of his drawing room. Henry was asleep in his bed as the officers burst into his bedroom. They allowed him to dress then he was led away in handcuffs. Police officers seemed satisfied that a news cameraman for a national TV channel was there to capture the entire incident on film. During the rest of the day, officers ransacked Henry's house from top to bottom for evidence and to locate any assets which could be immediately frozen with their court injunction.

In New York, I woke up at 8.23, late for me, but without a

hangover. I was slightly unsteady on my feet as I made it to the bathroom. I turned on the television, just in time to catch the end of the morning news, showing Mr Client being led away in cuffs. I could hardly believe what I was seeing. My mind struggled to comprehend what was going on. I was thinking in overdrive. I needed to act quickly. Really quickly. In no time at all, the authorities would discover that Henry had large sums invested with me, and the trail would quickly lead to my broker's account on the exchange floor, an account which now held in excess of $1 million. As he was led away into custody, I imagined Henry Bloomberg would try to keep a very close eye on me for the rest of his life. I still owed him over $300,000 after all.

I got under the shower, the hot needles penetrating my scalp as I tried to figure out exactly what to do. There was no choice in the matter, only one move to make. In a similar style to what I had done a year or so earlier, I was going to grab the cash and run.

Over the years, whilst travelling around the world, I always popped into the local bank, opened an account and deposited a few quid in there for a rainy day. It was useful to have accounts in various countries so that I could confuse the authorities when it came to an audit trail by hiding the money from the tax man and creditors. That day, paranoia descended upon me like a ton of bricks. I quickly arranged to have my entire broker balance transferred to one of these offshore bank accounts I had, thank God, kept open on the Isle of Man.

I wasn't even going to bother returning to Los Angeles to recover my possessions from the apartment or office: I was fleeing on the very next flight.

I wasted no time at all. I hurriedly withdrew the few thousand dollars I had in my current account, leaving a few hundred dollars there to keep the account live.

The Isle of Man experience had shown me that you can never have too many accounts, wherever they were in the world. I took a yellow cab directly to the airport, churning over and over again in the back of my mind whether I'd left incriminating documentation in my office in Los Angeles. Would the investigators discover it? Would it lead them to me via Henry? I had visions of getting stopped by the FBI as I boarded the plane, tomorrow's newspapers announcing, 'BROKER IN BOND SCAM HELD AT AIRPORT'. Maybe the SEC would intercept the wire transfer on its way to the Isle of Man? Maybe I'd make it home and start all over again, only to have it all snatched away from me as I began a new life as a millionaire, facing extradition to the US and a hefty jail sentence? My mind was racing, working overtime.

I arrived at JFK, looked around and headed for the BA desk. There was a 3.15 flight to Heathrow, so I bought a one-way first-class ticket. I had no luggage to check in, so I went to the first-class lounge to sit it out, longing for the day when I could properly relax before a flight. It seemed that every time I was about to make a long-haul trip I was running away from something.

By three o'clock, I was aboard the jumbo. I finally relaxed as we taxied down the runway and took off, the Big Apple stretching away behind us as we sped off into the sunshine. As I started to unwind, ready to doze off, I started thinking what I would do with all the money. Bright red Ferraris, thoroughbred racehorses, magnums of vintage champagne, spacious riverside apartments, horny, leggy chicks, gold coins, platinum cufflinks and titanium credit cards.

19

Henry Bloomberg found himself in prison. Reports in the media at the time and information from the private detective seem to suggest that Henry wasn't keen to turn in Irving Simpson when he was caught. The authorities, however, were desperate to know where the bonds had originated from. Especially the Feds. I was told that they had promised him that, with the right amount of cooperation, they could help him out of his delicate problem. It turned out they had also made him one other promise, one that deep into the small hours would have offered him some comfort. The Feds, the asset and forfeiture squad, and the SEC were keen to retrieve whatever funds they could, and were looking for Henry to point them in the right direction: would Henry gladly give up all his ill-gotten gains to get himself out of the cage? I am to believe he made a full confession – the bank accounts, the safe deposit boxes, the stocks, the investments. But not the futures. Not his account with me. I wasn't a registered broker, so I would be able to keep that quiet, he must have thought. He also turned in Irving, as well as all the ex-clients who had helped him launder the bonds. He had decided to tell it all, exactly as it happened, keep his fingers crossed, and hope for the best.

The result was a plea bargain deal, where he would assist fully, plead guilty to the lesser charge of 'handling' the bonds and get a short sentence, suspended even. Otherwise, it was to be ten to fifteen mandatory. In the afternoon, he made bail.

He most probably headed straight to my office in Century City to liquidate his futures investments. When he got there, he found no screens, no phones, no traders – no money.

Back in the UK: Operation Grandslam

20

I was now back in London, safe and sound, the money likewise safely deposited in the Isle of Man, earning 8 per cent, tax-free. I say *the* money, rather than *my* money. My money is not the sort of money that normal people earn in salaried jobs, the kind of money most of the population pick up every month in brown pay packets, with tax and national insurance deducted at source, to be spent on the mortgage, school fees, summer holidays, the pension plan and the Christmas catalogue. So I call *my* money, *the* money. Mine's easy money, ill-gotten gains, *schwarz geld*, because it wasn't really my money to start with. If I really thought about it, which I tried not to do, I would probably have surmised that it wasn't really Henry's money either. Someone who lavishes their money so easily should always be held with some suspicion in my book.

I didn't know at the time, but when I walked through Heathrow, I had been recognised and followed by one of Her Majesty's Customs and Excise Investigative Branch officers who was aware of the outstanding balance I owed his department. He was already prematurely celebrating his discovery. Not everyone at Customs shared his jubilation, however. HM Customs and Excise had other ideas in mind than my immediate arrest for the default. At my VAT trial, it was revealed that a senior investigative officer at the London office had decided that I should be kept under surveillance, convinced something major was about to unfold. On and off for the next four years, Customs would invest millions of taxpayers' money in a long-term covert operation of Kafkaesque proportions, culminating in one of their biggest Excise operations ever.

I pitched up at Richard Evans's for a couple of days, my house just down the road having been repossessed by the bank. I went to visit my father who was pleased to see me and glad I was back. Then I got invited to stay over at the Hamptons' country house. I pitched up there for a few weeks, transferred some money from the Isle of Man and decided what to do as I lazed in the countryside.

If a scam works, it is rational to do a repeat, the only trouble for me being the tarnishing of my reputation within the bullion business after my sudden departure in 1980. I was surprised to discover just how forgiving people can be.

I dined out a lot with the Hamptons and old friends. One evening we went to Liberty's nightclub and to my delight, I was recognised and welcomed by everyone. Walking into Liberty's was like being in a time warp, all the regulars at their usual positions at the bars, asking me what I was drinking, as though I had just popped out to the loo for a couple of minutes.

Within a few weeks, I re-established myself in Birmingham as though nothing had happened. I bought a superb luxury flat in Petersham Place and took over some smart offices next to the stock exchange in Great Charles Street, Queensway, from a jeweller contact who was vacating his city offices in favour of other premises.

I formed a new offshore company and called it International

Gold Bullion Exchange (IGBE). I started advertising our services in investment magazines all over the world and dealt in gold bullion bars, gold coins and the full range of futures and options. I opened a trading account with a firm of brokers in London and, with my New York experience under my belt, started to take on quite a lot of straight client business. Although my company was based on the Isle of Man for tax purposes, we were, of course, registered for VAT in the normal way in the UK, and I was curious to discover how Customs and Excise would handle the matter given my previous reputation. I didn't have too long to wait to find out, a phone call confirming a routine visit to inspect the books taking place after only six months of trading. Of course, given my previous experiences at their hands, I made absolutely certain that all my records were complete, straight as a gun barrel, and computerised. During his visit, I contrived to rifle through the VAT man's briefcase, which gave me the opportunity to photocopy my entire Customs file.

I took the copy of the file home with me that evening. It was only a few pages thick, but it sure made interesting reading. 'HANDLE THIS TRADER'S AFFAIRS WITH CAUTION – PREVIOUS COMPOUND SETTLEMENT DEFAULTER' was printed on the front page. There then followed a list of the cheques I had issued to Customs late in 1979 in part settlement for the sixty grand I owed them, and a second list, with photocopies, of the ones that had bounced after I had fled to America. Some twenty-eight grand remained unpaid. A note stated that the department was 'endeavouring to recover a proportion of the balance outstanding on the unpaid cheques as preferential creditors through the official receiver, but it appeared that a large proportion of the company's assets had been removed by the director when he fled suddenly, without warning, to the United States of America'. No mention was made of the FNFC shares, which, incredibly, were now trading at over £1 each. The gut feeling I had had about them while in the States was proving to have been spot on.

Back in the UK: Operation Grandslam

The file went on to cover some observation and surveillance notes, and there was a rather disturbing entry from Heathrow Customs, noting that I was wanted for questioning by US Immigration for outstaying my welcome in America and working illegally whilst visiting the country on a B2 multiple-entry visa. There was no mention of the current account I had been using, the bonds or Henry Bloomberg, but another note on the file worried me: 'Believed to have substantial assets in North America.' I was about to rip the file into small shreds and flush it down the waste disposal, but I realised I might have been being a little hasty. I could always destroy it at a moment's notice. I locked it in a small safe, hidden behind the tins at the back of the kitchen cupboard.

The early to mid-'80s were turning out to be an exciting and successful time for me. IGBE grew from strength to strength. We were conducting more and more futures business, all straight, all kosher. We started to get pitched for business from respectable firms of London brokers, and by one in particular called 'City Investment Securities'. Their account executive was a chap by the name of 'Rupert Dansiger', and he came to see me in Birmingham after having pitched to me for weeks. Rupert and I immediately got on well. He was well educated, had a degree from Oxbridge and also had a great sense of humour. He loved a drink, as well. We hit it off, and IGBE opened a trading account with the company. City Investment Securities was a subsidiary of a larger organisation. A family business, it was one of the largest unquoted, privately owned companies in the States, and it also had interests in foodstuffs. Rupert used to delight in telling anyone who would listen that if you purchased certain frozen foodstuffs in the UK, there was a good possibility that they might be one of City Investments products. Rupert was a great hustler and was very good at generating big volumes of business for his firm. The good times rolled again, just as they had done in 1980. I was determined, this time, to make sure that they continued.

This was the era of rogue and unlicensed dealers, and broker domination of private clients. We were not required to be authorised or supervised by any regulatory body (yet). It was a period of the 'churn them and burn them' attitude. The heady 1980s.

Woody Allen once said that a broker was someone who kept investing your money for you until it was all gone. I was not about to disprove his theory. We traded in everything – gold, silver, platinum, coffee, cocoa, potatoes, T-bills, S&Ps (future derivatives sold on the Standard and Poor index), freight futures. I traded the very first contract on every new exchange that opened on the LIFFE (London International Financial Futures Exchange). We were taking the piss, but loving every minute of it, as long as the large commission cheques kept rolling in at the end of every month. I was great on the phone. One day, I even paged a client at the airport. He was about to board a plane, but I got him to wire transfer a large amount of funds to trade on the Dow Jones Index. He missed his flight, did his brains and that was that. We were reckless, cavalier. We were to be one of the very last unauthorised firms to trade in futures, although having the weight of City Investments behind us gave us considerable respectability and allowed us to continue in business long after a lot of other firms were being shut down by the Department of Trade and Industry.

In 1985, I was approached by a firm with whom I had done a lot of business over the years called 'Cyclical Bullion Ltd'. The company was run by 'Victor Russell' and 'James Owen', who had been in the precious metals business together for years. They had a serious proposition to put to me. They could obtain large quantities of .999 fine gold bullion bars, weighing 1kg each. I was initially told that the gold bars had been obtained from a leading bullion house in exchange for scrap gold, and I chose to believe their story. I was asked, what with my extensive contacts in the precious metals and futures markets, if I would be able to place these bars on their behalf. The carrot was that they could supply me at a discount of 3 per cent of the current spot price.

Back in the UK: Operation Grandslam

They were talking in terms of being able to supply me with up to £100,000 worth of bars a day. However, they would need to be paid for the bullion plus VAT at the standard rate of 15 per cent.

I immediately contacted Rupert. Could City Investments, with their huge contacts, place this bullion on the London Gold Market on IGBE's behalf? A meeting was convened in City Investments' boardroom the very next day. Seated at the table were Rupert Dansiger, Robert Jones (the City Investments MD) and an American, who seemed quite cautious and didn't appreciate the ins and outs of bullion dealing. He was, however, high up in the City Investments hierarchy.

Their answer, to my delight, was positive. City Investments would purchase from IGBE at 99.5 per cent of the spot price and pay us the VAT. City Investments, in turn, would sell the bullion on the London Gold Fix via 'Julian Paxton Merchant Bank', who were one of the members of the London Bullion Market. For this service, City Investments would charge $100 for every 400 ounces of bullion traded (a percentage of which would be rebated to me), and they would want the bullion delivered to Paxton's on their behalf. After all was said and done, the deal would net me about 2 per cent, or £2,000 a day, for the amounts that we were talking about.

It worked like clockwork. Every morning I would go to the bank IGBE used and withdraw a banker's draft for £100,000, payable to Cyclical Bullion. Then, 12 shiny kilo bars of fine gold would be delivered to my office, wrapped in brown sticky tape.

Securicor would then collect the bars from us and deliver them to Julian Paxton, on City Investments' behalf. Julian Paxton didn't know at any time that the bullion originated from us; they thought they were dealing exclusively with City Investments. After the morning gold fix at 10.30, Julian Paxton would wire transfer the money to City Investments, who in turn would wire transfer me. I would then issue my clients with a small cheque to complete the purchase – the invoice invariably came to around £105,000 in total – and I would pocket the £2,000 profit every morning. Nice work if you can get it, and it was to get even better.

Soon, the volume went up. Instead of delivering 12 kilos a day, we were handling 24, sometimes as many as 36 kilos a day. The profit on the deals was now as much as £6,000 a day. This one deal now dominated my whole day's trading, and I was keen to make sure that all went well, without any hitches. After the wire hit the bank, usually around midday, I would go to lunch, often at Club 64 in the Hagley Road, an exclusive private members club which served expensive champagnes and wines. I was making very serious money and, with the commissions I was generating on the private client futures business, I was on target to make in excess of a million and a half that financial year. I purchased a Lamborghini Countach in bright red and kept it parked on double-yellow lines outside the stock exchange all day. I left the price sticker in the window. Sensibly, I thought, I invested in a pension scheme and dropped a six-figure sum into it.

Unknown to me, Customs and Excise were taking a very keen interest in my affairs. I was hardly low profile, after all, but ironically it wasn't my extravagant lifestyle, or their current alert on my activities, which had sparked their full-scale investigation. The whistle was blown by the Bank of England, who were keeping a watchful brief on Julian Paxton: it was them who had alerted Customs and Excise to the potential VAT fraud.

Julian Paxton were in difficulties, a major Asian player having defaulted on them for millions, and the Bank of England were making sure that they could fulfil their obligations. In order to preserve the integrity of the City, the Bank of England would later rescue Julian Paxton with a multi-million-pound package, but for the time being, the authorities were just observing their activities.

The physical gold bullion deal with City Investments was raising eyebrows and concerns with the powers that be for a number of reasons. First, this trade was unusual in the UK. Surprisingly, very little physical gold bullion trading takes place in Britain, most of the millions of ounces of gold that trade daily are on paper, bank to bank. Second, this deal just didn't make commercial sense. It shouldn't have been possible to deliver kilo bars of fine gold below or at the gold price – all the major bullion dealers charged a premium over the spot price. Third, the source of the gold was worrying. Could this gold be the proceeds of the recent Brinks Mat robbery? If not, there was only one other explanation – it was smuggled gold, brought into the UK without VAT being accounted for, and there was one almighty fiddle going on.

The Bank of England quickly discounted the idea that the gold could be from the Brinks Mat robbery, so that left the smuggling option open. They immediately contacted senior officers at Customs, who could hardly contain their excitement at having a second chance to convict me. A full-scale Customs investigation was soon under way.

This is how our little scheme worked. In Belgium and Luxembourg, gold bullion is not subject to any VAT at all, but the metal trades at just over the spot price of gold. A sophisticated gang of smugglers would buy the gold for 2 per cent over the spot price, smuggle it into Britain, sell it to Cyclical for 95 per cent of the spot price (losing 7 per cent), add VAT to the invoice (recouping 15 per cent, leaving 8 per cent net profit), tear up their copy of the VAT paperwork and not account for any of the VAT with Customs. Of course, Cyclical reclaimed their input tax on these invoices in the normal manner, and then simply passed the bullion on to us, plus VAT, making themselves a turn of 2 per cent.

What Customs couldn't figure out, however, was City Investments' role in the affair. Why, they wondered, were they needed at all? Couldn't the smugglers, or Cyclical, or us, simply deliver the bullion to Julian Paxton, get paid and cut out all the middlemen? And why did the smugglers drive the bullion all the way up to Birmingham in the early hours, only for it to be sent all the way back down the motorway to London with Securicor a few hours later? What they had failed to realise was that Julian Paxton wouldn't have entered into this transaction with any of the players other than City Investments.

The bullion deal continued to flourish throughout the summer and into the autumn of 1985. I flashed around town in my Lamborghini, up and down Richmond Hill Road without a worry in the world, blissfully unaware of the interest the police and Customs and Excise were taking in me. It was soon Christmas again, and I took an expensive cruise in the Caribbean alone, returning refreshed for the new year. Volumes soon went up again, and I was back to regularly making £5,000 or £6,000 profit a day. I also started dealing on my own account in the futures market, through City Investments, and took on large positions in the gold, silver and platinum markets, often concluding some monster-size deals. Rupert installed a direct line to my office, and we were on the phone to each other all day long, wheeling and dealing. I was also trading in ever-increasing quantities of stocks and shares, often running huge positions in speculative stocks, all on lines of credit generously provided to me by local firms of stockbrokers. Amazingly, FNFC shares were now trading at over £3 each. If I had held on, my investment would now have been worth £10 million, the dividends alone coming to over £600,000 a year. Soon, I would have another multi-million-pound trading opportunity in my hands.

I partied every night, wined and dined a string of smart girlfriends, became friends with the 'in' crowd, dressed immaculately in designer suits, but generally found it tough to make severe inroads into the money. I tried hard, though, I can assure you.

21

Operation Grandslam was a multi-pronged Customs and Excise Investigation. It targeted International Gold Bullion Exchange and myself, Victor Russell, his son Richard, James Owen and

Back in the UK: Operation Grandslam

'Jason Brown' from Cyclical, their suppliers, Julian Paxton and City Investments, as well as a string of other bullion dealers, coin dealers and associates, including Richard Williams.

As far as the Birmingham side of the operation was concerned, my VAT man was in charge of surveillance coordination – much to his delight, I should think.

Covert Customs and Excise operations are a fine art and include observations over a long period of time: telephone and premises bugging, the trailing of people and vehicles, and a large amount of photography and video recording. Assisted by the special operations department in London, sophisticated electronic bugging and surveillance equipment was hurriedly shipped up to Birmingham.

I suppose my first inkling that something out of the ordinary was going on should have been when I arrived home one evening and found the apartment had been burgled. In light of the Customs file I had read, I should also have been wary. There was no sign of forced entry and, although my flat had been given a thorough going-over, the only property to have been stolen was the television and video from the sitting room.

By chance, I used the phone to call my solicitor later that night and when I hung up, it rang back at me. I picked it up and, to my amazement, heard a recording of the previous conversation. I called my solicitor back immediately from a phone box outside and he told me to call BT, who duly informed me that, on this particular day, Customs and Excise had obtained permission from higher powers to tap the phone. I surmised that they had secretly bugged my house during this false 'burglary'.

By this stage, September 1985, Operation Grandslam, one of Customs' largest, most-expensive and daring excise operations to date, was in full swing. I didn't realise at the time, but I was being followed around town most evenings, the undercover officers having some difficulty in keeping up with the non-stop, thrill-a-minute life I was leading.

High Stakes

At an exclusive luncheon held at the Strathallan Hotel to celebrate the launch of the new Ferrari, I was invited, as a guest of Ferrari UK, to participate in the Beaujolais Run – an annual car race for lunatics and eccentrics which commences in France at midnight the day the new wine is released. The luncheon was sponsored by a well-known local interior designer called 'Rodney Marks', who had come good from nothing, and had just taken delivery of his new Mondial convertible, on show at the hotel. My friend James Steventon, who dealt in Ferraris, was organising the trip to France and my co-driver was to be Russell Bray, a prominent motoring journalist. It was at this lunch that I was also introduced to Jenny. We were to stay friends for quite a while.

We set off for France in the Lamborghini a couple of days early, the idea being to soak up the atmosphere in France before the race started. I was terribly seasick on the ferry crossing and took a few hours to recover. It was snowing heavily when we arrived on the Continent, but after a few glasses of good French wine I was feeling better. Later, during my VAT trial, Customs representatives told the court that they had followed us to Dover, convinced that the Beaujolais Run was part of the bullion-smuggling operation. They had even instructed their counterparts in France to keep a discreet eye on us.

On the day of the race itself, Russell, who took the whole thing very seriously, insisted that we visit the vineyard from where the race would start, so that we could practise our getaway and the first few kilometres to the autoroute. Having accomplished this, we felt satisfied that we were more prepared for the race than anyone else. Our car was the fastest, and we knew the route. All we had to do was sit it out until the off at midnight and not get too drunk at the dinner party, which James had organised for that evening. Soon, midnight approached, and we were in the car, at the entrance to the vineyard. A Volvo estate appeared on the scene with a large digital watch on the roof, ready for the start of the race. Russell had a clipboard on his lap, with all the pit stops mapped out for refuelling. We were soon revving up and off.

Back in the UK: Operation Grandslam

We were first out of the traps, and I floored it. Through sleepy French villages in the dark, into the town and then onto the autoroute to Calais, where I got up to about 160mph. As I glanced in the rear-view mirror, the pursuing white headlights of a chasing Ferrari slowly melted into the distant horizon.

We could actually see the fuel gauge move on its downward journey towards empty – this was six to eight miles a gallon territory. Russell put on a tape and Bonnie Tyler came on singing 'Lost in France'. He had calculated the first pit stop for petrol and as we pulled in to refuel, the freezing weather conditions hit us. Soon we were off again, but this time the roads were dangerously icy, so I slowed down – 120mph, 100mph and soon a mere 70mph. Then a Ferrari sped past us, then a Porsche and then a whole fleet of other British cars. About a mile down the road, it happened. The tyres lost their grip on the ice and there was one almighty pile-up. Mercifully, no one was badly hurt, but there was a good amount of damage to some rather nice sports cars. We all limped to a nearby hotel where we revised our plans. Russell was happy to drive back and I decided to fly. I got a taxi to Charles de Gaulle, which was rather like hailing a taxi in Park Lane and asking for Manchester Airport. I eventually made it, but just missed a direct flight to Birmingham, so flew to Heathrow and took a cab to the reunion lunch at the local Holiday Inn. I was the last one back. I later found out that the lads had restarted from the hotel and made the ferry after all. For coming last, James presented me with an overnight airline bag, which included toothpaste and comb, and a BA timetable for the Paris–London shuttle.

Customs, carefully observing what was going on with the car trip – the change of drivers and my sudden disappearance in France – were now more confused than ever. On occasions, I would send my courier down to London on the train with consignments of gold for delivery to the London Bullion Market. Later, in court, we found out that there had always been three Customs officers on board the train during these trips. If only I'd

99

known, I could have saved a fortune in insurance premiums.

Like a bubble surfacing to the top of a champagne flute with a pop, confirmation that I was under surveillance came in January 1986. I was being watched, photographed, indexed, filed, numbered, followed, *investigated*. A friend, whose office was across the street from me, had been to a dinner party where a Customs officer, unaware of our friendship, had let slip that officers were staked out in his office building, investigating a major gold-bullion fraud suspected of being in progress right across the street. Customs had stepped up their surveillance and were recording all the comings and goings in my life. My friend had also found out that they had parked a car near to my apartment, with high-tech, remote-controlled surveillance equipment installed. They were closing in on me.

The morning after this information had been relayed to me, I felt like putting on my jacket, marching across the street into the building, up the stairs, finding their 'offices' and pulling the plug on their operation – maybe grabbing reels of film from their cameras, crushing it up in my fists, destroying their surveillance notes, disposing of the evidence. Like the Mafia characters used to do in B-movies.

But I didn't. Instead, I convinced myself that I wasn't doing anything wrong and carried on with my life as normally as possible. Easier said than done. Something in my persona had shifted as a result of being investigated; I felt as though my whole operation was on a very short lease of life, and that IGBE, my empire, was heading for a brick wall. I became obsessed about security and started to suspect that all my staff were leaking confidential information to Customs. My futures trading began to suffer. I started taking on bigger and bigger positions in the market, for comfort, hoping that their company would isolate me from prosecution. I didn't care if I was doing lucrative trades or not, all the discipline and the techniques I had acquired in the States were going out the window. I began taking on monster positions in markets I knew little or nothing about, using the tiniest of excuses to trade up massive numbers of contracts. I even authorised Rupert at City Investments to use discretion and trade on my behalf, if I was unavailable. I was on tilt. A fellow coin and bullion dealer from Yorkshire, who I'd known for some time, once told me that we all have panic buttons, self-destruct buttons. I had pressed both of mine at once.

The year 1986 was to become one engrained in my memory. It was the year when my tiger stormed back into the picture with a vengeance, after such a long hibernation. My trading account with City Investments was looking like a comedy of errors. I started off the year with a big thing about platinum, but it came to nothing, and I exited the market with no loss, just a largish commission payment to Rupert for the privilege of the trade.

In one instance, I picked up my direct line to Rupert at City Investments' trading desk: 'What's hot today, fat man?'

'I'd go into sugar at the moment. You can buy at £160 – it'll be £180 by the end of this week, big boy.' I pursed my lips.

'OK – buy me 200 contracts, March, at the market.'

Rupert whistled to himself. 'Two hundred contracts.' (City Investments charged me £15 a contract and he got 25 per cent of that.) He tapped out some figures on his calculator. He had just made himself £750.

'And work it slowly, it's for a good client.'

'Booked,' said Rupert. 'Who's the client?'

'Me.'

Twenty-four hours later, sugar was down to £148 a ton. Rupert had pulled me out of sugar and switched me into copper. Within three hours, copper had dropped by £30. Without telling me, he liquidated that position and reinvested it in gold on the New York exchange, and by the time the first member of City Investments' staff had arrived at work the following morning, he had already switched my position back to London. In this way, I avoided parting with cash-deposit requirements, which I could ill afford as far as City Investments was concerned, and which were always appearing on their equity runs as a day trade.

High Stakes

But our luck wasn't in. By the end of a fortnight of trading, we had succeeded in dropping half a million of IGBE's net worth. I wasn't amused, and Rupert knew that unless he pulled something out of the bag, and pulled it out smartly, he was going to be minus one very big and long-standing client – a client who was worth to him personally, quite apart from what the firm made out of me, about £100,000 in commission a year.

I summoned Rupert up to Birmingham to see me, and we had a meeting at my apartment. I settled into my favourite chair, and Rupert went to the bar. He poured me nearly half a tumbler of Hine Antique cognac from my Baccarat cut-glass decanter and handed me a cigar.

I stared at him straight in the eye, then took a large pull on my tumbler. I needed enough drink for courage, but not too much that I would lose what little concentration I had remaining. I then carefully cut the end of my cigar with my cutter. Rupert nodded slowly, 'You have this margin money readily available, I presume?'

I pulled out my matches and lit the cigar, slowly, deliberately, rolling the tip over and over in the flame, sucking gently, sucking deeply, caressing and nursing the end into an even, bright-red glow. The smoke tasted sweet, reassuring, rich and beautiful. I took one large mouthful, let the smoke curl up for a few moments from my bottom lip, then blew it hard, straight out in front of me. I looked at Rupert briefly, then stared down at my exquisitely polished Lobb shoes. 'No, Rupert, I haven't.'

'Nor the £175,000 you need to complete the building purchase from Betts?' he enquired.

A chill went through me. Nobody had actually spelt out the enormity of the mess I was in before. This chill subsided, and I was left with a damp mixture of frustration and despair. I lifted my eyes to meet Rupert's. 'No, I don't have that either.'

'How about fifty quid for cocktails tonight at Liberty's?'

Rupert's tone had suddenly become warmer again. He grinned back.

Back in the UK: Operation Grandslam

'I think I can just about run to that,' I said.

'Well, that's a start.'

I picked up the glass for another sip, but to my surprise it was empty. 'Drop more?' asked Rupert.

'Just a drop,' I said, conscious that I was beginning to slur my words and fighting hard to feel sober again.

Rupert refilled my glass. 'I think of you as one of my family. If it's within my power to help, then I will.' He paused and lifted his glass. 'Your health.' I lifted mine, and we both drank. Then Rupert continued. 'Now, you seem to be in a lot of trouble. The sums of money you owe are fantastic – in anyone's terms – almost £1 million altogether. Everyone dreams of being a millionaire. Even today, with all the inflation we've had over the years, to be a millionaire is still to achieve a magical status. You owe more money than perhaps one man in a hundred thousand will ever make in his entire lifetime. You are a bright fellow. You have enthusiasm, energy, youth, ability. I don't know – maybe you also have rich relatives – but if you don't, you will need an awful lot of hard work, and luck, to ever pay back even a portion of that sort of money. It will be a millstone around your neck, that you will carry all your life. Instead of earning money to enjoy, you will be earning it to pay back your creditors. Of course, you could always go bankrupt, but I doubt that you would ever work again in the futures or precious metals industry with a bankruptcy behind you.' I was starting to despair at this lecture.

Rupert continued, 'I am, however, privy to some information that, if acted upon correctly, could enable you to recoup the money.' I eased up a little now, listening intently to every word Rupert said. 'I am aware that there will be a severe shortage in the potato futures market for the deliveries due under the April contract. I am about to arrange a serious team of investors to try and corner the market. I can put you in. City Investments will allow you to go long a couple of hundred contracts with very little margin, as the market has been very steady for a long time, and the official exchange deposits are only £200 a contract,

103

anyway. I hear, believe it or not, that April could go up as high as £300 or £400 per ton. It's in the high 80s at the moment.'

Despite being rather over the top, I managed to do some quick calculations. If I bought 200 contracts of 40 tons each – 8,000 tons – and we went up to £200 a ton, I would make £1.6 million profit, enough to bail me out of my hole and give me a profit of £600,000.

'When do we start buying?' I asked eagerly.

It's a funny thing this, but when you are out of form, things do go wrong. In the same way, when you are on a roll, and have your extra dose of luck handed to you on a plate, you just take it for granted. I was starting to believe that I had run out of good luck. I had agreed the previous year to purchase a large freehold building in St Paul's Square, in the heart of Birmingham's jewellery quarter. The building was a bargain, but because of my losses in the futures markets, I had to sell it to a local property developer, and I sublet back from him the part I needed to run my business. Shameful. A bullion dealer in Leeds, who I conducted a huge amount of business with, went wrong for millions, bounced cheques on me for £130,000 and fled the country. I later found out that this had something to do with my spud position refusing to budge in value for a while, as he had also built up a large position in the market. When he disappeared, his broker was forced to slowly liquidate his position, which was another factor that helped to keep the lid on the market. I had to make up the most unbelievable lies to keep my bankers happy.

I had an appointment with my bank manager, 'Hugh McIntosh'. He was canny and could tell that I was pushed. The appointment was not at the bank, but at the Highfield Club, a casino and dining club in Moseley that Hugh liked to frequent. Somewhere between his fourth pint and his third snifter of cognac, he agreed to lend me £100,000 for three months, at six over base. This was to be secured by a charge on the part of my apartment in Petersham Place that my building society didn't own, a loan on my £40,000 Ferrari and by holding custody of my certificates of stocks worth £25,000.

Back in the UK: Operation Grandslam

With the exception of a £1,500 Piaget 18-carat gold watch, a wardrobe of various Armani and Hugo Boss suits, several dozen Turnbull and Asser shirts, three pairs of Lobb handmade shoes, some gold cufflinks and an assortment of modern furniture, artefacts and inessential trappings, I had hocked my entire worldly goods. I blamed Customs. I had to massage my stock figures and lie about the amount of bullion I held in the vaults to my accountant, Monty Levi. I blamed Customs. Bills weren't getting paid at the office. I blamed Customs. My futures trading was becoming a nightmare. I blamed Customs. The only light at the end of the tunnel was my potato position with City Investments, but even that stubbornly refused to shift upwards in value. The bullion-bar business with Cyclical was quietening down as well. When I asked what was going wrong, Victor Russell made some excuse about ferries being late. I was now seriously beginning to wonder whether their previous explanation of the source of the bullion was true, and had a strong suspicion, a gut feeling if you like, that all was not well. I had strong ideas about what kind of trouble or scandal would blow up if Customs and Excise stumbled onto this. Gold is a strange material – it infects most men who touch it with a reckless greed.

Luck did shine favourably on me one day, though, amidst my quagmire of financial nightmare. One morning, I woke up feeling on top of the world, got dressed and drove in the Lamborghini to the office, full of beans. It was one of those glorious summer mornings, and I switched on the price monitors to follow the markets. I noticed gold starting to creep up in the Far East. For some reason, I was convinced of a major bull move. It was 6.30 a.m. I was unable to trade much for my own account, as my equity run at City Investments was right to the limit, so I racked my brains for someone I could call at that ungodly hour of the day to have a punt. I went through my lists of regular customers, called most of them and put them in the market for a quick trade. My eyes hovered at the name of Harry Conway, an American numismatist who ran a very successful coin and antiquity emporium opposite the British Museum. Harry and I got on well, and I knew he secretly admired the chaos I sometimes caused. Although he didn't trade in the market very often, I wanted to put him into a position that I just knew would make him a few thousand bucks profit in the short term. I decided to call him, and surprisingly he wasn't upset at being woken so early.

'Harry, gold is moving up swiftly in the Far East, I think you should be in for a quick punt. I think you could be in and out of the market before you leave your house to go to work.'

He instructed me to buy him some contracts and, within an hour and a half, the market had rallied by a few dollars, and I sold his position for him, taking great delight in phoning him over his breakfast to inform him of his windfall profit. If only I could have done that well for all my clients. Harry would never forget that early-morning trade, and it helped seal a mutual friendship and respect for one another that would remain solid throughout my ups and downs in the years to come.

Ambition, however, like most of the characteristics that make up a person, is best acquired young. If you are going to run your own company, then you have to spend years working on it very hard, almost to the exclusion of everything else. But the worse things got, the less I worked, and the more I included everything else in my hectic, chaotic life. I was determined, on a personal front, to try and keep up my image. The luxury apartment, the Lamborghini, the gold cards. Late nights, champagne. The default mode of haggard paranoia is not the correct expression for the driver of a Lamborghini, unless you are a rock star, which, plainly, I was not. I hadn't earned this car. I was an interloper, a thief, a fraud. People can tell. I was the ultimate '80s man – a financial high-flyer with large aspirations and even larger lines of credit. But like the 1980s themselves, I didn't train on. My empire was about to vanish in a puff of smoke.

In Court with Customs and Excise

22

Long afterwards, many still remember those three days in the last week of February 1986 with vividness and anguish. Had I accepted an early-morning breakfast invitation, though, the events of the hours, days and months that followed could well have turned out rather differently.

The phone purred by my bed. I glanced at the alarm, it was 6.48 a.m. on Thursday, 26 February 1986. 'Come and join me for breakfast at the Plough and Harrow,' the cheery Italian voice said. It was my pal Fran. We had been up late partying at Liberty's the previous evening. I passed on the breakfast invitation, put the phone down and rolled over to a get a few more hours shut-eye.

At 7.18 a.m., teams of Customs and Excise officers, in 15 different locations all over the UK, were given the go, go, go signal to swoop. Operation Grandslam, the culmination of many months' work, was about to come to fruition.

From unused court evidence, which described the actions of the nine Customs officers who were assigned to my case, I have been able to piece together a picture of what happened that morning outside my apartment. The officers gained entry to the block via a neighbour of mine, who let in someone supposedly delivering a telegram to their address. The Customs men then took the stairs to the second floor, quickly found my highly polished whitewood door, complete with brass knocker and spy hole. At 7.22 a.m., a series of sharp raps sounded through the apartment. When I slung on a robe and went to check who it was, I observed a young male figure dressed in a business suit and carrying a briefcase. He held an identity document, and I noticed the portcullis logo of HM Customs and Excise. I inspected the document, unlocked the door and the young man stepped inside. Then, before I could close the door, a proliferation occurred, as unexpected and remarkable as a magician's trick. Where there had been one individual with briefcase and preferred credentials, suddenly there were three, behind them three more, with still another phalanx at the rear. Swiftly, like an inundation, they streamed into the apartment. A man, taller than most of the others, and emanating authority, announced curtly in a Scottish accent, 'My name is "Chris Wilson", we are officers of Customs and Excise. We have a warrant to search these premises. Are you Nigel Goldman? Are you alone? I'm arresting you on suspicion of evading value added tax. You do not have to say anything, but anything you do say will be taken down and used in evidence.'

Wilson continued, 'You will notice that this search warrant allows four officers to be present on this search. With your permission, we would all like to participate. That way, the matter will be concluded more quickly. If you have no objections to the extra officers being in your premises, please sign the bottom of the warrant.' I signed, and went to my bedroom to get dressed. One of the officers followed me and stood at the bedroom door while I washed, shaved and got ready.

I had been busted. Again. This time, though, the matter seemed to take on much more significance than my previous run-in with the department. I felt that I would need all the luck in the world to get out of this hole. As I was getting dressed, the officer at my bedroom door said, 'I'm really glad that this arrest is over with, Mr Goldman, I was one of the officers on night duty, following you around town over the past few months. I was having difficulty keeping up with you, I must admit – nightclubs till two in the morning, the casino, and then off to the office at 6.30. How do you do it? I've suffered from high blood pressure, and my marriage is on the rocks, thanks to all this.' I gave him a wry smile.

Once I'd dressed, he followed me into the sitting room. I went to the bar and poured myself a large brandy. Officers were searching the whole apartment thoroughly, drawers were being emptied, the sofa cushions were being examined, the curtains ruffled. In the kitchen, one officer was attempting to smash open some frozen fish from the freezer with a large wooden mallet.

'You'd be amazed where we find our clues, Mr Goldman,' he said, as he smashed the helpless haddock, sending pieces of frozen fish flying all over the kitchen floor. Another officer was removing tins from the shelves in the kitchen cupboards and piling them up neatly on the work surfaces. He would soon discover the small safe, containing the photocopy of my Customs file that I had been storing for months. My God, why on earth hadn't I had the sense to destroy it?

Almost on cue, I was asked if I had a key for the safe. I took the small Yale off my bunch and handed it to him. On seeing the safe's contents, he summoned a couple of his colleagues into the kitchen to examine his discovery. I half expected them to cheer. Meanwhile, my phone was ringing off the hook – friends, staff, anyone, having heard of the swoop on the morning news. Every time the phone rang, Wilson picked it up and replaced the receiver without saying anything. Outside, in my garage, a team of Customs mechanics were taking the Lamborghini to pieces, while another couple got to work on my Ferrari.

I later found out that in other parts of Birmingham, teams of Customs officers had swooped on the homes of Victor Russell, 'Richard Russell', James Owen and Jason Brown. In London, they arrested Richard Williams and 'Peter Simmons'. Accompanied by armed police, they also arrested 'Simon Ford', Cyclical's supplier. Officers also attended the premises of Julian Paxton and City Investments. In Leicester, the homes of some Asian bullion dealers were raided and in Bilston, Wolverhampton, Manchester and Leeds many other coin and bullion dealers were apprehended.

By mid-morning, officers had completed their search of my apartment, and they escorted me to my office premises to continue their search there. Only the previous day, I had been proud to show someone around my new building, now I felt ashamed. Though no one knew it, it was to be the last time I would be present as part of IGBE. I could barely face my staff; the expensive dealing room unusually quiet, the boardroom empty. They bagged up all the paperwork, and my secretary handed me a cup of sweet tea. My father turned up out of the blue, having heard the news on the radio, and complained bitterly about their treatment of his son. Then, their search complete, the Customs officers drove me to London to be interviewed. As we left the jewellery quarter in Birmingham, I noticed, to my horror, a group of photographers clicking away, eager to get a scoop for the evening papers.

HM Customs and Excise investigation department is situated in New Fetter Lane. From the outside, the Customs building looked like any other. No one would have guessed that this was a government building, there were certainly no name plaques or signs as clues. They took me inside. 'That sounds like our Nigel,' a voice shouted from halfway up the stairs. Walking towards me was Colin Peters, gloating – he had watched my arrival from his upstairs window. I began to wonder if these people attended training courses on how to psyche out interviewees.

The building was grey and dreary inside, pretty much like its sister office in Birmingham. The walls were covered with charts, names and lists of officers. But what no charts showed was the drive and determination which all the officers possessed and which, with their added ingenuity and boundless energy, had led to these arrests. I was shown into an interview room on the first floor with reinforced windows, just in case. The room was quiet. I was seated at a table in front of two officers who had been present during the raid on my flat, 'Stuart Hill' and Chris Wilson. Wilson clicked the tape into action. 'My name is Chris Wilson, an officer of Customs and Excise. Also present is Stuart Hill, a Customs officer, and Nigel Goldman. There is no one else in the room. The time is 11.43 a.m. and the date is 26 February 1986.'

Wilson continued, talking to me this time: 'As you know, you have been arrested on suspicion of conspiracy to evade VAT. You may be interested to know that we have also arrested a large number of your associates. I want to ask you some questions about a very large quantity of fine gold kilo bars, .999 fine, that you have been dealing in with Cyclical Bullion, a deal which we don't think is entirely legitimate, if you get my drift.' He cleared his throat before continuing. 'Do you know how many kilos of gold you have handled in total?'

'I don't work in kilos, I work in ounces,' I replied. 'I'm old fashioned.'

Wilson sighed, 'Very well, have it your way, how many ounces then?'

'I don't know,' I replied.

Wilson shrugged and tried a different tack. 'This is a most unusual bullion transaction. As you are no doubt aware, the volume of gold physically traded in London is normally very small, yet you have been trading in enormous quantities of gold. Do you have any idea about the origin of this gold?'

I have been told, over the years, never to answer any questions put to me by the police. Peter Kinsley, my solicitor friend from the OCs, used to make a point of emphasising this to me, Scotch in hand, banging his free hand on the bar, no doubt aware that I could find myself involved with the law at any time. Customs obviously came into the same category as the police, but for some strange reason I didn't think they had too much to go on and felt in control of the situation. So, the more questions they asked, the more I played along. I soon realised that they were well wide of the mark. They had considerable suspicions, sure, but the more they probed and quizzed me, the more I realised two things about the situation. First, never overestimate the opposition – most of their interview was pure guesswork, with questions designed to get to the bottom of a mystery. Second, they really didn't have a clue about what had gone on – after all their painstaking investigations and surveillance, they didn't, couldn't, appreciate what had happened. There were lots of pieces missing from their large jigsaw puzzle. They would have to do a lot better than this to secure convictions in Crown Court, which was presumably where we were all heading.

Wilson shifted his stance again, and I noticed that his colleague, Stuart Hill, was starting to look a touch uncomfortable. Wilson spoke clearly, but was a little less sure of himself. 'So, let's just go through this once again, shall we? The bullion gets delivered from Cyclical to yourself, then you deliver it to Julian Paxton. Can you explain why the Securicor paperwork we have uplifted bears City Investments' name on it and not IGBE's? We suspect there were two separate consignments – one for City Investments and one for you. What happened to the paperwork for the second IGBE consignment, and where was that consignment delivered to? Let's assume your paperwork gets ripped up [he got hold of some blank scrap paper from his desk drawer and ripped it up for effect] where does the second lot of bullion go?' Now, I couldn't believe what I was hearing – Jesus, these guys didn't have a clue! Hill was nodding in agreement with his colleague and the crazy suggestion that there was a mystery consignment and missing paperwork, both of which didn't even exist. They continued with their questioning, tying themselves up in knots, contradicting themselves from question to question, probing, trying desperately to understand what had gone on in this exercise of evasion of the public purse. They had plenty of clues and suspicions – indications of fraud, if you like – but did they have sufficient evidence to bring charges or secure a conviction? At the moment, I doubted it, but I didn't want to count my chickens. They still had plenty of paperwork to examine, and there was also the possibility of someone in custody 'coughing'. I didn't even know some of the people they had hauled in.

There was a knock on the door. Wilson addressed the tape again: 'Mr Poland enters the room with coffee at 2.46 p.m. Mr Poland leaves the room at 2.47 p.m.'

They carried on with the interview. This time it was Hill's turn to hold up pieces of paper which had been taken from my office for examination and were now labelled as exhibits in clear plastic. 'Mr Goldman,' Hill said, 'you are an intelligent man. It is quite obvious that something untoward has gone on here. Help us on these points, and we can make things a lot easier for you. Give us a cough, if you like, and we can have you give evidence for us against the other conspirators. You could turn Queen's evidence and get a shorter sentence.' I ignored him.

He had discovered a disturbing item of paperwork, a document now labelled: 'DAVIDSON G' (named after the Customs officer who had seized it from my apartment). This was a piece of paper, in my own handwriting, with my thoughts on how the chain of supply might have taken place with regard to the gold deliveries. I could remember jotting this out one evening after a conversation with Victor Russell. It was a flow chart of how smuggled bullion could end up on the gold market, and whether I, as a receiver of the bullion, could be implicated in a VAT fraud. The paper read as follows:

> Gold kilo bars – smuggled gold? Imported illegally? Delivered to Cyclical.
> Cyclical – IGBE – Julian Paxton
> Funds Julian Paxton – IGBE – Cyclical
> Do I know bars could be smuggled, therefore VAT fraud?
> If I know – guilty. If suspicious only, innocent?
> If smuggled, fraud obvious, but are IGBE, City

Investments, Julian Paxton in conspiracy if we don't know?

As long as proper VAT invoices, continue operation, as before.

There then followed a note, with an asterisk:

Chase up Victor Russell for outstanding VAT invoices, well overdue.

Hill replaced the 'DAVIDSON G' document in a clear plastic folder. It was his prize exhibit so far. I cursed myself; why on earth had I left that in my desk, and the file in my kitchen? Without these documents, they would have had nothing on me. Nothing at all. Hill waited for a few seconds for the implication to set in, as he had been trained. 'What have you got to say about this document then, Mr Goldman?'

There was no sense in denying that it was mine, that the handwriting was mine (they could easily produce an expert to confirm that), so I used the Kinsley back-up tactic and said nothing. 'No comment, no comment, no comment.' Fuck them! Let them prove their goddamn case against me. Let someone else turn Queen's evidence. I wasn't going to incriminate myself, or grass anyone else up for that matter. Unfortunately for me, in a different part of the building someone in custody had taken a slightly different view of the situation.

There was another knock on the door, and this time Wilson and Hill were motioned outside by a senior, official-looking figure. Wilson clicked the tape to pause, while Hill bundled up his paperwork and took it out with him, including his prized 'DAVIDSON G' document. Had he left it behind, I would gladly have eaten it.

Where the room was quiet before, the silence was now intense. Exterior sounds intruded faintly: air conditioning, a car horn from outside on the street, typing from further down the corridor, a jet whined as it climbed high above the city. Oh, to be on it and to be free.

It was a few hours later, certainly after six o'clock, when they returned, and they looked quite pleased with themselves. Hill spoke. 'The investigation is still ongoing, and there are a number of people who remain in custody. We are keeping you overnight for further questioning tomorrow. We will shortly escort you to a police station where you will spend the evening.'

My property was brought in, in sealed transparent bags. A wallet full of gold credit cards and charge cards, a wad of cash (which they had counted out and totalled at just over £800) and my flat keys. I noticed that the Lamborghini keys had not materialised, and as if reading my mind, Hill assured me that they would be returned to me tomorrow. Next, they took me out to face one of their senior officers, who authorised my detention past the 24-hour mark, and I was escorted, on foot, by Wilson and Hill, to Snow Hill Police Station.

'You're not going to try anything stupid, are you?' Hill asked, obviously concerned that I was thinking of doing a runner. It was the last thing on my mind. We walked on, heading towards Hatton Garden.

The pubs were open for their crisp, spring-like evening trade, drinkers spilling out into the lukewarm pavements with their pints and glasses of wine, not a care in the world.

I longed to be able to walk into a pub and order a round, something I would normally just have taken for granted. At that moment, Hill enquired again if I would cough, and indicated a drink wasn't out of the question if I did. I took this as a confirmation of their weakness, passed on their offer and we walked on to the police station.

Snow Hill is one of London's oldest and quaintest cop shops, situated near Hatton Garden. Many City crooks, swindlers and fraudsters have spent their first night in custody there, awaiting charge, remand, bail or release. In the future, it would become a temporary home to some high-profile defendants, but tonight a reception committee awaited my arrival, Customs having buzzed through to reserve a cell for a multi-million-pound VAT swindler. Hill and Wilson walked me in and deposited me at the duty sergeant's desk for my first evening in the clutches of the City of London Police.

The desk sergeant fondled my sealed property bag, bursting with cash and plastic, and sighed, I assumed at the prospect of having to count all the money and enter all the cards onto a property sheet. He was about to break open the Customs seal when I volunteered that I had no objection to the bag remaining sealed and intact, and simply being listed as 'one sealed bag, contents unchecked' on the property sheet. The sergeant immediately brightened up at my suggestion, made a comment to his colleagues that they had 'a reasonable one, here' and instructed them to place me in the ladies' cell, for a bit of extra comfort.

I felt a sense of relief when the cell door clicked shut, although common sense told me the relief was surely to be only temporary, and that the wretchedness of the day would resume and be just as bad, even worse maybe, the next day.

Customs officers were trying to complete their jigsaw puzzle. For them, Simon Ford, who earlier that afternoon had agreed to turn Queen's evidence against Cyclical, would have been a useful piece in their mystery. No matter how hard he was pushed on the subject, however, he could not confirm any knowledge of dealings with IGBE or me, his business being restricted to Messrs Russell and Owen. It was to be the precious 'DAVIDSON G' document that would play a role in my case.

23

'This is IGBE,' the young trader snapped crisply into the telephone, which was cradled expertly between his shoulder and ear, leaving his hands free to thumb through the long computer printouts. My apparently trustworthy employee was seated in my chair in the high-tech dealing room, alone. (The rest of the staff had probably left early, or not turned up at all, at the news of my continued detention in London. The doorman was no doubt happy to let the familiar faces into the office block.) 'I want to sell 400 contracts of April potatoes, what's the quote?'

From the GAFTA [Grain and Feed Trade Association] market in the Baltic Exchange, the voice of the City Investments trader drawled, '98 to a half – I can sell 20 and work the rest.'

'Sell 'em,' the IGBE man said, and on that one simple command, like a game of high-stakes electronic poker, a multi-million-pound trading windfall evaporated from the company's ledgers onto the equity runs of the other eager players in the market.

This is how I imagine things panned out that morning in my office, as I languished under the long arm of the law. It seems, from what I could glean from my financial records, that the trader dumped the company's currency and treasury positions, then the soft commodities, and finally the precious-metal contracts. Whoever was responsible had acted in the company's worst possible interests by liquidating all the open positions at the earliest opportunity. The phones, the office equipment, the petty cash tin and a photocopy of the client list also disappeared from the office that day.

24

'We now accept,' Wilson continued, 'that there was only one consignment of bullion delivered to Julian Paxton, after all. But can you explain to us, as we asked you yesterday, where you thought this bullion originated from?'

There were now four people in the interview room, my solicitor Chris Miles, at last being allowed to listen in to proceedings. Miles stood up and looked at his watch. He was a tall figure, bespectacled, his hair quite unkempt – a college haircut.

'My client has nothing to add to the statements he made yesterday. The time has come, gentlemen, for you to either charge or release him. He has now been in your custody approaching 36 hours. I would like to remind you that he is a businessman and has a company to run. A company, incidentally, which will not hesitate in suing your department for loss of profits over this wrongful arrest. If you still maintain that there has been some impropriety, may I suggest that you charge him, otherwise I intend to apply to the court immediately for his release.' Wilson turned to Hill. They both looked tired, worn out, their eyes bloodshot from lack of sleep.

Hill then addressed Miles: 'The decision as to whether or not to prefer charges is one which is being taken at this moment in time, at the most senior level. We propose to terminate this interview now. Copies of this tape, and the previous tapes, will be made available to you in due course.'

He then clicked off the tape and removed the cassettes from the machine, which he proceeded to place in their cases and label with tamper-proof security stickers, which I was asked to sign.

Hill and Wilson got up and left us alone in the room. I turned to Chris. 'Well, what do you think?'

'First, they do actually have more time. The clock starts ticking when you arrived here, not when they first arrested you in Birmingham, so they could, theoretically, hold you for a further few hours without charge. But I think they will charge you – that's my view. Now, the question is bail. Have you made any plans for bail to be put up for you? How about your father, would he be prepared to stand surety for you? I don't know how much they would be looking for, Nigel, but they are bandying around some horrendous figures out there.'

'Here's my father's number. He knows what's going on, he came to the office yesterday. Give him a call, I'm sure he will help.'

The interview-room door swung open once again. Where before they had looked tired and drained, Hill and Wilson walked in with what seemed like a spring to their step and a twinkle in their eyes. I was led out to reception to be formally charged. Their charging officer was a huge, bearded figure, who leant over a small desk. It looked as though it could collapse at any moment under his weight.

'Nigel Goldman, you are charged under the Customs and Excise Management Act with conspiracy to defraud HM Customs and Excise of £1.8 million in unpaid VAT. You will be held in custody overnight and will appear before Guildhall Magistrates' Court tomorrow morning.' Wilson and Hill took me out for another walk and another night in police custody, although this time we went to a different police station. The following morning, I was woken early. I was desperate for a shower and a shave, but these luxuries are denied to you in the hands of the City of London Police. I did ask, though. The officer's reply was along the lines of: 'This isn't a bloody hotel, you know.'

At Guildhall Magistrates' Court, I was placed in a holding cell in the basement. The cell was quite roomy and modern, and the bars at the front stretched from the floor to the ceiling with narrow gaps in between them, so that you could see out and communicate with people in the other cells. After a few minutes, there was some activity and Jason Brown was brought in, followed by James Owen, Victor Russell, Richard Russell, Peter Simmons and Simon Ford. They were each allocated cells. This was the first time I had seen any of them since the arrest. They seemed in reasonable spirits, and we started to talk to each other about what had happened, and the events of the past few days. They all admitted that we were in a bit of a delicate situation, but encouraged me by saying that throughout their interviews I had come across as being on the periphery of the conspiracy. Some small comfort there, I thought. I was beginning to believe that the charges against me might be dropped, or at least they wouldn't stick in court.

Their words of encouragement lifted my spirits, I must admit. Then something else happened to cheer me up: a team of solicitors arrived to attend to us. Chris had brought all the morning papers with him. We were headline news in all the broadsheets, but I grabbed the *FT* from him and turned to the commodities page. April potatoes had closed the previous day at £103.50, well up on the previous day, in heavy trading. I did a quick calculation. I was £160,000 better off. Not bad for two days in custody, although of course at that stage I didn't know that I had been sold down the river by a resentful employee.

Chris told me that he had spoken to my father, and that he had agreed to stand surety for me. With these three bits of good news, I was now feeling quite pleased with myself, content even. However, the euphoria I was enjoying was going to be extremely short-lived.

The court called us, and we were led in, one by one, up the narrow, winding staircase to the dock in the modern courtroom. We all stood close by one another in the dock – nervous, unshaven, smelly, dirty, unsure of our fate. The three magistrates walked in attired in ostentatious black velvet gowns. We were in one of the most elite magistrates' courts in the country, where the old traditions had not yet been updated. I noticed that they also wore regalia – this was more like a medieval star chamber than a court – but it was evident that they took their duty very seriously indeed. To our left, some journalists were seated, ring pads and pencils at the ready, and a court stenographer was also present. To our right, on a bench, sat all the defence solicitors and the brief for Customs. Surely, we would be granted bail? The prospect of a long remand in custody didn't bear thinking about. I saw myself as just a small cog in a bigger wheel.

The Customs brief stood up. The court went very quiet, you could hear a pin drop. All eyes turned to him. He was quite a young man, soberly dressed in a dark-grey single-breasted suit, white shirt and quiet tie. When attending Crown Court these days, it is advisable to look your best: choose your most expensive suit and polish your shoes. Stand out. I was still wearing my Armani suit and a loud pink tie. I was beginning to wonder if I had overdone it. I tugged on my sleeve, to keep my Piaget watch out of sight.

'If it may please the court,' the Customs man began, 'allow me to introduce everybody. To my right is Mr Fletcher, he represents Messrs Russell senior and junior, and Mr Owen; Mr Wilson next to him represents Mr Simmons; Mr Denton represents Mr Ford; and Mr Miles [Chris bowed slightly to the Bench, the only one to do so, I was pleased to see] represents Mr Goldman. He's the defendant seated in the centre of the dock, with the pink tie on.'

He paused while the magistrates surveyed everybody.

'The allegation is one of conspiracy to evade value added tax over a long period of time, on fine gold bullion bars. All of the defendants are involved in the bullion business to some extent or another, Mr Goldman being top of the tree as chairman and managing director of the International Gold Bullion Exchange.' At this I went white. They were trying to make out that I was the ringleader. I glanced over at Chris nervously, who stared back at me, shrugging his shoulders.

High Stakes

'The prosecution estimate that the amount of VAT evaded by this gang amounts to several million pounds.' I noticed the journalists scribbling away at their notes. 'This is a sophisticated conspiracy, involving all the defendants in the dock, although the parts they played are varied and differ in seriousness.' This was obviously their 'get-out' clause as far as Ford was concerned in turning Queen's evidence. 'With regard to bail, we would oppose it in view of the seriousness of the case. In the matter of Goldman, we would oppose it for two further reasons. First, we consider him to be a flight risk, he has a history of such conduct in the past, having fled the country in 1980 owing substantial sums to his creditors. Second, we believe that he still has substantial assets in North America. The other defendants, although lower down in the pecking order, if you like, still represent a flight risk, and in view of the fact that the investigation is ongoing, could well prove to be in danger of interfering with potential witnesses. Your Honours, if the Bench does decide to grant bail, we would submit that sureties be of the highest possible amount and that conditions of reporting be attached. We would also submit that all the defendants surrender their passports. Your Honours, this investigation is not yet concluded by any means, and we envisage that further arrests and charges are likely.' The prosecuting solicitor sat down. I glanced over to Chris again, and he looked back at me, concerned, then stood up and addressed the Bench.

'My client has not yet been convicted of anything and strenuously denies all these allegations and charges. He owns his own property and runs his own company, as you have heard. He is entitled to bail, that is his right, and we disagree strongly about what has been said about flight risk. However, he is prepared to surrender his passport and report to the police, if necessary. His father, a respectable member of the community, a retired dental surgeon, is prepared to stand surety.'

The other solicitors stood up to address the Bench, all saying something similar to Chris, and the magistrates finally rose and went out to deliberate. We were all led out of the dock and back down the stairs again, to the cells.

About half an hour later, we were ushered back into court. The magistrate at the centre of the Bench addressed the court. You could tell from the tone of his voice, the second he started, that it was a downer. He spoke in an upper-class whisper. Almost failing to hear, despite listening intently to what was being said, I heard him say the Bench was allowing us all bail to varying degrees. My bail level, I noted glumly, was the highest of the lot – £100,000. My father would have to put up the deeds to his home and some of his investments. While Wilson and Hill may have been concerned about their lack of hard evidence against me, the rest of HM Customs were surely prematurely celebrating their victory. I was going down.

We were escorted down the stairs again, but this time we didn't return to the cells. We were led into a waiting van, which had been expertly parked right up to the outside door, so that there were no escape gaps. We climbed in. We were on our way to Brixton Prison, on remand awaiting bail papers. As we pulled out of the confines of the court, a large group of photographers clicked away and a camera dollied in for the evening news. This was the second photo call.

Apart from my couple of nights in police custody, Brixton Prison in 1986 was my first proper taste of jail. It was the saddest place I had ever been to. Victorian, dreary and depressing, long, dimly lit corridors, painted in drab colours, led to the cells. I was put in a cell with a middle-aged man, who had already spent eight months on remand, facing a murder charge. The cell was small and claustrophobic, probably originally designed for one inmate, but now forced to house two because of overcrowding. There was no sanitation, a plastic bucket in the corner our shared toilet. This was where prisoners, unconvicted on remand, and convicted, had to live, eat and sleep, for 23 hours each day, behind a locked door. Prison conversation is a world of broken promises about a chimerical future. I ignored most of what my cellmate had to say. This was going to be his fourth sentence. He had done three, five and eight years at different points in his life. He had spent the bulk of his adult life in jail. Now, he was looking at life. I was starting to feel rather depressed, anxious. Surely my bail would be sorted out soon? Chris had promised to get the documents to my father for signature, and then to the police in Birmingham, as quickly as possible. Meanwhile, I had to sit it out in this stinking hellhole with the graffiti decorating the walls to keep me company. I lay on the top bunk.

At about 4.30 p.m., the cell door flew open. A young screw informed us it was time for tea. My cellmate made his way to the canteen, and I was about to follow him when a couple of other screws appeared and instructed me to follow them to reception. I had made bail, and had to receive my rail warrant and get discharged.

After my confinement, the day outside was dazzling and bright, the sky a glowing blue. It felt brilliant to be free. At Euston Station, I was embarrassed as I handed over my HMP rail warrant to the ticket clerk and paid the difference to exchange it for a first-class single. I was out, but the real battle had only just begun.

Serving Time:
Insurance Fraud

25

It was quite clear to everyone in the room that IGBE was insolvent, unable to meet its (considerable) liabilities. It was April 1986 and I was broke. Bankrupt. But whichever way he looked at it, Monty Levi just couldn't figure out how the company had ended up with such a black hole. Sure, there was the cost of the new dealing room, the extravagance of the cars, the expensive lease back to the office block, the advertising. He added up and subtracted all the columns of figures again, just to make sure. He arrived at exactly the same figure – or negative figure, to be more accurate. A million. One million pounds sterling. Deficit.

Everyone in the room was looking to me for an explanation for the deficit. How it happened. Why? All eyes turned to me – my accountant, my solicitor, my liquidator, my banker, the insurance broker. They all looked to me, the man in charge of the International Gold Bullion Exchange, for an explanation. And, just like so many high-profile businessmen before and after me, I tried to conceal it, cover it up. Stubborn pride, call it what you like, I would not admit to the losses. Of course, I should have said, 'I've been a fool. I've blown the million on the futures markets. Sorry, chaps. I'll be on my merry way.' Or something along those lines. I should have admitted everything and said, 'Sorry, I've been a fool and made a dreadful error of judgement.'

Don't ask me why, but what I did instead was unforgivable. I dug myself into a hole so deep that I would find no escape. Once I started on this trail of deceit, the whole thing just spiralled out of control. I know I should have owned up to it, told the truth about all those bum trades in the market. The coffee futures, the S&Ps, the gold and silver, the currencies. Rupert's recommendations, my tickles, my fancies. Hindsight is wonderful. I was beginning to wish that I could have traded instead of blowing all the money and trying to lie my way out of it.

Of course, Customs hadn't quite twigged yet that there was no money left. Their legal department had made a quick, rather expensive, *ex-parte* visit to the High Court in the Strand and obtained various injunctions and writs, which they sent round to Petersham Place with the process server. He hand-delivered a Mareva injunction freezing all my assets, and IGBE's, and for good measure I was handed a writ to the tune of £1.8 million for their assessment of the unpaid VAT. They should have saved their money on the court fees and process commissions. And to crown it all, on the morning of the meeting, another caller popped by to relieve me of my gold cards, which she took considerable delight in cutting in half with a pair of valuable retractable antique scissors, which she wore around her neck on a gold chain.

I glanced around my sitting room. Although it was only 11.30 in the morning, drinks flowed freely. It was quite clear to everyone that the million was missing. In a flash, I conjured up the most ridiculous explanation imaginable. I blamed Customs. Accused them, to be precise. I accused Customs and Excise of helping themselves to £1 million worth of gold bullion from my company's vaults during their search of the office. Can you believe it? I told you gold had a strange effect on people.

I waved the writ at all those in attendance, trying to convince them that the sheer gall of issuing the writ was proof that Customs were 'at it'. After all, they had failed to account for anything that they had removed from the office – paperwork, gold, anything else for that matter. Hadn't they behaved badly?

The law always catches up with you, the pretty lawyer had warned. It always gets its sweet revenge in the end.

'We are living,' I said, 'in the era of a police state, where bureaucracy has gone mad. It wouldn't surprise me in the slightest, if the bullion is to be wheeled into court as an exhibit to strengthen their case. After all, they haven't got much else, have they?'

'Do you know,' I addressed the gathering, enquiring of no one in particular, 'how few members of the public have actually ever seen a fine gold bullion bar?'

Everyone that morning had a sneaking (or strong) suspicion that I wasn't telling the truth, but were too polite to say so. They would soon find out that there was no gold, and that Customs hadn't uplifted anything other than voluminous quantities of paperwork. But I had bought a few days, in which I could work out a plan. I was in so much trouble, anyway, that I foolishly believed this extra hole I had dug myself into wouldn't make the slightest bit of difference in the overall scheme of things. An extra line on the rap sheet, a further charge for the jury to consider. These people didn't deserve, on paper, the havoc that I was about to introduce into their lives, but they were to get it anyway. I sent them on their way and was left on my own to contemplate my future. I couldn't decide whether to leave the country, or stay at home for the next few weeks, drink the bar dry, and wait for them to unravel the mystery and arrest me again.

I must admit, it did take them a while to figure out that Customs hadn't touched a single bar of gold on the visit to my offices. What with all the reconciliations, audit trails and invoicing, there just couldn't be the missing million in bullion anyway. But the strangest sequence of events was about to unfold, as though each one had a life and personality of its own.

Discussions took place to enquire if the company was insured for such an eventuality. It was. An insurance broker subsequently insisted that I complete an insurance form for the loss. When he came to see me with the document I was rather heavy handed with the vodka and £100,000 was written in the relevant box for the value of the claim, instead of £1,000,000. I signed the form and it was duly sent off to the insurance company. With that slip of the pen, one of life's ironies was about to unfold. What I had done was a bad thing. A very bad thing. A stupid, senseless, cavalier act of madness. Maybe I really was going nuts. But there were saving graces. I didn't expect to see any money; I didn't expect the insurance company to even consider coughing up. Even if they did, I wouldn't get any money, the claim was in IGBE's name, and IGBE itself was subject to a number of court orders and Marevas. What had I done wrong? You can't send a company to prison, and all I did was fill in a bleeding form.

What I had done, what I had filled in, unwittingly, was my own warrant to go to jail, directly, without passing 'Go'.

I imagine Customs weren't in the least bit pleased when they discovered that their visit to the High Court was to prove fruitless. They were probably even more dismayed when they discovered that IGBE was about to be put into liquidation. Customs contacted West Midlands Police and instructed them to re-arrest me under the Bail Act. It was the intention of Customs to haul me before the Stipendiary Magistrate and request that I be held in custody until my trial. They sent one of their undercover officers to Birmingham Magistrates' Court to handle what they thought would be a routine application. It looked as if he had been on a drugs bust the previous evening, wearing his leather jacket and jeans.

'We have information that Mr Goldman has sacked all his staff and is liquidating his company, therefore we believe he presents a flight risk. The department believe that he has substantial assets hidden in North America [that old chestnut again], and we have received information that he holds a second, Israeli, passport.' Nothing could have been further from the truth.

Author with his father Gerald

Author aged four, trying to look like a 1960s bookmaker

Author with cousins Jeremy (left) and Jonathan

The Rare Coin Investments plc stand at the Dubai Money Show

The Rosso Corsa Ferrari at Old Bridge House

The Lamborghini outside the International Gold Bullion Exchange offices

The author at Folkestone Races after Go With Bo wins

Goldfinger Nigel makes Penny Pay

One penny became worth £28,750 when Birmingham's 22-year-old tycoon Nigel Goldman paid a world record price for a 1933 coin.

Man is cleared in VAT case

A Birmingham business-man, accused of taking part in a £3.5 million VAT fraud has been acquitted.

£1.6M GOLD SEIZED IN FRAUD PROBE

Midland men held after Customs raids

Dealer cleared

A Gold dealer accused of being involved in a £3.5 million bullion fraud yesterday walked free from court.

Judge Thomas Dillon directed a Birmingham Crown Court jury to find Nigel Goldman, 31, not guilty of four charges of conspiracy to cheat Customs and Excise of VAT on fine gold bars.

The judge said there was insufficient evidence against him on any of the charges.

Goldman, of Petersham Place, Edgbaston, Birmingham, had denied all the charges.

Bo's No Go

The Jockey Club have dropped the Bo Knows Nigel case against trainer Geoff Lewis.

Heavily backed Bo Knows Nigel failed a dope text after being withdrawn from a race at Folkstone in August.

But on Lewis' instructions a similar test was taken in France and they found the sample to be under the drug threshold.

Some of the headlines that featured in the media during those heady decades living the high life

On holiday in Mauritius, 1992

A night on the town during day release from HMP Ford

The author with Jane
Thompson at the
Lanesborough Hotel, 1992

The author with American futures trader Drew McHail
in Brighton on day release from HMP Ford, May 1999

Fit after my release from prison

Enjoying a glass of vino
on the Costa del Sol

An evening out with Anthony Worrell Thompson,
my girlfriend Caroline and friends

Serving Time: Insurance Fraud

Chris Miles stood up to address the magistrate. 'The Bail Act, as I am sure you are aware, comes into play, if you like, when someone is arrested at the airport with tickets to Mexico in his pocket. My client has done nothing of the sort, and the liquidation of his company was forced upon him by the issuing of Mareva proceedings by Customs themselves. With regard to the allegation of the Israeli passport, we would like to enquire where that information has come from. I have today spoken with the Israeli Embassy in London, and Mr Goldman has never been issued with such a passport. In fact, in order to qualify for an Israeli passport, one has to have visited the country, something my client has never even done.'

The magistrate saw right through Customs and declined their application. I was back at home again, free on bail, but bored to death. Every other Friday, I would go and sign on, initially with the Lamborghini, which I must admit was a treat for those waiting in the DSS queue. The following Tuesday a thick, brown envelope stuffed with giros would arrive to pay the mortgage and service charges on Petersham Place. Of course, I didn't spend a penny of the money on household bills (the apartment was about to be repossessed, any time). I used the money instead to try and maintain some sort of lifestyle, while the wheels of justice slowly turned. It took a while for the police to cotton on to what exactly I had been up to, but when they did and came round to arrest me, it was almost a relief. I was in such a state, in such terrible trouble anyway, that a short interview at the hands of the West Midlands Police would make a pleasant break from my enforced boredom and panic. Little else happened that year – 1986 came and went, soaked in drink and vague memories of falsified insurance claims, police and Customs interviews, and pending trials. I felt strange, intolerably lonely, staying at home awaiting my fate, drinking my bar dry while IGBE was lying in state, shrouded in its Mareva injunction.

Still no date was set for my Customs trial, but by March 1987 the police had got their act together, and I was due to appear before

129

Birmingham Crown Court, charged with attempting to obtain £100,000 from a well-known insurance company by deception.

Just before my court appearance, my bank secured the repossession order on my flat to clear their overdraft, and I was forced to move out to a small maisonette in an unfashionable part of Birmingham. But soon, when the judge had finished with me, even that location would appear luxurious, compared to the new surroundings he had in mind for me.

Snow was lying on the ground as I took a cab to Birmingham Crown Court. The case was being held in the old court building; the new courthouse, under construction, was due to open soon after. The building was Victorian, foreboding and sinister; high ceilings echoed murmured conversations between defendants and their briefs, as they huddled in small groups near the doors to their allocated courtroom. An airport-style metal detector that you walked through at the entrance was the only intrusion of modern life into this cobwebbed morgue. I had a hastily convened conference with my barrister, Michael Grey, who was also to be my junior counsel for the forthcoming VAT trial. It had been agreed that I would plead guilty and, in that way, the fact that I had intended to obtain £1 million as opposed to the £100,000 would be overlooked.

'I'm going to ask the court to impose a suspended sentence, but I think that the chance of a non-custodial sentence is very remote,' he said.

I was very nervous, but grateful that the charge wasn't ten times what it should have been. We went in, and I entered the dock and was immediately frisked by a prison officer. I was soberly dressed in a dark-blue, pinstripe suit, on my solicitor's instructions.

His Honour Judge Jowett entered the courtroom. Everyone rose. Everyone sat. My counsel stood up and began his plea for a suspended sentence, only to be interrupted by the judge.

'There's no question of a non-custodial sentence in this case, Mr Grey.'

Serving Time: Insurance Fraud

My eyes met those of Chris Miles. I was going down, but for how long? Mr Grey did his best to take the sting out of the charge, and then the prosecution had their turn to have a go. They went on and on. I thought that by pleading guilty I would be saved the embarrassment, but they went into every little detail. How it was premeditated, how I was highly intelligent. On he droned. All I wanted was to get the formalities over and done with and to find out how long I had to do. How long was I going to prison for? The judge looked me straight in the eye. I got the impression he had a heart of stone.

'I would be failing in my duty if I failed to impose a custodial sentence in this case, so I'm sending you to prison for 12 months.'

That was it. I was led down the stairs from the dock, down a long, narrow corridor to the cell block.

Initially, I was banged up in a cell under the court with someone who had just got eight years. He laughed my sentence off as a walk in the park. Then I was unlocked and taken into another cell where a prison officer was sitting behind a desk. He started to take down my details, then I was examined for tattoos and scars. I was in a trance; everything was a blur. Then Chris Miles and his assistant solicitor, together with Michael Grey, appeared and we had a few minutes together. They all assured me that I would be out within six months on parole, and that I would serve my sentence in an open prison. I imagined that Customs would be celebrating the news of my incarceration, but I didn't dare imagine what schemes they would have up their sleeve for me during my sentence. My legal team urged me to get fighting fit for the VAT trial, reminded me that we had a tough case on our hands, and Michael Grey wished me good luck for the future.

I was taken back to my cell and within a few minutes we were on the move again, to Winson Green Prison. I was handcuffed to the chap doing eight years, and we were ushered onto a coach for the journey to jail. I couldn't help looking out of the window as we made our way to the prison, observing people going about their routine and everyday chores – shopping, standing on the pavements chatting, pushing prams, not a care in the world, taking everything for granted. I made up my mind there and then that if I got off the VAT trial, I would never get myself into that position ever again.

I went through the prison reception procedure like a zombie, as if in a daze. I was weighed by a black con (108kg). 'You'll be 88 kilos by the time you get out,' he said. Apart from this encouraging weight-loss estimate and months of enforced clean living, there was little else to look forward to. After being supplied with a bed pack, change of kit and some basic toiletries, I was banged up in a cell with two other cons. One was a young Irish guy who was doing three years for cannabis offences, and the other was a Birmingham burglar who was just finishing off a two-year sentence. I was preparing myself for the worst, having had a small taste of prison life in Brixton. My Irish cellmate chain-smoked strange roll-ups and was pouring a hot drink out of a flask, into a blue plastic, prison-issue cup. 'Here, drink this.' He offered me the cup. I climbed onto the top bunk and sipped the tea. Then everything went blank. My gritty eyes opened under a strip light in a ceiling far above human reach. I was still lying on the top bunk, on a mattress so thin it was as useful as a piece of cloth would have been to soften the grind of hip-bone on slab planking.

Underneath, on the bottom bunk, lay Sean, who gave me my 'tea'. Lifting my head, which felt as though it weighed two tons, I saw a heavy door, with an eye-level latch. Behind me was a window of thick, opaque glass, held firmly in place by a strong metal frame. I could not even remember being locked up.

I was wrapped in a leprous green-coloured blanket, with more holes in it than blanket. It had a stench which was almost visible. It had obviously been used for many years, a mockery of comfort for scores of frightened nobodies, numbered and filed into the care of HM Prison Service. Taking care not to let the accursed rag actually touch my bare flesh, I jerked my hips until it slithered to the green-tiled floor.

Serving Time: Insurance Fraud

I flopped back, angry. Fuck them and their stinking blanket. The movement of my body against the hard wood under the mattress was so uncomfortable. I started feeling vulnerable. I could turn on a display of manically concentrated violence, just to let them know I was not a disposable nobody, but that would have been stupid. You cannot afford to leave your mark on a prison cell. Black marks get noted on your personal file, follow you from establishment to establishment and usually end up with you losing the chance of parole, or serving additional time.

Your skull would fracture, smash and flatten, before it could add a single hairline crack to these concrete walls. No boots made for man could dent the door. The mattress had a texture unknown to man. I was a prisoner. I was in jail.

There is only one way to beat it all – stay cool. Do not give the guards one inch of satisfaction. I moved my eyes this way and that, fast then slow, trying to analyse my unusual surroundings.

Staring along the ridges of my nose, I saw, for the first time, a message crudely scratched on the cell wall, now faint in its definition.

Please God
Just one
more chance
10 years
Oh Jesus

Somebody managed to make a mark then.

I hate people who whinge.

I lifted my wrist high enough above my chest to see my wristwatch. It said 5.56 a.m. In order to go to the lavatory, I had to stand up, there seemed no other way about it. My heart had become a stable for a small, violent horse. The greys and greens, the brown sheets, gloomy lighting, the confinement, the stale second-hand oxygen, the scrawled graffiti messages – all of them made me feel like I was drowning at the bottom of a goldfish bowl. The lavatory was a plastic bucket in the corner, choked and overflowing. The stink was revolting. I switched to mouth breathing, but the taste was worse than the smell. My contribution cascaded over the edge of the full bucket onto an already very wet floor. Wet footprints marked my route back to the bunk. Every time I breathed, there was a fearful sense of doom. The doom seemed to grow inside my body.

I stretched out on the bunk again and told myself that it would all be over in eight months, maybe six, and that in just over two hours' time I would be out of this hellhole for at least fifteen minutes when I went to join the queue for breakfast. I could then make an application to see the governor, doctor or chaplain, which would free up some more time.

The hatch slammed open and a screw looked in to do a head count. A few minutes later, the door was unlocked. The corridor swarmed with noisy inmates, shuffling in line with their buckets to slop out in the crowded recesses. Those short of money begged roll-ups from the barons. Others held plastic bowls to fill up with tepid water for a wash and shave back in their cells. Screws in uniform stood at various vantage points, bored, ensuring good order and discipline. Once those chores were completed, we lined up for breakfast at the canteen. Long-term prisoners ladled out the stodge. Runny porridge, two slices of stale bread, a pat of butter and stewed tea. The food was slapped onto a metal tray, the porridge running onto the bread, rendering it an inedible mush. Instead of eating, I binned the lot, climbed the stairs back to my landing and lay down again on my bunk. My two cellmates hadn't stirred out of bed during the whole procedure, oblivious to early-morning prison life.

Later that day, I was taken to be photographed for my prison file. I was then told that I was to be interviewed at 2.15 that afternoon for allocation to a long-term prison to serve my sentence. The time came and went, and I remained locked up. I started to panic, wondering what had happened to my valuable appointment, but I was soon to learn that in prison nothing runs to plan. I discussed with my cellmates the conditions in other prisons and where I should aim to get allocated to, much like I used to discuss the attributes of different first-class hotels around the world with friends over gin and tonics.

It was three days before I got my appointment, and I was taken into a cell which had been decked out as an office for use by the senior officer in charge of allocations. He sat at a desk with a colleague at his side. An inmate, their orderly, hovered around in the background brewing tea. The senior warden began.

'I don't see any reason why you shouldn't serve your sentence in an open prison, do you?' This was, without doubt, the nicest thing anyone had said to me for the past few days. I tried to conceal my eager excitement as I agreed to his suggestion. I asked to be transferred to Sudbury, an open prison which had been recommended by other cons, but I was informed that I was going to Ashwell instead, because there was single accommodation available, instead of dormitories. I was told that I would be shipped out within a few days.

Again, the timetable slipped, but after three weeks in 'the Green', I was told to pack my kit. I was off. This time, I was ushered out into the prison courtyard, with the other transfers, mainly short-term prisoners who were categorised as low risk, and we went into a minibus for our journey. I noted with some satisfaction that none of us were handcuffed, and it became obvious that we were about to be transferred to a regime that was much more relaxed and trusting than the closed environments of the local prison system. Our journey was full of optimism and hope, most of the cons asking the screw who accompanied us questions about visits, work, food, phone calls and accommodation.

'It's like a holiday camp, you'll have a great summer with us.'

The screw was right. The place was heaven compared to Winson Green. We had our own room with a key, there were shower facilities, a TV room, a library and the freedom to roam the fields surrounding the prison. There was even a mini-golf course, and I started to play golf with other businessmen who, like me, had fallen from grace. Even the food was palatable. If I had to do time, this was the way to do it. The summer was approaching and the weather was glorious. I was starting to lose weight and get fit. The forthcoming VAT trial, although uppermost in my mind, seemed somehow less significant than before. I was starting to feel confident that I could beat the rap.

I was then moved from Ashwell to Wormwood Scrubbs. Whilst it would of course be virtually impossible to prove, I suspected it was because the powers that be felt conditions were too relaxed and open for me there, bearing in mind my pending VAT trial and the temptation to abscond.

The Scrubbs was pretty much the same as the Green, except that it was worse. There was very little to do, and I spent around 23 hours a day banged up. There was no work and little 'association'. I was starting to get seriously depressed. Then, out of the blue, a screw came to my cell. He had a message for me from the discipline department. I was required as a witness in a civil court case in Manchester. I was to be shipped out to Strangeways the following day. I didn't have a clue what the case was about, or who the parties involved were, but I wasn't going to complain about my free ticket out of the Scrubbs. With a bit of luck, once the Manchester episode was over, I might be able to persuade the authorities to return me to an open prison, without informing Customs.

At Strangeways, I had an interview with a solicitor who had been instructed by City Investments to come and see me. Apparently, a group of investors, capitalising on my incarceration, had decided to get together and sue City Investments for the money they had lost in the futures market, and blame me for recommending bum trades to them. The solicitors for City Investments didn't think the claim stood a cat in hell's chance, but to be on the safe side they briefed me about what questions I was likely to be asked in court.

A week later, I was transported to the County Court to give my evidence. Dansiger was in attendance, together with a senior representative from City Investments. I wasn't due to go up and give my evidence until the afternoon, so Rupert kindly volunteered to go out and buy some goodies for us. He came back to the holding cell with sandwiches, beer, crisps, chocolate, a bottle of wine and some fruit. I had the best nosh up of my life and a good drink, too. The screws who had escorted me kindly turned a blind eye to me drinking, as they were invited to join the feast. In the end, I wasn't even required that day and had to appear the following day as well. This time, the screws didn't take me in cuffs and, since they had warmed to me, promised that I would have a good job waiting for me when I returned to the nick. I gave my evidence (badly), had another booze up and some nosh. City Investments lost the case and faced a compensation bill of tens of thousands of pounds, and I was returned to the nick. I was offered a job in the officers' mess, the best job in the prison, which I gratefully accepted. About a week later, though, it was decided that I had to go back to Winson Green, as that was the prison I was originally sent from. I didn't complain too much, as I had a strange feeling that I might be able to talk my way back to an open prison again. My thoughts were to be proved right and, within a week of being back in the Green, I was on my way to Sudbury Open Prison to finish off my sentence.

At Sudbury I got fit, lost a ton of weight, used the gym and did a lot of walking in the grounds, taking full advantage of the fresh country air. Booze and tobacco flowed freely, and some friends arranged a drop for me, containing champagne, whisky and cigars. I had a glass of champagne for breakfast and a few Scotches as a nightcap. My time was passing quickly; I was to be out soon. As that day grew nearer, though, I became more and more apprehensive about the VAT trial, and I was very much aware that if I lost that trial, I would be straight back inside and serving a considerably longer stretch than I was doing now.

As my parole date approached, I was handed a form to fill in with my reasons for requesting early release. I filled it in, listing my enormous sense of remorse, my intention to rehabilitate and my sorrow as the main features for being released on licence. A couple of days after handing in the form, the Home Secretary announced that all short-term prisoners would be released at the halfway stage of their sentences to ease the overcrowding in the prisons. I was to be let out in less than a week.

The day I was set free was glorious. I hadn't slept all night, thinking of the things I wanted to do when I got out. I got weighed in reception, 88 kilos as predicted, so I had lost a total of 20 kilos in just 6 months.

I headed straight to Horts wine bar, a newly adopted favourite of mine. All the regulars were in their usual places. The lads noticed how well I looked. An old flame, Jenny, was there too, and we started chatting and drinking. I ended up spending the next four days with her.

26

I had come out of my prison experience well – fighting fit with a positive mind and feeling years younger than when I went in. Probably better, and cheaper, than any health farm. I was certainly feeling a whole lot better than my various co-defendants, who, I had learnt from reliable quarters, were finding the long delay on bail intolerable.

During my first meeting in chambers with my trial barrister, Hugh Mayor, QC, I had even more reason to feel cheerful. 'We have a good defence to this conspiracy charge, Mr Goldman. If this was indeed a conspiracy, why were the gold bullion bars transported from London to Birmingham, only for them to be shipped all the way back down the motorway again a few minutes later by IGBE. Would it not have been simpler, and indeed cheaper, to just get the bullion delivered by your co-conspirators direct to Julian Paxton on your behalf?' Hugh Mayor, like all good criminal defence barristers, had located and homed into

Customs and Excise's Achilles heel in one fell swoop. I was glad my chair had arms; they prevented me falling out of it.

As any lawyer and any acquitted crook will endorse, guilt had nothing to do with whether I actually committed the offence in question. Guilt is a technical relationship between charge and evidence, and must be established beyond reasonable doubt by the prosecution, who have to persuade a jury that the evidence is consistent with only the prosecution's version of events and not any other. Hugh was ingeniously going to propose that I was out of the circle, making up just a small innocent part in a larger jigsaw, which saw gold travelling up and down the land. Why otherwise would such a risky and time-consuming project be implemented by one of the main players? Hugh Mayor was certain that he could beat the charge. We were pleading not guilty, and we were going to win.

The trial soon started in the newly opened Birmingham Crown Court building. On the advice of Peter Kinsley, my old friend from the OCs, who I had drinks with most lunchtimes during the trial in the Gazette Club next to his offices, I spent the first few days of the trial sitting in the dock with my co-defendants, arms folded, looking up to the ceiling and doing my best to make out the entire proceedings had nothing to do with me whatsoever.

It had been agreed with my counsel that I would not go into the box to give evidence and that after the prosecution case was finished, my QC would ask the trial judge to dismiss the case against me through lack of evidence. We still had one obstacle to overcome, though. The Customs document 'DAVIDSON G' was still on their list of exhibits. Hugh Mayor made an application to have the document removed from the case, and the jury bundles, as it was prejudiced against me, and the jury should not be invited to consider its significance. The application took a whole morning, in the absence of the jury, and was, needless to say, vigorously opposed by the prosecution. The trial judge retired to his chambers to consider our application. When the judge returned, he threw the document out. The Customs case against me was collapsing.

High Stakes

Nevertheless, I had to sit through the rest of the prosecution's case and pray that Hugh Mayor's gamble would pay off, and that we would win our argument at the end of their presentation.

With a couple of days to go to the end of the prosecution's innings, I was again *in situ* at the Gazette Club. Many of the legal boffins came up to congratulate me on winning the trial, yet the case was far from over. It seemed they had all heard whispers that I was going to win. I had to question whether it was some kind of sophisticated wind-up, or if they really did know something. I returned to court that afternoon, desperate for the case to end, praying that some legal technicality wouldn't turn up all of a sudden and shatter my dreams.

On the last day of the prosecution's case, Chris Wilson was called to give his evidence. He looked terrible, his face ruddy and his eyes as bloodshot as a hunter dog. It looked as if he knew he had lost.

On my way out of court, I passed a senior Customs officer sitting in his car. He wound down the window to tell me that he knew I had beaten them. The following morning Hugh Mayor delivered his argument to the court. The judge ordered a verdict of not guilty against me. I watched the jurors shake their heads in disbelief and amazement. The Customs brief smashed his fist down on his trial bundles.

I'd beaten the system. My lawyer had exploited Customs like some soppy submissive puppy dog who rolls over on his back to have his tummy tickled. I had stuck two fingers up at the government, been acquitted of being the ringleader of the largest-ever gold smuggling operation in the UK at that time. The charges had been brought by the elite squad of HM Customs and Excise. It had been their biggest-ever case. I doubted they would ever forget me.

PART TWO
The Touch

1988–99

Starting Over with Rare Coins

27

We were driving eastwards down the M4, it was a blazing hot afternoon. Although normally a good driver, my performance was particularly bad that day because the girl in the seat beside me was trying to remove my trousers. I held onto the leather steering wheel tightly. The cockpit of my Mercedes Sports had a smell of new leather and expensive perfume.

'Not here!' I shouted, wriggling and trying to move upright in my seat. I took my right hand off the steering wheel and tried to refasten my fly zipper. I put my hand back on the wheel, and her hand pulled down the zipper again. At the same time, her tongue burrowed into my left ear.

'Why don't we pull over?' she said, seductively.

'We have to get to the races. Ouch!' A very cold hand slid down inside my trousers. Her mane of expensively highlighted blonde hair descended onto my lap. I pulled over.

Vanessa eventually pulled my fly zipper back up, and we drove into the car park of Windsor Racecourse just in time for the start of the evening's racing. I displayed the Racehorse Owners' Association car park badge, which Tom McLoughlan, a friend of mine, had given me the previous evening, and the white-coated car park attendant ushered us into a space in the owners' and trainers' car park right next to the entrance gates to the course.

In this car park, smartly dressed upper-class owners, trainers, thespians and villains climbed out of their Porsches, Mercs and Rollers, some already talking to their bookmakers on mobile phones, while others sat in the cool of their air-conditioned cars studying the form in the *Sporting Life* and *Racing Post*.

I locked the car, and we headed in. Complimentary badges for owners were being handed out in a hut, and we joined the short queue. 'Name, sir?' enquired the badge man, who had a race card open in front of him and was ticking off the names of owners and runners as he dished out the badges.

'Sir Nigel Goldman, we have a runner in the third race, although you won't find my name there, as I have only just bought the horse.'

'No problem, sir,' and he handed my guest and me each a deep-purple badge with matching twine.

'Fancy pulling a stroke like that,' Vanessa said, as she wrapped her arm around mine and looked over her shoulder to make sure that no one could overhear her. 'As if you own racehorses.' Somehow, the suggestion of actually being an owner did hold some appeal. I had always dreamed of a horse passing the winning post in first place in my racing colours. If you want something badly enough, you can make it happen, I suppose.

We walked into the course. Some lads were leading horses around the paddock on the right, in front of us was a Tote betting hut and to our left there was the grandstand where the restaurant and bars were situated.

We decided to go and take a look at the horses. A racehorse close up is exactly like a supermodel close up – its legs are too long, it is riddled with sinews, and it looks as though it could do with a good breakfast. Like those catwalk models, the horses seemed sullen; they were whinnying in a slightly hysterical manner, each with its own initialled coat.

Starting Over with Rare Coins

We followed the horses as they were led out of the paddock into another enclosure, nearer to the course. A sign was displayed at the entrance of the paddock:

Parade Ring
Only owners and trainers with horses involved in the next
race allowed in this area

Quite a few owners stood around in important-looking groups at the centre of the parade ring, chatting with their trainers, awaiting the arrival of their prized bloodstock. Then the jockeys arrived in the ring in a plethora of colour, twirling their whips. Peaky with starvation, they touched their caps as they were introduced to the owners and took their race instructions from the trainers. I was beginning to think that racing wasn't about winning – more about keeping underweight. The jockeys were then given a leg up, to settle into their saddles, and take their charges down to the start. While Vanessa was taking all of this in, inquisitively studying her racecard, I overheard one of the trainers instruct his jockey: 'Settle her, get her balanced, keep her covered, then push the button at the distance. You'll cruise up.' This sounded like a pretty good tip to me, and the jockey jumped on a horse with a number 8 on its saddlecloth. I turned to an older man standing next to me who was studying a *Timeform* guide. 'Eight looks good to me,' I volunteered, hoping for some expert confirmation, so I could justify a decent wager.

'You don't want to go betting heavy on fillies,' the old man warned me. 'They don't run true to form, and they're liable to spit it out in the last furlong. Pass the action, kid.'

Reluctantly, I passed and Vanessa and I strolled over to the champagne bar under the grandstand. A fat man was selling shellfish at exorbitant prices, and the bar was situated next door. I purchased a warmish bottle of Veuve Clicquot and was a little surprised to be handed plastic tumblers to pour it into.

A badly dressed Greek stood at the bar drinking Campari and

soda. He sported trousers that were three inches too long for him and frayed around his heels. He was busy ripping up a fistful of losing Tote tickets. He noticed me frown at the plastic tumblers. 'So you don't throw 'em at the losing 'orses!' he said, dryly. It did cross my mind that one could always chuck the entire glass bottle at a horse, if one felt so inclined.

We settled down at a table to sip our drinks and watch the race on television. Eight sluiced in at generous odds, and there were no queues at the books.

We went out to the paddock to look at the horses for the next race, then made our way into the ring to have a bet. This was my very first experience of racing, but I was already beginning to enjoy the atmosphere of the occasion. Board bookmakers chalked up their prices, while the larger layers on the rails shouted out the odds on offer. White-gloved tick-tack men conveyed action from the rails to the books, so the smaller players could hedge. I ignored the favourite in the race, which was on offer at around even money by most of the bookmakers, and took an interest in a horse called Golan Heights, quoted at four by everyone – except for one chap who was offering seven and a half. I went up and had £40 on it with him, and had unwittingly taken 7–2 on a 4–1 chance. I even stayed his hand when he attempted to sponge off the 7–2 and change it to 4–1. 'No, it definitely said 7½,' my voice quavering. 'I'm really certain about that.' I have to say, he seemed pretty certain it didn't. In the end, it made no difference at all; Golan Heights trailed in fifth, a 10–1 shot beating the favourite by a neck.

The following race was the seller, and we watched the winner being walked around the small parade ring in front of the auctioneer's stand. The auctioneer picked up his mike. 'This horse is offered for sale by auction, having just won the last race impressively by five and a half lengths.' The horse was being led round in circles, still blowing quite hard after its exertions in the race and sweating up under its blanket, unaware of the interest surrounding it, or indeed which racing stables it was going to that evening. A large crowd had gathered around the auctioneer's rostrum as he continued in his plum tone, 'I will remind you that this horse is to be sold under the rules of racing and that we will not accept any cheques drawn on foreign banks, as they take so jolly well long to clear, if indeed they clear at all. What am I bid? Five thousand? At three thousand, thank you, sir. At three, three and a half, four and a half, at five now. At five thousand. All done, at five thousand? At five thousand guineas. All done? One more?' I resisted the urge to put my hand up and bid. Just. 'At five thousand guineas for the last time. Sold.'

So, that's how bloodstock changed hands. I imagined being the buyer of the horse, following its progress for the rest of the season, watching it being trained, betting on it at the races. Going for a touch. Yes, racing was certainly growing on me and held considerable appeal.

That evening I took Vanessa to dinner at the Bell and Dragon, a seventeenth-century pub in Cookham High Street which boasted a magnificent restaurant. The pub was run by a wealthy, elderly Swiss couple and frequented by the Thames Valley clique. The wine list was fabulous, and the owner told me that the Roux Brothers ate there every evening at one stage, while they were opening the Waterside Inn at nearby Bray-on-Thames, so that they could negotiate the purchase of a portion of his wine cellar. After dinner, we walked by the Thames, taking in the beauty of the summer evening in the country. Some boats had put up along the reach, and there were barbecues and drinks being served on deck.

As we walked along the towpath that summer evening, holding hands, I thought about how my life had been smashed to pieces over the previous couple of years, about all the knocks and blows, and the despair. I thought back to the six months I had spent in prison, when I had had nothing. Vanessa looked up at me and smiled, and I smiled back. I thought about how, after just a few short months, the pieces all seemed to be slotting back together very nicely.

28

After winning my VAT trial, I had decided I needed a change and so moved down south to start life afresh. Rupert introduced me to a small German brokerage company he was doing business with called 'Mark Butler & Co'. Mark ran the business with 'Stephen Kay', whose family were ring-dealing members of the London Metal Exchange.

Mark offered me a deal which I couldn't refuse. They would provide me with an office, a trading desk with Reuters screen and phones, all expenses spared. In return, I was to get clients to open accounts with the firm, make all the investment decisions and do all the trading. I would be paid £300 a week pocket money while I got things under way, and we would split the commissions 50/50 on all the business I introduced. I immediately grabbed the opportunity and signed a lease on a small flat in Cookham, Berkshire, a picturesque village by the River Thames in the heart of the Thames Valley.

At Mark Butler's, I immediately got on the telephone to everyone I knew – ex-clients from IGBE, friends, contacts. Flush from my success at Birmingham Crown Court, I was in good form, opening one trading account after another. Mark and Stephen couldn't believe it. The account opening forms and enclosed cheques were arriving in large numbers every day. I hit the phone hard, was full of enthusiasm and seemed to have boundless energy. Within a month, I had opened over 50 accounts and soon we had in excess of £1 million under management.

I started to generate huge amounts of commission income and was turning this small brokerage company into something quite phenomenal. I would regularly pocket over five grand a week in commission, and I talked Mark into letting me use the company account for entertaining clients. He was quite happy to let me have the run of the place. I opened an account, filled in my occupation as 'commodity broker' (the in-vogue occupation of the time) and to my surprise the manager gave me a gold MasterCard almost immediately. My financial history still lay buried in my dim past. At the weekends, I used Mark's Mercedes to run around in. I was back with a bang.

I felt happy and relaxed in Cookham; it was the first time in many years I had done so. It was a new world, the promised land, a world finally free of magistrates, juries and QCs. I had five girlfriends on the go all at once. Debbie, a legal secretary from Birmingham, who wore too much make-up and had written me long letters while I was in prison; Jane, also from Birmingham, who worked in a casino, and whose sister worked as a secretary for Chris Miles, my lawyer. She looked and dressed as though she was a teenager. Lovely. They came to stay on alternate weekends. And in Cookham, I discovered Janet all by herself in the pub one evening. She had such a lovely wardrobe and lots of interesting friends. And there was Suzanne, an estate agent who showed me round lots of cottages I pretended to be interested in buying. And then Vanessa, who loved going to the races. I was a one. I succeeded in keeping them all secret from one another.

Although I was earning good money working for Mark Butler, the gravy train was about to end. Mark paid little or no attention to the regulatory bodies under whose auspices licensed dealers operated and who were in charge of cleaning up the City. Eventually, their umbrella would cover all aspects of City activities, but in the late 1980s their prime objective was to target small derivative firms who were operating on small capital bases. Firms like us. In Germany, where derivative business was outlawed, Mark had a team of agents who introduced huge volumes of options business at premiums which bore no resemblance to the actual quotes prevailing in the London market.

High Stakes

The demise of Mark Butler & Co. began innocently enough, with an almost questionnaire-style enquiry from the Association of Futures Brokers and Dealers. We filled the form in, returned it second-class post and kept our fingers crossed that we would hear no more. But it was quite clear that further enquiries would follow, especially when it came to the matter of the firm's cash reserves, which Mark was draining out of the company almost as soon as he was earning them. The powers that be were also taking a close look at Mark Butler's affairs for two other reasons. First, Stephen Kay was involved in a prolonged and nasty law suit with an overseas client who had deposited a huge amount of money with the firm, which Stephen had managed to dispose of entirely in a fortnight's orgy of trading. Snippets of this pending case leaked out to me over liquid lunches at the local wine bar in Chalfont St Peter, run by a colourful local woman who got in smoked salmon and bagels to keep us nourished during our long, boozy lunches. Second, the powers that be were a little alarmed, to say the least, at the considerable ease with which I had managed to slide into such a powerful position in the futures industry so soon after being discharged from prison and in the aftermath of the VAT trial, from which there was still huge dollops of smarting in the higher echelons of the Establishment. We were hardly 'fit and proper' in the eyes of the City regulators and, like so many small brokerage houses in the late 1980s, we were about to be closed down with not so much as a hope and a prayer for the directors and staff. How I hated the authorities for their complete lack of understanding. I was beginning to wonder if the regulators were working in conjunction with the large firms to corner the market all to themselves.

Just before the demise of his firm, Mark got married to a woman who already had children. Jane and I attended the wedding ceremony in Gerrards Cross, and we enjoyed a slap-up lunch at the Bull. Financially, though, Mark's lifejacket had been punctured, and he was destined to sink or swim. In one final attempt to float, I found him one Friday evening sitting at his desk, chain smoking, bottle of Scotch half empty, eyes glued to Reuters, trading in vast volumes of S&P futures. In a rare bull market correction, the Dow spewed up, taking Mark and his clients with it. After that we parted company amicably and went our separate ways.

Over the previous nine months, other brokers in Mark's office had earned an average commission of £25,000. The volume of my business was such that I had netted £150,000. After tax and overheads, such as my champagne bills at the wine bar, which Mark was not interested in splitting with me, I had stashed away some £105,000. By lucky investments in the stock market, I had managed to turn that sum into £190,000. I was also in the process of taking legal advice from counsel as to whether I had a claim against Customs and Excise for their failed case against me. I was assured that I had, and Michael Grey submitted an opinion that we could successfully sue them for wrongful arrest, false imprisonment, malicious prosecution and about a million on top of all that for the Mareva injunction and writ for VAT, which had caused the demise of IGBE, the loss of my reputation and, of course, the repossession of Petersham Place. I was beginning to feel rather pleased with myself and was coming round to the opinion that the time was right to set up my own company and get back into business on my own account. I was itching to get started.

29

When starting a business or forming a company, especially one designed to relieve Joe Bloggs of his savings, form a company that appears to be already well-established and trading from rock-solid foundations. Choose a name with Investment, Imperial or International in the title. When advertising, list your phone number and put 20 lines in brackets after it, even if you are sitting in your spare room with only one line. Get a fax and telex number, and invest in a cable address. Issue a million quid's worth of shares, even if none are paid up. Publish a glossy brochure, with pie charts and graphs, illustrating how investors fielding money in your company's direction will do ten times better than in the building society. On paper, at any rate. Promise huge tax-free returns on clients' investments, employ a team of hungry, commission-only salespeople to pitch for business over the phone. Teach them the nuances of selling, persuading and coercing the gullible public over the phone. Make them stand on chairs while they give good phone to the mugs in suburbia. Take stands at major investment shows and exhibitions all over the world. Send out mass mailings to gold-card holders and investors in high-risk stocks on the AIM (the Alternative Investment Market). Invest in mailing lists of mug punters. Beg, steal or borrow lists of mugs from other bucket shops in the investment industry, or from bookmakers and racing tipsters.

With all the above in mind, Rare Coin Investments plc was born in 1988, shortly after I parted company from Mark. It was possible then, and still is now, to form your own unlisted plc company inexpensively. Those three magical letters – plc – conjure up images of self-respect and financial stability, and open lots of doors when it comes to obtaining credit.

Of course, most members of the public think that your company holds the same status as a fully listed public company, like ICI or Courtaulds, and I for one was not going to persuade them otherwise. The only legal criteria to be fulfilled for one of these plc companies to obtain a certificate of trading is that they issue shares worth £50,000. However, I was quick to exploit the loophole in the law which stated that only 25 per cent of this figure had to be paid up. So, for a mere £12,500, I was off and running.

Although most of my previous business ventures had ended up being riddled with fraud and dishonesty, wound up insolvent or generally sucked financially dry, I was full of good intentions when I formed RCI plc. I was returning to my roots as a numismatist. My philosophy, or my corporate plan, if you like, was quite simple. We would supply portfolios of rare coins to investors and take a nice percentage for the privilege. This kind of scheme was tried and tested, and had worked very well in the States, where boiler shops of salesmen pedalled huge quantities of high-grade coinage to investors either through direct mail or on the phone. In order to entice potential punters in my direction, I decided to design a corporate brochure, which I would puff up to make the idea of rare coins as an investment a marketable idea. I didn't really intend to tell porkies in the brochure; it was just supposed to be a bit of sales hype. A few charts and diagrams would help to prove the point, and I scoured through some old Seaby coin catalogues to show price increases over the years to reinforce our promise of unrealistically high returns in a speculative venture. 'Nothing ventured, nothing gained.' I spent hours designing the brochure, conjuring up an image that I would want to see if I was to be persuaded to invest in a new project. There is a saying that the best salesmen are the easiest people in the world to sell to themselves, so with that in mind I went on a crusade of designing a corporate brochure that I could really believe in.

I must admit, it did take me some time to get it off the ground, what with all the dummy runs and all those graphs and pie charts, but eventually a smart, fawn-coloured brochure dropped on my desk from the advertising agency. I was back in business again. There was just one little matter to attend to before I put my energies into my new company.

I had heard on the grapevine that a man in Leeds I knew quite well, called 'Julian Green', who was also a close pal of 'Guy Michaels', had acquired a stake in a quoted public company called 'Bearwater', with the idea that he reverse his ever-expanding successful property business into it. I had spent quite a lot of time as a guest of Guy and Julian, and over the years had conducted quite a lot of business with them both. Julian would sometimes even come down to Birmingham to stay with me, and we would often take positions together in the stock and futures market. I respected him as a shrewd businessman, even though he seemed a bit of a maverick, and felt certain that if he had acquired a stake in Bearwater, bigger and better things were to follow. Consequently, I phoned up my stockbrokers, 'Harriet Ward & Co.', and purchased a quarter of a million shares at 30p each. By a sheer fluke, he took my instruction down by mistake as a quarter of a million pounds' worth of shares and when the contract note arrived the following morning, and the share price had already rallied to 38p, I kept shtoom. My intention was to hold onto these shares for a few months, see what Julian was up to with the company, then sell the shares on. I didn't have quite enough money to pay for these extra shares, but Harriet Ward was a very understanding and accommodating firm, and I knew I would have little or no difficulty in getting them to extend me some credit.

My views on Harriet Ward were spot on – not only were they quite happy to accommodate me, but they were taking an active interest in Bearwater's share price themselves. Quite a few of the company's directors had invested their own money in Bearwater, so whenever I phoned, they were always keen to hear my views on the company. I became more and more bullish, and when the share price hit 50p, I added to my position. Bearwater had also agreed to take over the Rodney Marks Design Company, a company based in Birmingham which specialised in the upmarket interior design of hotels worldwide. I knew Rodney Marks quite well. I had met him when I was invited to participate in the Beaujolais Run. He was still a flamboyant character and lived extremely well in Bell Hall, a grand mansion near Birmingham which I had gone to view with him in 1985. The other arrow in their quiver was Moyses Stevens Flower Shops. I had visions as a major shareholder of walking into their upmarket florists in London and ordering bouquets for everyone at no cost. The more I looked at the Bearwater deal, the more I fell in love with it. Again, I thought about England Futures and became convinced that I was taking part in the trade that would get me back into the millionaire league, where I was now firmly convinced I belonged. I even had visions of appearing in *The Times* 200, along with the wealthiest people in Britain.

So, when a large manilla envelope from the bank which was acting as registrar for Bearwater arrived in the post, I eagerly opened it. It contained a bunch of share certificates in my name for the shareholding. I got my calculator out and added up the total number of shares on the certificates. I was a little dismayed to find that it only came to just over 600,000 shares in total, not the

Starting Over with Rare Coins

800,000 that I had purchased. I thought maybe that the difference was because I still hadn't paid for all the stock, but a couple of days later another envelope arrived with another batch of certificates, about 800,000 this time. Unbelievably, the registrars had mailed my holding to me twice over.

By now, the Bearwater share price had risen to 68p. I went for a walk to think through what to do about the windfall of share certificates, dropped on my lap like manna from heaven. I had already made up my mind that the bank weren't getting them back, but I had to figure out a way to try and realise their value without getting nicked for fraud.

I figured that if I sold the extra shares I would be easily guilty of obtaining the money by deception. I was painfully aware how carefully I had to tread, only so recently having walked away from the VAT trial. Instead, I hatched a plan which would allow me access to the money value of the shares, without actually selling them. I contacted my private bank and made an appointment to see the manager. I explained that I had just formed a new company, RCI plc, and that I wanted to inject sufficient capital into the company to enable it to trade profitably and issue a large number of paid-up shares. I made up a story that I was prohibited from selling my Bearwater shares for three years, as a condition of my shareholding, and I impressed him with a printout showing the price performance of the stock over the previous few months. My request was quite simple. I wanted to lodge all my shares with the bank and borrow 80 per cent of their value in the form of an overdraft, to inject into RCI. The loan would be repaid after three years, when I would liquidate the holding, hopefully at a price considerably higher than the shares were trading at that time. Amazingly, the bank bought my story. It was typical of the cavalier attitude for which the late 1980s would be remembered – the bank were greedy for the interest on the loan and, within a week, my current account had been credited with £650,000. The day that happened, I was off to Windsor races where I had arranged to meet up again with Tom McLoughlan. The following morning, I would be penniless.

155

Gambling on a Winner

30

My first couple of visits to the roulette table of racehorse ownership were to prove expensive and unsuccessful adventures, but, like most dry wheels, it would lay the foundations and tease the taste buds for an interest in racing some years later, which would bubble and froth over with unprecedented success.

Anybody who buys a racehorse out of a selling race is either very silly or very clever indeed. All punters expect stables to pull the occasional stroke and getting a moderate horse ready to win a selling race is taken as part of their calculations – or guesswork, as it is otherwise known.

The calibre of horse entered into a selling race in the first place is the worst kind. The horses are generally poor performers, condemned animals, with strings of duck eggs next to their name in the formbook. They are a liability. There are worse kinds of races, though. Where? At illegal flapping tracks somewhere in Ireland or in unpronounceable regions of the world where work riders go out bareback at 100 degrees in the early morning sun. There are worse horses, too. Where? Lame in fields at permit holder's yards, or virally infected animals condemned to their boxes, unable to race, labelled and destined for the knacker's yard. Group calibre bloodstock these horses are not. These are sellers. Platers.

Tom and I met up at Windsor in the champagne bar as usual and, after attending quite swiftly to our third bottle, went out to watch the seller, which was won convincingly by a horse called Order of Merit. We ventured out to the auction ring. The now-familiar group of onlookers were gathered round, and the auctioneer tapped his mike into life as the horse was led in. The trainer eyed his animal dourly, like a banker weighing up his chances of recouping a loan to a recession-hit South American country.

Tom suggested we buy the horse between us and that I should go into the ring to bid, since I had auction experience. He instructed me not to pay more than 8,000 guineas. The auctioneer tapped his mike, ready to begin. Tom slid his Coutts chequebook out of his jacket pocket, and smiled and nodded at me to go in the ring.

'At five thousand, five thousand guineas, fifty-two, fifty-five, fifty-eight, six.'

Tom nudged me on. 'Go on, bid for it,' he whispered. I raised my hand at 6,800 guineas and caught the auctioneer's eye.

'At 6,800 guineas for the last time. Sold!' I had just bought my first share of a racehorse.

Of course, the purchase price of a horse is a mere down payment: the annual training fees alone come to twice the cost. Then there are the entry fees, gallop fees, vet and blacksmith bills, transport and insurance. If you want a pet, get a dog. Racing is a hungry animal that eats deep into your pockets.

'Do you want him?' Tom enquired of a shortish, unkept-looking individual who had wandered over to the vicinity of the auction ring.

'Yes – I'll take it, Tom,' he drawled in his Ayshire accent. At first, I thought that we had just flipped the animal for a quick profit, and that this fellow was the lucky new owner. No price tag had been mentioned, though, which I thought rather odd. It turned out that this character was going to train our horse at his yard. I was quickly introduced to the man, our new trainer. We broke open another bottle to celebrate our acquisition.

On our way out of the racecourse, a man in a white coat was selling the late edition of the *Evening Standard*. 'Tomorrow's declared runners, tomorrow's declared runners,' he pitched. Had I purchased a copy, I would have seen an article which would have warned me of the dire scenario about to unfold.

That evening, while Order of Merit made his journey in the horsebox to his new stables, a different kind of horseplay was unfolding in deepest Yorkshire at the offices of Julian Green and Bearwater plc.

31

On my way into RCI's offices the next morning, feeling slightly hungover, but still excited at the purchase of our new toy, I stopped the car and popped into the local newsagents to purchase some newspapers. When I went up to the till, I slyly folded the *Sporting Life* into my *FT*, out of the view of other customers.

I remembered once, when checking into Champneys, an expensive health farm, that an overweight man was also checking in and was asked at reception what papers he wanted. '*Express* and *Sporting Life*,' he replied. I cringed at the mention of the *Life*. It seemed such a spivvy paper to request, almost embarrassing – to me, a bit like pornography – but I was excited to see if we featured.

Back in the safe sanctuary of my car, I slipped it out from its respectable cover and eagerly opened it to scan for the report from Windsor the previous evening. It was on the last page. 'Order of Merit was purchased out of the seller for 6,800 guineas by Nigel Goldman and Tom.' I burst out laughing noticing that the hack had completely forgotten to ask what Tom's surname was.

I walked into the office quietly content and switched on the price monitors as usual to keep me abreast of the markets, in particular Bearwater's opening price. I saw that they were unchanged on the previous night's close, but it took a few moments for the asterisk next to the share price to sink in. I looked again to make absolutely sure that I wasn't imagining it, but it was there all right. An asterisk right next to the quote. My stomach jumped up to my heart as the implication sunk in. The consequences caused me to hyperventilate and endure a serious panic attack. Bearwater had been suspended from trading on the stock exchange, and I had a gut feeling that this was a suspension of the worst possible kind – not a takeover bid or good news. The news report which was being flashed to brokers and banks all over the country read as follows: 'The Directors of Bearwater plc have asked the stock exchange to suspend their shares, pending a clarification of the company's financial position.'

At a certain time in one's life, various events and occasions take on monumental importance. Exams, marriage, deaths, moving house. That day, the suspension of Bearwater shares on the stock exchange was one of the most important things in my life. I was left wondering how on earth I was going to wriggle out of this one. No doubt my bank would soon get hold of the news and freeze the money in my account which was now secured by worthless paper.

I went for a stroll by the river outside my overpriced, picturesque, serviced office in Bray-on-Thames to work out a survival plan. Just along the river, I saw the jetty lead down from the Waterside Inn, another overpriced establishment. Then the task crystallised in my mind, an endeavour to which I could sternly commit all my passion and energy. I was going to fuck the bank up.

I decided that I would have to milk my account for as much as I could and keep my fingers crossed that the sleepy suburban branch hadn't got hold of the news. I also made up my mind that if I was challenged about the shares, I would feign ignorance of the news. I deliberately avoided speaking to anyone at Julian Green or Harriet Ward and jumped in the car to pay a visit to the bank.

On the way, I made up a list of who I could have some drafts made out to, people I could trust to look after some funds for me. By the end of the day's business, I had milked my account for £230,000 in banker's drafts and had arranged to withdraw another chunk of drafts and a substantial amount of cash for the following morning. Incredibly, the withdrawals went like clockwork the following day too, and I succeeded in running the account down into the ground. It would take my local branch an incredible three months to actually pinpoint what I had been up to, by which time they wouldn't get a single penny piece back.

I was now technically insolvent, but I had salvaged sufficient cash from the wreckage of the Bearwater disaster to continue trading, and to continue to lead my extravagant lifestyle. Funnily enough, RCI started to do really well and I was putting together some pretty decent deals. When I got home each evening, though, there were always letters from the bank, demanding the repayment of their loan, each letter getting nastier than the last – more threatening, more legal, less trusting. There were also an endless stream of messages on the answer machine from the manager requesting, pleading, that I call him. 'We can sort this out together,' he urged in broken tones. 'Come in and we'll discuss it.' Little did they know I was worth nothing. I, of course, ignored them all anyway and set about organising my funds in a clever and secret manner, so that when the eventual, inevitable day of bankruptcy was upon me, I would be well provided for and would be able to continue to trade in coins until my discharge.

The inevitability of bankruptcy crept up on me like a heavy, thick fog. Debtors about to visit, or who are already resident in Carey Street, may cry in their sleep to try to make things get better, but nothing happens. Nothing. Just rotten positions, enormous overdrafts, stacks of unpaid bills and red reminders in brown window envelopes, bin-ends of once-expensive lots of premier Krug from the salesrooms, dreams of receivers, trustees, County Court summonses, unrepairable poor credit ratings, blacklisting.

I was crying in my sleep about all my wasted opportunities, how I had messed up my business life. I cried in my sleep and nothing changed, certainly nothing got any better. Bearwater plc remained frozen in its suspended state while the directors awaited the auditors' clarification of their financial position. The bank remained light to the tune of £700,000-plus on my current account, while interest accrued at a rate of £183.37 a day (their statements, reminders and, lately, writs were an almost daily reminder to me). My emotions were on a roller-coaster ride of their own, turning my life inside out and upside down. I couldn't be happy or sad any more, only smashed up to pieces or going mad.

All this was going on, then one morning in 1989 I woke up with gritty eyes and drove to Slough to attend the County Court. I purposely parked up around the corner from the courthouse in a housing estate, keen to keep the Merc out of the sight of bailiffs, court officials and ushers. I walked up to the court building, past working-class mothers dragged their howling and yelling kids down to the shops in buggies. The first two glass swing-doors I tried to the court building were locked shut. A printed cardboard sign reading 'Please use other door' had slid down behind some Citizens Advice Bureau posters and was virtually out of sight. I made it in through a glass door which had 'C UNT   COURT' stencilled on it in black capitals. Someone had scratched out the 'O' and 'Y' in 'COUNTY'. In the foyer, typed lists of plaintiffs and defendants were pinned to green baize noticeboards – matrimonial, bankruptcy, repossessions, default, judgements to be entered for non-payment of hire purchase agreements and leases. I scanned the lists and noticed that the bulk of the plaintiffs were High Street household names –

suppliers of electrical goods on easy terms – banks and finance houses. This was where the mighty public companies took their revenge on their defaulters.

A bespectacled lady in her early 50s, who exuded an air of authority and wore black robes, called parties to attend Court 2 for the start of a case. Hardly anyone took any notice. A man shuffled off an overcrowded bench and crumpled up a chocolate bar wrapper as he made his way to the courtroom. The whole building had an atmosphere of lethargy and defeat about it. I wandered up to the enquiries counter and joined the queue of miserables waiting to be weighed off by inefficient civil servants, isolated from the public they were supposed to serve behind protective glass screens. It wouldn't have surprised me if they were bullet-proof. A young man with acne and thick glasses was manning the first position, counting dirty banknotes handed to him by a defaulter and issuing a receipt and change. What a life. I tried to arrange my position in the queue so that I would end up being attended to by the pretty girl on the third counter, but my luck just wasn't in and I ended up with four-eyes. I asked for all the details that were available on bankruptcy, and he handed me some forms and a booklet issued by the Insolvency Service, part of the DTI. I smiled as I noticed on the top of the form that a fee of £135 had to be paid before you could declare yourself bankrupt. It was abundantly clear on the form that only cash or postal orders were acceptable methods of payment for this fee, which I suppose is understandable given the circumstances. I took the forms with me and went back home to study and attempt to complete them. That evening, over several large drinks, I filled in the columns of creditors and assets. My biro hovered unhappily over the column marked assets, my expression morphing into confusion. I thought about my Rolex, the wardrobe of Hugo Boss and Armani suits in my bedroom, the Merc and my shares in Abbey National. My biro returned to the relevant column, and I considered writing in 'nil'. Instead, I wrote 'legal claim against HM Customs and Excise: £800,000'. Under the column marked creditors, I listed the bank, a few credit-card bills, store-card bills and my home utility bills. Assuming my claim succeeded against Customs, I would be about square. I had made sure the rent on my flat in Cookham was now in the company's name, and also the lease on the Mercedes, something I had hastily arranged through a company in Reading called Vehicle Solutions, who sent a very good sort round to sign up my documents. I got a company called Landhurst Leasing to provide the finance for me. (Ten years on, the chairman of Landhurst and myself, the lessor and lessee of this particular agreement, both at the time directors of public companies, were to meet up under rather different circumstances.) Once I had my house in order, I returned the form to the County Court in Slough, handed it in sheepishly with the cash and waited for the phone call to book my examination by the official receiver in Reading. I was about to pay my first visit to Carey Street. I decided to keep this particular visit secret from all my clients, friends and new-found racing contacts, and hoped that I could sneak my bankruptcy through quietly unnoticed (and with a minimum of column centimetre lineage in the local press) and carry on life as normally as possible in spite of it. When it came to the time to register myself as an owner with The Jockey Club, and list my racing colours, I noticed to my horror that one of the questions they asked was if I had ever been, or was about to be declared bankrupt. I obviously lied on the form and never heard another word about it.

32

'The horse will win, Tom,' our trainer assured my partner in crime. 'I'll get Elaine Bronson to ride it in an amateur event up at Beverley. Have your boots on it.' I was starting to feel 100 per cent convinced by the trainer's enthusiasm for Order of Merit, which seemed to become more and more bullish as extra rounds and further bottles of wine were ordered over dinner at the Jade Fountain, an upmarket Chinese restaurant situated just off the High Street in Ascot.

'The horse will win pulling a cart, Tom. It will win by ten lengths.'

At our table for dinner that evening was a man whom Tom had introduced me to at the races called Bernard Bates, a former stockbroker turned bookmaker, who had a betting shop in Bracknell. He was a jovial fellow and was a regular racegoer on the Southern Circuit. Bernard and I immediately got on well and, soon afterwards, I would meet up with him and his wife Margaret at Windsor on Monday evenings, and I would regularly go racing at Sandown Park, Ascot, Kempton and as far afield as Chepstow with them. They also had horses in training and had enjoyed some success as owners. Obviously, as a bookmaker, any information that Bernard could glean about the ability of horses in forthcoming races was priceless, and he was quite flexible in playing both sides of the fence – a happy layer at the odds, and he wasn't frightened to have a tilt at the ring on his own account when the opportunity presented itself. He was well respected in the ring and maintained hedge accounts with the leading firms. He was to play an important part in my success as an owner in the forthcoming years.

In anticipation of landing a coup with Order of Merit, I got myself prepared by opening accounts with the leading bookmakers and, by the end of the summer, I had credit accounts with Ladbrokes, William Hill and Coral. There was now just a few days to go until Order of Merit was due to run at Beverley and, as the time got closer, I felt excited at the prospect of possibly landing my first touch as an owner.

I met up with the trainer and Elaine at Epsom, and gave them both a lift up to Beverley. Tom couldn't make it to the track that day because of business commitments, but had given me £1,000 to put on the horse for him when I got there. With the investment that I intended to make – £1,500 win and £500 place

– at estimated odds of 20–1, I was looking to have something in the region of a £3,000 win and £750 place on the animal, which was a huge bet by any standards for an intimate, amateur-riders' ladies' race up north.

One of the horses in the race was being ridden by Her Royal Highness, Princess Anne. I asked Elaine to report back to me how she conducted herself in the weighing room and whether she swore at the other jockeys during the race.

As soon as I entered Beverley racecourse, I realised that I was going to have great difficulty in getting any serious sort of money on the horse. With pockets full of readies, neatly counted out and folded into hundreds, ready for action, I wandered round the ring to observe the betting action for the race before ours. Someone went up to a prominent boards bookmaker on the front line and requested a £600 to £400 on the favourite and got his bet cut down in half. Large layers these guys were not. I had visions of asking for £100 on our horse at odds of 14–1 or 16–1 and being offered a pony at the price. A pony, a monkey. Cockle and hen, ten. Why the animal imagery for proletarian money? Lady Godiva, fiver. Then the back slang: Rouf, four; a nevis, seven; a carpet, three; or a gimell, if you've any Jewish blood in you. Double carpet, thirty-three. Six is half a stretch and a stretch is twelve. This was type-talk and prison-talk, and you shouldn't use it. Trying to put a few grand on an outsider at this meeting could easily end up with the horse starting a virtual short-price favourite. I also noticed to my horror that, of the three firms that I had opened accounts with, only Ladbrokes were represented on the rails. I got on my mobile phone to Tom to explain what was going on at this backwater meeting, and he told me to do my best and get on what I could.

I watched the favourite get stuffed in the race before ours, and then hovered around the ring to start work on backing Order of Merit for the next race the minute prices were chalked up on the boards.

If you or I toss a coin and bet on the outcome, I'll have a quid heads and you'll have a quid tails, and one of us will win and one of us will lose. A quid. If a bookmaker offers odds on heads or tails, he will offer 5–6 the outcome, so that in the fullness of time, with the law of averages on his side, he will show a profit. Luck doesn't come into play in the long run as far as the bookmaker is concerned; he will consistently offer just under the true odds for the outcome of an event, and let the punter do the guessing. Profit is sometimes considered a dirty word in Britain, hushed in upper-class circles of guilt-ridden aristocracy as something bordering on the obscene, almost pornographic. Whispered in the same tone as words like cancer, bankrupt and Holocaust. Profit is also a bookmaker's sacred cow, cleverly calculated mathematically to an over-round percentage.

Of course, very occasionally, bookmakers do make the odd mistake and price up the outcome of an event with rather too generous odds. This is bound to happen from time to time, with the huge array of races and events being priced up each day, but when such a mistake does occur, the bookmakers have two powerful weapons left in their defence armoury: first, they can (and do) refuse all or any part of a bet; second, they can slash the odds in an instant. Few members of the public realise that even the big three – Ladbrokes, Hills and Corals – use these tactics in their high-street shops. On occasions, they will reduce the maximum that a punter can have on an event to twenty-five or fifty quid if it looks like they have dropped a clanger.

On the track, the smell of hot money for a horse, especially a large-priced one, rings alarm bells and gets the jungle drums beating in an instant. That is exactly what happened as I walked into the betting ring to back Order of Merit at 16–1. I did my best to wear an expression of eccentricity on my face as I went up to the bookmakers to back my horse, and I did manage to get the odd folded tenner and score on at the price – I even managed to persuade a game bookie, who wore a very loud, checked jacket and Trilby, and chewed a King Edward, to let me have forty quid, and then the price just evaporated, being sponged off the boards as rapidly as I could stride around the ring. Gingerly, I wandered up to a Ladbrokes representative on the rails and got a further £250 each way on at 8–1. By the time I got back into the ring, Order of Merit was down to sixes, and I got stuck in again. I still had plenty of action left to do when the horses went behind and were under orders, so I retreated to the stands.

Trainers have a large catalogue of excuses readily prepared up their sleeves to offer the awestruck owners for the poor running of racehorses, which include the going, the trip, whether the track is right- or left-handed, the horse's blood count, the pace and so on and so forth. Logically, in a seventeen-runner handicap there is only going to be one winner, so sixteen trainers have their explanations prepared well in advance of the race in an attempt to pacify their owners. And, of course, to ensure that the next month's training fees are settled. Even jockeys are in on this. They often get off their mounts breathless, offering quick advice to the owners about the trip, or encouraging them with comments like 'could do with further; would appreciate a step up in the distance, but ran on well,' before legging it back to the weighing room to get changed into another set of silks to earn the fee for their next ride.

I noticed that Order of Merit was sent off with eights and nines generally available in the ring again, as the layers tried to get their satchels stuffed with mug money.

I focused on the action through my recently acquired Zeiss miniature bins and noticed Elaine being pushed out by none other than Princess Anne. Maybe my mind was working overtime, but I could have sworn that I noticed HRH mouth something to Elaine as her mount galloped past her. As the race progressed further, our horse seemed to be going backwards, treading water. By the time the winner had passed the post, the AA were looking for Order of Merit and were having difficulty finding him with their radar.

In the end, he came in with only two behind him. The bookmakers had got their original pricing right after all.

High Stakes

Out of breath and obviously disappointed, Elaine came back to unsaddle. She confirmed that Princess Anne did indeed indicate to her in no uncertain terms to get out of her way. Girls will be girls. There was going to have to be better progress if Elaine was to achieve her aim of becoming leading lady amateur jockey that year. I wondered what the odds were for that eventuality after this disaster. Maybe Tom and I could get out of trouble by backing Elaine to win the championship and hope that the trainer could work the oracle. I went back up to the Ladbrokes man on the rails, who seemed even more polite this time, and I had £500 on Elaine Bronson at 7–1 to win £3,500.

Rails bookmakers have seen it all before – punters coming into the rings as lions and leaving as lambs, many ending up with prison sentences. Even the shrewd have dropped millions in racing. Terry Ramsden, the high-flying '70s Japanese-warrant trader reputedly dropped tens of millions of pounds in the ring. In the end, they knew they had found a mug from Essex and were queuing up to take him on. Like me, Terry was to find out the hard way years later that the Establishment often won the day, as he would also end up serving a term as a guest of Her Majesty.

Our journey home was a long one, but I was hooked and longed to be travelling home from a racetrack as a winning owner, with a trophy and substantial touch under my belt. Racing, though, is one of the hardest games in the world. I would have to pay one further visit to the cash desk for more chips, have one more taste of the medicine, before I was introduced to someone quite extraordinary who would beat the odds for me. Never in my wildest dreams did I believe or anticipate the huge success and thrill racing was going to present to me as an owner in just a few seasons' time.

33

'Can you name these people?' the examiner at the official receiver's office in Reading kept asking me. Their offices were located opposite TGI Friday's, where I had just finished a liquid lunch with the girl from Vehicle Solutions. The examiner sat at his regulation-issue desk, which was littered with steel trays containing printed bankruptcy forms and analytical paper for listing details of bankrupts' assets and liabilities. The examiner was a young man in his late 20s or early 30s, cheaply dressed with a spotty face. They were obviously causing him some considerable discomfort and, every minute or so, his hand would wander up to one for a scratch, before he thought better of it and went back to his form filling.

By now, my concentration had evaporated almost completely, and I started gazing out of the window at the nearby railway track. A goods train was busy chugging into a siding with its load of open-top wagons.

'These people, Mr Goldman, can you name them?'

'Sorry, which people?' I said.

'These people from Customs and Excise, the ones you are allegedly suing for £800,000. Can you name them? If we are to take this claim seriously, we are going to have to check with their department.'

I should have realised right away that the possibility of one government department suing another was extremely remote, to say the least, but having this ongoing matter in my file would distract the official receiver's office from my case and maybe allow my bankruptcy to quietly take place almost unnoticed. I put the examiner in touch with my lawyer, who I explained had all the case papers in his possession regarding my action against Customs and Excise, and I then tried my best to explain how I had ended up in such a sorry financial state. Yet again, I blamed Customs. I was told that I would have to attend the County Court for an oral examination in the near future, which sounded very much like a visit to the dentist. As I left the official receiver's office, I drove the Merc around TGI's car park about half a dozen times, so that if they were spying on me through their Venetian blinds, they would be totally confused.

The only cavities which were probed during my oral examination at Slough County Court were the huge financial gaps in my statement of affairs. The hearing took place in open court in front of a judge, the official receiver bombarding me with questions about my finances. He was thorough and was determined to explore all avenues about my financial affairs leading up to my bankruptcy, using his powers as an officer of the court to great effect, constantly reminding me that my answers had to be truthful, and that I risked being in contempt of court or guilty of perjury if I lied. He went on and on about my stake in Bearwater, trying to get me to admit that the purchase was speculative, or a gamble. There is a little-known section of bankruptcy law which states that if a bankrupt has gambled or indulged in speculative activity prior to his bankruptcy, then he is guilty of a criminal offence. At the time, seven years was the maximum imprisonment on conviction, or a £5,000 fine, or both. The fine option struck me as odd – how is a bankrupt supposed to cough up five grand? I had read up on the law a couple of days before the hearing, so I was prepared in advance for this line of questioning and was conscious of not falling into the numerous traps that the official receiver had laid for me during his examination. Fortunately, I came across well in court (my mother was right – maybe I should have become a barrister) and I certainly availed myself better than the guy who had taken the stand before me. When he was asked why he hadn't paid any tax for 20 years, he answered that he paid loads of tax every day 'on his betting, drinking and smoking'.

In the end, the official receiver looked like he was starting to bore the judge: he was over-egging the pudding and getting nowhere. Fortunately for me, there were a large number of other unfortunates waiting at the back of the court to be put through the mill, also for ten o'clock hearings, so the judge let me off the hook, and I was free to leave the court, the official receiver having failed to make any real progress with my case. As I left the court, the spotty examiner was hovering in the foyer. He informed me that my ordeal was over for the time being, but I should inform him if any windfall sums of money came my way in the next three years, or if my earnings at work exceeded that which I required to maintain a reasonable standard of living. Whatever that meant.

He also told me that a trustee in bankruptcy would be appointed to monitor my business activities over the next three years and to realise any assets which came my way.

It was abundantly clear to me that I would have to tread carefully, and I hastily arranged for my father to be appointed as director of RCI, so that I could take up the position of a mere employee working for a salary. A few weeks after the court hearing, the trustee got in touch, and I arranged to meet her at the RCI premises, where she could interview me about my post-bankruptcy activities. A chain of events over which I had no control was about to unfold. Disaster was looming.

34

'I think we should get rid of Order of Merit,' Tom decided over lunch. 'He's fucking useless.'

We were dining at the Clermont Club in Berkeley Square, an upmarket, private members' casino which I had just joined. Paul

High Stakes

Saidelbaum, a colleague of mine in the coin business, and I had been introduced to the club by 'Michael Holt', an American businessman who was a high-roller in London in the 1960s. He insisted that the Clermont gave us both honorary membership. On Michael's introduction, they were extremely happy to oblige. The club was once owned by John Aspinall and was infamous in as much as it was previously frequented on a daily basis by Lord Lucan, who used to entertain his regular group over lunch before staying on to gamble in the evenings. London casinos are great places to entertain because the food and wine are the finest in Europe, and heavily subsidised by the gambling action in the casino. In my particular case, lunches and dinners were complimentary as I was a high-roller on the tables; on each occasion, I was extremely grateful to note the pen being presented to me to sign the bill as compliments of the management at the end of my numerous marathon boozy lunches and dinners. I have always given the appearance of being much wealthier than I am and this is the image to portray to casino managers when you change up a couple of grand to play roulette or blackjack. They will happily entertain you for a number of months, hoping to relieve you of a sizeable lump of money. I used to keep careful, accurate records of how I fared with my gaming – I was to find out at a later date, they did too.

I toyed with my lobster. Tom continued, 'I think that we made a mistake buying a horse from a selling race at Windsor. I believe you would do a lot better buying a horse out of a breeze-up sale. There's one coming up in a few days' time at Ascot. If you are interested, I have been introduced to an up-and-coming new trainer. He will assist you in picking a horse with potential, and his training fees are very reasonable. I won't be able to get involved financially, as I'm fully committed in business myself, but how about having a go? I'll offer you all the help and advice that I can, and I feel sure that this new trainer will be able to get a horse ready for us to go land a massive touch.' I didn't need much encouragement as I was already gagging to get involved again, so I agreed with Tom to sell Order of Merit and meet him at Ascot the following Friday. I ended up making a couple of thousand loss on Merit, but still, was glad to move on.

Our lunch bill came to over £500, what with two bottles of Cristal and the cigars, but again it was complimentary. I felt obliged to play the tables with some action after such a splendid lunch and climbed the stairs to the gaming rooms. Tom went to the loo to freshen up, and I headed straight to the roulette table. I bought £500 in £5 chips. I had by this stage refined my play around number 31, my lucky number, and had arbitraged 22 and 9 in my bets, as they were 31's neighbours. If I hit, I learnt to be quite ruthless and pressed for all I was worth for the repeat. Go for the chandeliers. I covered 31 with a sizeable bet and had smaller bets on 9 and 22. The ball spun. It was a short spin, purposely so by an experienced croupier trying to get her first customer of the day on to a wrong footing, but miraculously she hit nine. I had £15 on the number straight up, which resulted in a payout of £525. I pressed for the next spin and nine came up again. This time, I copped over two grand. Spin three, can you believe it? Nine, nine red.

Nine, red, odd. Lovely nine. The croupier leaned over and counted my chips, which were piled high on the number. I had placed over two hundred quid and won just over nine grand. I covered 31 and 22 again for the next spin, pressed 9 just ever so slightly and watched her spin miles away.

I got up to cash in my winnings. Nine grand, nine lovely sealed packets of crisp £20 notes. I was about to cheekily enquire if the house had any difficult games I could play, remembered our free lunch and thought better of it. I went downstairs just in time to bump into Tom, who was coming out of the gents'.

'I thought you were going to play?' he said.

I told him I already had as I grabbed hold of his arm and ushered him out of the front door of the club as quickly as I could. 'Let's go for a drink, and I'll tell you all about it,' I suggested.

35

My second visit into the roulette table of racehorse ownership involved Tom introducing me to another trainer, one John White of Wendover. He predominantly trained horses over the jumps and proudly included George Michael's father amongst his list of owners. He was keen to expand his training operation at Wendover, so when Tom introduced me to him, he was eager to welcome me as a new owner to his yard and suggested that we purchase a nice two-year-old horse for around ten grand that he could train up for a quick touch. I liked what I heard from John White and had visions of not only recouping the cost of Order of Merit in one fell swoop, but also landing a touch to put me ahead in the hardest game in town. I had been here before – hard games, that is – and had always fared well against the odds.

John White suggested that we go to the Ascot breeze-up sales in around three weeks' time and a choose a horse there. The breeze ups are auction sales which are held at the racecourse. The entries run past potential buyers in pairs, over a couple of furlongs. This sprint-past enables the buyer to have a fair idea of the potential of the bloodstock that is being viewed. They are preferable to buying a horse out of a regular auction ring, where it is simply led round in circles and sold on appearances and bloodlines only. As the day of the breeze ups was approaching, I remember feeling the excitement building up in me. What did the future have in store for me? Could this be a wonder horse I was going to purchase?

Soon, the day of the Ascot breeze-up sale arrived. It was a crisp, frosty morning. I woke up early, full of enthusiasm. Tom met me at the Ascot racecourse, and Bernard Bates turned up to join us and watch the proceedings. I viewed the proceedings attentively from the grandstand and two horses caught my eye as they breezed up. One was a beautiful black colt. He was well-defined for a two year old and certainly looked older. He behaved well, going down for the start of his little sprint up, but ran a little green over the short trip. The second horse I fancied was a chestnut filly, who had a shorter tail than normal. Some gypsies had cut her tail when she was a yearling in a field, and it hadn't grown back properly. She was also a very attractive horse and ran well in the breeze-up. I preferred the colt to the filly, but had unwittingly chosen the two most expensive horses in the sale. In the end, it was going to be a matter of luck. The colt fetched £14,000, and I settled for the filly at £9,500.

I paid for my filly with a cheque drawn on RCI's account, assigned it to John White's yard and sat tight, ready and waiting for a training miracle to develop. Through training miracles, great gambling coups are landed, and Tom and I were determined to see this one through. While my horse was being prepared for a touch, Tom and I were conscious of the secrecy we had to maintain in preserving a well-planned betting coup. We went to enormous conspiratorial lengths to ensure our plans to land a touch ran smoothly. On our frequent, early-morning visits to the yard to watch the filly do her work, we were careful to keep the stable staff and work riders in the dark. Buttoned-up lips were the order of the day, too many touches having been thwarted in the past by eager lads spilling the beans in the pub just before race day. Or by colleagues, girlfriends or City traders placing unusual track or ante-post bets on horses you are trying to do an SP job with. So Tom and I decided to put everyone away – and that meant everyone. We also went to the trouble of recruiting Tom's two brothers-in-law into the scheme to assist us in getting our bets on at the track. We were starting to plan our coup with military precision. We had just four weeks to go until the filly was to run, and we were being constantly updated with encouraging work reports from John White. I, meanwhile, was busy beavering away at my coin business and putting away large chunks of cash, ready to have a huge bet on race day. I was even careful with the various accounts I had opened at bookmakers, making sure that my credit limits remained intact for the mammoth investment. I was like a kid with a new toy. I filled in the forms for The Jockey Club to register myself as an owner again. I thought long and hard about a name for the filly and decided on naming her after a high-denomination and valuable Charles I antique gold coin, Triple Unite.

In an almost identical scenario to the Order of Merit disaster, John White soon had serious misgivings about the ability of my horse. Fillies are very delicate animals; they run with fear. They have no purpose, they don't know they're passing the winning post, they run until you stop them. Mine, however, was working poorly against the other two year olds in the yard and was very green. She was a bit of a madam to say the least, playing up in her box; she even bit one of the lads and kicked her legs double-barrelled at White's missus on a couple of occasions, narrowly failing to crown her. She was none too keen to participate in stalls training either, an essential prerequisite for racecourse appearances. The chances of her giving a good account of herself seemed remote, to say the least. Tom and I went to the yard one morning, unannounced, to watch her do some work. Triple's work looked impressive. However, we would later find that she had flattered to deceive us.

After Tom and I had visited the stables, we were even more convinced that we were on to a good thing. We just couldn't contemplate not thinking about Triple Unite, all other matters compartmentalising themselves into insignificance compared to the touch we were about to try and land. The waiting before the race was unbearable. I stuck a picture of my horse on my desk, looking at it every day as the race drew nearer. The knowing arrogance in it took my breath away every time I looked at it. Life seemed to be a magnificent business, full of power and delight and mystery.

Gambling on a Winner

I awoke early on race day full of beans. Apprehensive, nervous, butterflies in my stomach; a powerful cocktail of fear and greed overwhelmed me.

Tom came to collect me around 9.30, and we drove up to Birmingham and checked into the magnificent Plough and Harrow Hotel. I was back in familiar territory, my old stomping ground. Our plan was quite simple, actually. We were going to back Triple Unite off the boards at Wolverhampton racetrack that afternoon, land a massive touch and retire to the sanctuary of the hotel that evening to count our winnings. Over coffee in the sumptuous lounge, I noticed that only one of the morning papers had tipped the filly, the column inches focusing on a two-year-old colt that had run well on its two previous outings. A good price for my filly was assured, the tissue indicating 16–1 or better.

All good gambling coups have to be well prepared in advance, and as far as the backing of Triple Unite was concerned, Tom and I were taking no chances. The market at Wolverhampton was quite strong in those days, and Tom had arranged to meet his two brothers-in-law at the track and give them instructions, together with a large quantity of my neatly counted and bundled readies, so that our coup could be landed with military precision.

We pulled into the old car park at Wolverhampton, the new stand and facilities still some years away. Despite the dry mud underfoot and the poor facilities, I was in no doubt that fortunes had changed hands over the years at this venue. I was smartly dressed in a double-breasted dark-blue Armani suit, light-blue poplin shirt with button-down collar and a trademark Missoni tie. I trod carefully to avoid getting my handmade Lobb shoes muddy. Tom was also dressed well in a dark pinstriped business suit. It was obvious to anyone who saw us that we were taking our business seriously. We had come up here from down south to give the northern bookies a slap.

We met up with Tom's men in the bar and I gave them their instructions. I would go into the parade ring with my trainer and lad, and Tom and the boys would quickly and efficiently go down the rows of bookmakers backing my animal. They knew that they had to grab the big odds while they were on offer and, with any luck, the bets would be on at generous odds before the bookies tumbled to what was going on. I could feel the excitement bubbling up inside me. Tom and I were planning to take out over a hundred grand from the ring, each. My nerves were calmed by a couple of glasses of champagne, but soon it was time to lead the horse out into the pre-parade ring and for our men to get to work on the layers. As I walked to the racecourse stables with John White, I noticed a couple of the more prominent boards bookmakers already chalking up the odds for our race. I smiled to myself as I saw Triple on offer at 14–1 with the mean guy and 20–1 next door. Those prices weren't going to last for too long.

The filly was saddled up and, for a change, she seemed quite at ease. The travelling head lad told me that she had behaved well on the way up to the course. He said 'travelled like a Christian' actually. Now, what do you make of that?

As we led Triple into the parade ring, I glanced over my shoulder just in time to see the ring explode into a noisy commotion. Tom and his men were causing havoc, backing my horse into oblivion. The bookmakers didn't know what was hitting them. '2,800–2, Triple Unite, ticket number 38', '7,000–5 Triple, down to myself', '2,000–2, ticket number 68', '1,000 –1 Triple'. They were getting quite hefty sums on at biggish odds, before the market just fell apart.

'I'll lay 5–1 Triple Unite,' one brave Midlands bookie yelled. Tom descended on him, clutching a handful of cash. '4–1 now Triple.'

'I'll lay 7–2 Triple. 3–1 now Triple Unite.' We had caused a mini avalanche, everyone wanting to back my filly. Meanwhile, the favourite had drifted out from 7–4 to 3–1. If the volume of money continued for my filly, we would soon be favourite.

Within a minute, we were. '5–2 Triple, I'll lay a 5,000–2 Triple,' a rails bookie screamed. And we took it, mopping up everything on offer. My horse was now clear favourite and, as the runners began loading into the starting stalls, her price hovered at 2–1 in the ring.

Racehorses, of course, don't know what price they are, and Triple Unite ran as though she didn't have two bob riding on her. She missed the break, got a brief mention during the first furlong, but from that moment on didn't worry the commentator. She ran so green it was embarrassing. There was possibly some power there, but she had no idea what to do with it. She veered from the rail to the centre of the course like a drunk driving a Ferrari, while out with the washing, forcing her jockey to change his whip to his left hand in order to straighten her out. It was all over in under a minute – weeks of dreams shattered in an instant. For a moment, however, unless my mind was playing tricks on me, I noticed that she found some power to her surge well inside the final furlong and, at the very instant of doing so, her ears pricked up, as if she had suddenly realised the point of what she had been doing. But it was far too little, far too late. She finished seventh. Out of eight.

I attempted to maintain some composure as I slowly retreated, wounded, past the jubilant bookmakers to the sanctuary of the bar. I met up with Tom near to the books. Much to our horror, we were jeered off the course by the local bookies: 'Yow cum up 'ere from down smoke in yowr pinstripe suits trying to 'ave us over with a touch – be off with yow.'

'Bugger off back down smoke where yow belong,' another joined in, grinning broadly as he sucked on his Havana.

So, bugger off we did, back to the Thames Valley, after some serious drinking in the Plough and Harrow, then a visit to my old haunt Liberty's, to re-group, re-form and re-build. She had looked such a lovely, promising filly.

36

There was some consolation, of a perverse kind, when I returned to my office. Through my adverts in the Yellow Pages and local press, a customer brought in a spectacular coin collection which I bought and promptly made twenty grand on. I was recovering much-needed sangfroid, pulling something from the wreckage of my betting disaster.

Unable and unwilling to take refuge in self-pity, I immersed myself in work. The coin business was treating me kindly with profitable deals popping up out of the blue from the unlikeliest of sources at my premises in Bray-on-Thames. I began to attend the London salesrooms regularly, picking up quality coins at Sotheby's, Christie's, Spink's and the specialist coin house Glendining's. To my intense surprise, they offered me credit facilities, which I took up with relish. I was back in the swing and started to advertise extensively, not only in the numismatic press, but also in the odd investment magazine, looking for clients I could drop portfolios of coins onto at generous retail mark-ups. Margins on off-record gold-bullion coins and bars started creeping up once more, and I again quickly took advantage of my much-used loophole (selling gold for cash at a premium, over its true value, but without charging the customer VAT). I moved into a trendy riverside apartment in Barnes, opposite the River Café, which I rented from a local property developer. He lived a bit more riskily than I did, a lot more riskily in fact, and we often bumped into each other at trendy nightclubs and bars. I drove out to Bray-on-Thames every morning. There was method in my madness – while the whole of the Thames Valley was struggling to get into the City, bogged down in traffic jams during the rush hour, I cruised the 20-odd miles to my office in no time at all, always having a clear run to the office and a clear run home. I was having the best of both worlds: working away in the country and enjoying London life in the evenings. Unbeknown to me, these comings and goings were being observed and monitored by a well-organised gang of villains, who were determined to relieve me of my precious gold-coin stock.

I wasn't short of female company either. Various women joined me for my evening jaunts into the West End, some old flames reappeared on the scene and I regularly pulled at Motcombs, Mortons and Draycotts. During that period, an old girlfriend from my Midlands days introduced me to Suzy Watson, who was to stand by me for much-needed moral support years later when I got myself into trouble again. Tom introduced me to a girl called Ali who worked for a friend of his. I started taking her out, too. She loved a good drink and would regularly join me for dinners at local casinos and restaurants, and was also great fun to have around. Out of the blue, I was to receive a jolt, or rather a blast from the past. I bumped into Jane Thompson, fresh back from her disastrous engagement in Germany. I had always had this big thing for Jane and had been immensely keen on her, so I did my best to persuade her to move in with me in Barnes, dumping all my other girlfriends in the process.

I decided to take Jane away on holiday for Christmas and New Year at the end of 1991. We both deserved a good break, she was getting over her failed relationship and I had worked my nuts off all year. I wandered into a branch of Thomas Cook in Kensington and was shown into their VIP office. Within 20 minutes, I had booked a fortnight at the luxurious Le Saint Géran Hotel in Mauritius, often described by the cognoscenti as the finest resort hotel in the world. I couldn't wait to get away, but just a couple of weeks before we were due to jet off, the group of villains, eager to lock in their Christmas holiday money, decided to strike. Where they had got their information from is unclear to this day, but it wouldn't have been too difficult for them to establish my modus operandi, since, at the time, I was such a high-profile trader at various exhibitions, fairs and auctions. The gang had been watching and monitoring my habits carefully, and had hatched an incredible plot to hold me up in my car as I left my flat in Barnes, bundle me into a white van they had parked around the corner, tie me up and blindfold me, then drive me to my office and help themselves to my stock.

They got the first part of their plot spot on, and I will never forget my immediate shock and surprise as I gently eased my Mercedes out of its parking space that cold November morning. The passenger door flew open and a man jumped in. At first, I thought it must be someone playing some sort of practical joke on me, but the sight of the gun quickly confirmed my worst fears. The passenger, who had a scarf pulled up over his face, pointed the gun to my head.

'Do as I say, and everything will be all right. Otherwise, you're in for it. Get it?' I glanced over towards him in shock.

'Don't look at me,' he shouted in response. He then lowered the gun, sticking it in my ribs. I went cold, all the blood ran out from me. I must have been as white as a sheet. In my confused and scared state, I tried to figure out who this guy was, still unsure exactly what he wanted from me, what dreadful fate lurked in the wings. Was this payback time for all the liberties I had taken over the years? I thought about the gold coins in my case in the boot of the car; my eyes fell upon my valuable Rolex, expecting that it would be ripped off my wrist when the robber noticed it. I realised to my horror that our flight tickets were also in my case in the boot. The gunman told me to pull out, drive slowly and to follow the white van that was already manoeuvring out of its parking space a few yards ahead of us. To say I was shit scared would be an understatement. The gunman obviously felt my fear and enquired how I was feeling, momentarily putting my mind at ease by saying that they 'just wanted a little something from me' and that if I did as I was told I would come to no harm.

I knew that I had to react quickly, immediately, if I was to avoid being robbed blind, maimed, or worse. I was slowly following the white van now, probably at around five or ten miles an hour. Ahead of us, I could see the usual flow of early-morning commuters, funnelling into their queue at Hammersmith Bridge.

Out of the corner of my eye, I noticed a milk float pull up and park alongside us, the driver ready to make his deliveries, blissfully unaware of my unusual predicament. I focused on the milk float, finding some much-needed comfort in having a normal human being in sight. And then I made up my mind in an instant. I saw the milkman climb down from the float and go round the side of it to unload his crates. I floored the accelerator and crashed the car into the side of the vehicle with such force that milk bottles went flying. That very instant, I flung open my door and jumped out of the car, the gunman in the passenger seat still reeling from the shock of the crash. I ran for it, as fast as I could, back up the street, towards my apartment, but the gunman quickly got his act together, leapt out of the car and gave chase. As I looked over my shoulder to see where he was, I saw, to my amazement, that he was right on my shoulder, just behind me, swinging his arm and laying a numbing punch on my nose. I was almost knocked out, then I felt the warm trickle of claret gushing from my nostrils. The gunman ran back to the car, opened the boot, grabbed my briefcase, then ran past an astounded milkman towards his two accomplices, who were out of the van seeing what had gone wrong and what the hell was happening. Urged on by each other, they climbed back into the white van and screeched off towards Hammersmith Bridge and the snarled traffic jam.

I jumped back into my Merc and hit the central locking system. My immediate reaction was to follow them, but the blood was gushing from my nose, rapidly staining my white shirt and Missoni tie, not to mention the magnolia leather interior. I punched 999 into my mobile phone, the white van still in my sight, about 100 yards away, still desperately trying to negotiate its way onto Hammersmith Bridge. After what seemed an eternity, the operator eventually picked up my call.

'Fire, police or ambulance?'

'Police and make it quick. There's been an armed hold-up,' I answered.

'You are through to the police now. You are connected to a mobile phone, go ahead caller.'

Surely the police would act more efficiently than the mobile phone girl, but I was to be disappointed with their response action, too.

'What is your postcode? Where are you calling from?' I blurted out my details, gave them my location and was told to sit tight and wait for help to arrive. The whole thing seemed to take an eternity. In reality, I had probably got through to the police and given them all the details within a couple of minutes. I was still focusing on the white van with the three villains in it, desperately trying to make their getaway in the early-morning rush hour, knowing that their liberty depended on it. The driver seemed to be having second thoughts about negotiating Hammersmith Bridge, and then mounted the central reservation, facing the traffic the wrong way, and proceeded down Castlebar to the relative safety of a side street which would lead them out of the bottleneck. I was sorely tempted to give chase and redial the police on mobile, but my nosebleed was now so serious that I was starting to feel faint and thought I might pass out any moment.

Just then a police car screeched around the corner, the police having been stuck in the bridge traffic jam themselves. The robbers had missed a sensational nicking by seconds, and I was minus one rather smart Louis Vuitton briefcase, eighteen grand's worth of gold coins and two first-class tickets to Mauritius inside. God, did I deserve that holiday.

The police did their best to help: they took me home, made me some tea and patched up my nose which, mercifully, wasn't broken. Then came the long interviews and paperwork. Did I know who might be up to something? Who had I taken on in recent months as new members of staff? They made a big thing about my new salesman, 'Sidney Longman', who had joined me at about that time. He was particularly good at selling portfolios of coins to clients over the phone, and we understood each other and made good money together. He was fresh out of prison in South America where he had been serving a short sentence for an investment scam. I forgave him for that, and the police could see nothing suspicious about him at the time. The following year, however, he was to introduce me to someone who was to change my life, and maybe then I would become more reluctant in the forgiveness stakes.

Thomas Cook had replaced our tickets to Mauritius and a few days before we were due to fly off, the police had a touch. They had found the van, the scarf, the false number plates and the gang. They pulled them in for an ID parade, and I was asked to attend at the police station to try to pick the gunman from the parade. I was led into a long room with one-way glass covering one side of it; on the other side was the line-up. On clever defence solicitor's instructions, everyone in the line-up was wearing baker's hats and had their hands behind their backs to conceal telltale tattoos. It was impossible to recognise the gunman. The gang had got away with it. The police knew who they were, let me in on it and confidently predicted that they would be caught soon on another job. After all that, the holiday was much needed.

In scorching-hot Mauritius, on a white sandy beach with the gorgeous, pouting, bikini-clad Jane on New Year's Eve, I made some resolutions. I would always lock my car doors before I set off on a journey. I would work hard and prosper in 1992. I'd move away from London to a magnificent home nearer to my office. I'd buy a Ferrari, in Rosso Corsa, of course – that's bright red to the uninitiated – and I'd own a racehorse that would win in my colours. I wondered if I could make all my dreams come true the following year?

37

I knew deep down I should have been living in London and that I should have had retail premises in the West End nearer to Spink's and all the other auction houses where I seemed to be spending countless days sitting through hundreds of lots of numismatic items going under the hammer. I had been indoctrinated by those earnest men and women from BBC's *Newsroom South East* that the traffic had reached crisis point, there was enough air pollution in Chelsea to kill every man, woman and child within a week, there was anthrax in the Serpentine and a mugger in your wardrobe. It had all started to have an effect on me, so I decided to broaden my horizons. I still like this word, it sounds of adventures new.

One day, I picked up a copy of *Country Life* – the most dangerous magazine published today – and there, between the stories about straw-hat makers and some polo team, I read that for the price of renting a two-bedroom flat in Barnes, you could buy a home in Buckinghamshire. Instead of stepping out into a noisy, polluted street, you could have acres of daffodils, an Aga stove, a boathouse, and a wide and varied selection of 'reception rooms'.

Now, I know how this feels, because it happened to me. After an unswervingly happy life in London, and an excellent and varied sex life, I was exposed for no more than ten minutes to a copy of *Country Life* and within a month I was house-hunting in Marlow and on my way to Hackett for some tweed.

Sure, in Marlow there were the drinks parties like the ones I used to throw in London. And the marathon sessions in the Two Brewers in St Peter Street, where the malt flowed with bonhomie.

But it quickly became apparent that one vital ingredient was missing – nobody was flirting. Aged 35 in London, you only want to meet people so that you can get them into bed. Aged 35 in the country, you only want to get to bed.

Samuel Johnson was right, it seems. When a man is tired of London, he is tired of life. You go to London to live. And then you move out. To die. So why, then, was I there? Well, it's simple, actually. If you live in London, you can't have a Ferrari.

All these developments – my New Year resolutions – came one after the other. The new home. Some new customers. The new Ferrari (in red, of course, always red). A new love life. I let Jane loose after Mauritius, and she moved in with a film producer who'd been eyeing her up in the local pub and who lived down the road in Cookham. Easy come, easy go. I wished I'd sent Ali a Christmas card, after all.

The armed robbery had also started to have an effect on me and that had helped persuade me to set up home in the country. And Marlow was so near to my office, bowered in beauty, its surrounding hills a glory of beeches growing down to the Thames.

Old Bridge House, a fantastic property in the town, was owned by a local businessman who occupied the bottom floor with his girlfriend. She used the top floor of the building as a language school and the middle-floor apartment, the nicest one in the house, had been up for grabs at half a million, but had failed to sell, so it was now available to rent. The minute I walked in, I knew it was for me.

I stood in the beautifully carpeted and exquisitely appointed drawing room, gazing out of the window at the breathtaking view of the rapids and waterfalls by the Compleat Angler Hotel.

'How much are you asking?' I casually enquired.

'£2,500,' the owner replied and, as an afterthought, so that there could be no misunderstanding, he quietly added 'per calendar month, unfurnished'.

'I'll take it. Here's my company card. Please draw up the

tenancy agreement in my company's name, and if you would be good enough to call my secretary, I'll arrange to have a cheque for three months' rent issued in your favour.' Ten days later, I moved in.

What with all the activity and everything, I'd hardly had a moment to myself.

38

Sidney Longman was opening one account after another, and the money had started rolling in, in style, at RCI by May 1992. I began wearing extremely expensive suits to the office; the more stylish the better. Good suits from Savile Row and Giorgio Armani. Most days, cheques totalling twenty grand, accompanied by neatly filled-in application forms would arrive in the morning post and, on occasions, they would amount to fifty or sixty grand. We started to accept credit cards over the phone and volumes picked up even more. I put Sidney on 10, then 15 per cent commission. Nice work if you can get it. I would then spend the rest of the day busying myself constructing portfolios of coins for my hapless investors. Sidney persuaded me to publish a new colour brochure, to entice even more prospective clients, and introduced me to an advertising agency in London who were accommodating. There was quite a lot of sales hype and puff in my corporate brochure, graphs and performance figures and the like, and I took great delight in shoplifting a graph from *Moneywise* magazine, courtesy of MicroPal, and superimposing an almost straight line to the moon to illustrate how well an RCI rare-coin portfolio performed compared to traditional investments, such as building societies or unit trusts. Nobody cared, nobody complained and we continued to punt away at the customers. Our activities weren't covered under the umbrella of the 1986 Financial Services Act, which aimed to clean up the City, concentrating first on small-time brokers, putting many out of business and making it increasingly difficult for us to trade. I began to advertise even more heavily in the financial press, often booking entire pages in colour in upmarket financial glossies with freepost coupons. It was pretty obvious to anyone with a modicum of intelligence that we wouldn't produce the sort of returns we were promising, but as the promoter of any Ponzi scheme (named after the infamous Charles Ponzi) will tell you, there are literally thousands of penny stocks in obscure Canadian mining companies which don't even exist in the first place. As long as you have more front than Harrods, the respectability of an incorporated company behind you, the right bumf and the right salesmen on the phone, you can get away with it. For a while, anyway. How does the old saying go? You can fool some of the people all of the time . . .

There was one young lady who didn't quite believe what she read, though, and wouldn't be fooled: Sarah McConnell, a financial journalist for *The Times*. Although I had spent a fortune advertising in her paper, she went on a crusade to expose the fragility of the investments in certified coins that I was promoting as no more than a sham. Sidney's and my heart stopped for a few beats when we read the first article which she published one Saturday in May 1992. It was absolutely shocking. I will never forget that weekend, as we sat around contemplating our future, visions of all our existing clients cashing in their portfolios and all the cheques we were expecting being cancelled, or failing to materialise. At one stage, I even contemplated calling the whole thing off and closing down the operation. And do you know what happened? Nothing. Absolutely nothing. Despite our fears, we didn't lose one single deal – not one transaction in Sidney's 'lim' box (boiler-room talk for pending deals), which totalled over a quarter of a mill, failed to close, and all the money continued to flow in. Unbelievably, nobody phoned up to complain. One fellow, who must have been dyslexic, mad, or both even phoned up after reading the article to invest with us. We couldn't believe our luck, but realised that the gravy train wasn't going to last forever. We decided there and then to max out on our potential while the going was good.

Sidney kept harping on to me about 'loading' – a technique he had used a lot, having successfully milked it for all it was worth with his cronies in South America, before he got his tug over there for financial misdemeanours. Loading meant getting a powerful salesman on the phone to re-sell, usually for substantially more than a customer had invested initially, to existing clients. Stan knew just the man for the job and was prepared to introduce him to me for a 10 per cent override. Enter one 'Al Rubin' of Canada.

I had briefly read about Al's credentials in the financial press, usually in the 'questions of cash' columns in the *Sunday Times* or the complaints section of the *Mail on Sunday,* where he was invariably exposed as being the brains behind one scam or another and was described as a veteran wallet-thinner. He had promoted stocks and bonds over the years, usually pedalling penny stocks in non-existent companies, and had a reputation for raking in millions. Sidney had worked with him a few times, and they held mutually high expectations of each other. Sidney reached Al on the phone in Canada, and I arranged a meeting at the newly opened Lanesborough Hotel in London for the following week.

I arrived at the meeting unsure of what to expect from Al, but prepared to listen to what he had to offer. In my hotel suite, which still smelt of the recently applied varnish and where the minibar consisted, I was delighted to note, of cut glass decanters full of freebie spirits, I awaited the arrival of my new wonder salesman, my loader, the man who Sidney told me would turn me into the biggest coin dealer in the country. The minute he walked in, straight off his flight, I knew I had somebody quite extraordinary. He could even talk me under the table. After helping himself to a swift couple of Scotches from my bar, he sat down and explained that he liked my product, and I noticed that he had a copy of my brochure in his briefcase. He had done his homework on the flight and had quickly learnt the pertinent points of coin investment.

'I can load your clients right away, for sums of money that at this moment in time you can only dream of. Let me get to work on them right away. The key to this is timing, you cannot afford to wait another moment. They can get stale, they need to be loaded straight away. I want 20 points, my hotel paid for and expenses. Let me show you what I can do for you. Let me astonish you.'

Al, it quickly became apparent, had more layers to him than a Russian doll and he regarded himself very highly, preening himself as some sort of prima donna. But, in that half-hour session, I had been sold and was convinced I should give him a whirl. I had never met anybody so hyper before in all my life and wondered whether his phenomenal energy was natural or chemically induced. By taking on Al Rubin, I knew I was gambling with RCI's future, and potentially my own liberty, but this was a risk I was prepared to take in order to explore and probe the blue-sky phenomenon of investors' millions dropping into my lap.

Three days later, Al was installed in the office, playing the telephone as if it were a Stradivarius violin.

'Mr Simpson, "Ritchie Palmer" here from RCI. I'm so glad that I have been able to reach you. I have been trying you all morning. I have news of monumental importance for you. Your coins have rocketed in value, but the increase that you have seen is the mere tip of the iceberg. We are looking for them to double again by New Year. Now is not the time to sell, now is the time to add.'

Al would stand up, talking down to his client, delivering his speech like a president talking to Congress.

'Our principals, be it by astute business acumen or good fortune, have just acquired the Strathmore collection and our chairman, Mr Goldman, who as you know is one of the foremost numismatists worldwide, has authorised me to offer it to you as one of our preferred clients. Now, this collection comes to just over £1 million sterling, and you can take all or any part of it . . . Forty thousand? If you were to pull your belt in just a little, could you handle £68,000? I have a selection here that Mr Goldman has personally earmarked which comes to that figure, I know that he would be delighted if you could handle it. Excellent, well done, sir. Let me show you what I can do for you on this collection, you won't be disappointed. As we are finalising this transaction today, I want you to write a cheque for this sum and place it in an envelope with this reference number written on it: RCI323. That's my code, so that when your cheque arrives here at the office it will come straight through to me. We handle just *so* many cheques here, what with the mail-order side to our business and all. As I'll dispatch a bike to collect it, please stay in until the courier arrives. Thank you for the business, sir, and a very good day to you.'

Disguised under his Ritchie Palmer mask, Al pulled in a quarter of a million quid like that on his first morning and despatched bikes all over the country to collect the cheques. By the end of his first week, he had loaded my existing clients to the tune of £2 million and was in line for a commission rebate of £400,000. Sidney was up for a couple of hundred thousand override. Al knew that he had his followers horribly hooked, myself included. As I handed him the first pilot's case stuffed full of cash, which he was wiring to his offshore tax-free haven, I realised that I was becoming totally motivated by greed and was becoming reckless. My paperwork and invoicing were careless, and when clients opted to have their portfolios stored in our vaults for safekeeping, I breathed a sigh of relief and left the allocation of their coin portfolios on a long finger. Now tell me this, at the prices I was having to mark up my stock to cover all these overheads, how on earth could any of my customers ever expect to make a profit? In spite of the glowing charts and references in our new glossy corporate brochure (which I still had to pay the printers for), and what the salesmen were pitching to clients on the telephones, I was charging them the jackpot the minute they bought the lottery ticket. It was a system full of holes. I was beginning to wonder how on earth I had ended up in this marriage.

It may well have been that I wasn't playing with a full deck. If the figures wouldn't add up for me, the world wouldn't make sense. When I was young, I heard a wise man say: 'Give Crowns and Pounds and Guineas – But never your heart away.' God knows what would have been said if I had added VAT on to the coins as well. I was as mad as a hatter.

39

Con men have this thing for mature victims. They do. You hardly ever see them bothering with guys their own age. Elegantly clad in their designer-labelled suits, wearing hearts of stone, con men observe their victims from the sanctuary of their cunningly arranged stands at investment exhibitions, as they browse the tables of fellow con men who pedal their array of dodgy wares. Wines for the millennium, containers, sweet trades in futures, franchises, coins. Cons. You naturally associate investors with defencelessness, greed, gullibility. In the safe old days, when most Britons considered only two forms of investment – their home and their building society – money shows were a place you went to if you wanted to lose your shirt. But with ordinary savers now flocking to riskier propositions, the gulf between investment and gambling is becoming narrower. Nowadays, most investors love trade shows and exhibitions, they feel that they can be sure of a fair deal there. They just don't dream that they can get conned on a one-to-one basis, face-to-face and, besides, all the exhibitors are bona fide, vetted, with prestigious addresses, telexes, faxes and freephone numbers to ease enquiries.

I watched one of these investors the other day at an exhibition. He marched round one of these shows, polished brogues and dogtooth jacket, concealing the Coutts chequebook in his inside breast pocket. We call them civilians in the trade.

He was one of those civilians who had had neatly packed sandwiches wrapped in clingfilm in his briefcase every day for thirty-five years, so that he could ponder what to do with his six-figure nest egg, ten years ahead of retirement. I gently guided him over to my stand, sat him down and gave him my pitch.

Here's what struck him about coins. They were portable and easy to conceal. He could write them up and type them into his new home computer, together with their values and profit projections. He could cross-reference them by monarch, denomination, date and value. He could boast to his friends that he had a new hobby. He could watch them go up in price, just like I promised him. Investments. Don't you just love them? I took a cab directly to his bank five minutes after he left my stand to lodge his cheque and clear it before he had a chance to change his mind. And it was a decent lump, too. For a civilian.

Careful scrutiny of my business revealed that it was worth just over two million quid. My accounts looked good, but there was something lacking in my day-to-day routine. I longed to have another highly leveraged trade in the futures market. I had been keeping a careful eye on the new style of financial futures that were all the rage at the time, the height of fashion. Derivatives, such as bills and bonds, and the gilt contract on the LIFFE, which was the mirror image of what interest rates were expected to do in the UK. If you believed rates were going to go north, you went short; if you believed interest rates were heading south, you went long. I was of the opinion (don't ask me why) that interest rates were going up. Maybe I had read something somewhere and it had stuck with me. Not a massive move, but maybe an eighth or a quarter of a per cent or something. Enough of a move to show me a substantial profit if I traded in a large enough size. So I stripped a million out of RCI, debited my director's loan account and opened yet another futures trading account. I took on an enormous position, looking to make a quarter of a million quid if rates moved up a mere eighth of a per cent in my favour. The contracts ran until the end of September 1992, so I had six weeks for something to happen. Now I felt content, having a decent trade under my belt. It gave me an interest and justified the cost of the expensive Reuters equipment I had invested in. I also quite enjoyed the attention and non-stop phone calls to my office from my brokers. It made me feel wanted. This was my most highly leveraged punt ever, but I could well afford it. These were my halcyon days of enormous financial freedom. I could wander and roam, and do exactly what I wanted. It felt brilliant.

I had booked a short break at the Sans Souci Hotel in Ocho Rios in Jamaica for August, but just before I was due to leave, Tom was back on the phone with another bloodstock proposition for me. He had met up in London with a colourful bloodstock agent called Andy Smith, who had mentioned to him that a well-known trainer in Epsom called John Sutcliffe had a very interesting animal available for sale. This was a three-year-old gelding that had run a few times unplaced, but which Sutcliffe believed had far greater potential than his form showed. The trainer was keen to sell a half share in the horse for ten grand, to build up some new clients for his half-empty yard and to land a touch when he pushed the button. Tom could hardly conceal his excitement and told Andy to reserve the horse for me.

The drive up to Woodruffe House was a long and imposing one on that bright summer morning. The air of purpose that Epsom holds with such ease is reflected here and then strengthened to an absolute intensity. Everything is directed towards a single aim, a sole purpose: that of training a winning racehorse.

Of course, for a large majority of trainers and owners the kudos of winning is the only purpose, but for John Sutcliffe there was a further aim: the mouth-watering prospect of relieving the bookies of a substantial wedge. He had been there before, on numerous occasions, knew how good it was and held a formidable reputation as the head of a very successful gambling yard. All this got my adrenalin going. As soon as I met John that morning at Woodruffe, I knew straight away that we would get on well as co-conspirators in our mutual aim. His yard had an aura of style and class about it, the home of successful gambles landed over the years. I felt confident in his hands as I sat in his lounge that morning sipping his champagne. I somehow knew that this morning was to be the start of a long and mutually profitable association. Our discussion turned to the delicate question of training fees, Sutcliffe's other livelihood. They were £800 a month, plus VAT, blacksmith, vet and transport. I bought the half share of his gelding there and then, and we strolled out to the yard to view the bloodstock. Bo Knows Best was an unattractive, leggy thing, but he was cheeky and had a sparkle in his eye. Somehow, I knew he was going to deliver the goods for us. John was mega-bullish about his potential and reckoned him two stone in hand ahead of the handicapper.

'I'm running him down the field on Monday night at Windsor. Come and watch him run. If, after the race, you don't think he could have won, you can have your money back.'

Now you can't get much fairer than that, can you?

40

On the LIFFE, the gilt contract hovered around my entry point. Frustratingly, it would creep up a few ticks in my favour, then spit out its gains at the end of the day's trading, as the locals and large institutional investors squared up their books. I frequently popped down to London, to observe the trading on the exchange floor, paying particular attention to the pit my contract was traded in. My experience at the LIFFE was very similar to that of Comex and, as I observed the energetic young traders from the sanctuary of the visitor's gallery, I felt amazingly comfortable with such a huge position. The more I looked at the market, the more I felt certain that I was on the right side of it. Although the contract was relatively quiet in price movements, the volume traded was enormous and some serious positions were being built up by other players, who also shared my belief about the direction of UK interest rates.

I started to spend some time socialising back in London too, bored with my unadventurous evenings in Marlow at the Two Brewers, where I would regularly polish off a half bottle of whisky all to myself through boredom and spend endless hours talking nonsense to the resident bookmaker, who held court on the corner stool and took up my Scotch challenge.

In London, I would snoop around City wine bars, earwigging for clues about the market from young traders, who downed voluminous quantities of alcohol to wind down after their hectic days on the exchange. Usually, having failed to pick up any clues, I would then make my way to the West End to meet up with some friends for dinner, maybe punt a few grand in the casino, hit a club, pull a young lady (or two) and retire to my suite at the Dorchester or Carlton Towers. Then it would be an early morning start for the drive back to the office for letter opening and cheque banking.

Meanwhile, John Sutcliffe and Andy Smith were keeping me posted over the phone on a daily basis about Bo Knows Best's well-being and progress. It was like having a baby to look after. I had gone to Windsor to watch him run. He finished fifth, beaten by two-and-a-quarter lengths, and could easily have trotted up. He had come out of his Windsor race well, ate up (which I was told was always a good sign), and was ready for his big day next time out. John was planning to push the button on a seller up at Nottingham in August, and Brian Rouse was again booked for the ride. When he told me the date of the race, I noticed that it was a day when I would be on holiday in Jamaica.

I arranged to meet John and Andy in London for lunch to discuss the Nottingham situation. Tom came along too. He had now promoted himself and told everyone that he was my personal racing manager. The four of us went for another marathon lunch session at the Clermont Club in Berkeley Square.

Over large rounds of drinks, I popped the question: 'What concerns me, John, is how I'm going to get on, have a bet, if I'm stuck in Jamaica?'

'How much were you planning to have on him?' John asked.

Some advice I once heard flashed through my mind: never back a horse *in absentia* to win a particular sum of money – you never know what the starting price is going to be. I once met a man who instructed his bookmaker to back a horse to win him ten grand, thinking it would be even money. In the event, the horse went off at 7–1. On. And it got beaten, costing the punter a gut-wrenching seventy large.

'Leave it to me, Nigel. I'll back the horse for you on one of the accounts at SP, tax paid. We'll square up after you get back from your holiday. Andy will fax you at the hotel the day before the race with the tissue, the going and any other news about the horse. You will even be able to listen to the race over the phone. We'll meet up here for another lunch after you get back, hopefully to split up the winning cheques.'

Tom jumped on the bandwagon and backed Bo Knows Best too.

I decided to maintain my gilt contracts while I was abroad. Somehow, I wasn't particularly concerned about running this monstrous position while I was away. Call it gut instinct, or whatever. I had a feeling that not only would all be well with my contracts while I was on holiday, but that the money was also already safely in the bank as far as Bo Knows Best was concerned.

41

'Welcome to Jamaica, Mr Goldman.'

Immigration greeted me like James Bond, maybe on account of the cream Byblos suit and Panama hat I had changed into before we landed. Here's a tip: always look your best, wherever you go, otherwise you may be mistaken for some bum.

The driver for the Sans Souci was waiting for me by the carousel. He grabbed my bags and we walked out of the terminal building to the hotel's courtesy limo. It was still scorching hot, despite being just after six in the evening.

I settled into the back of the air-conditioned limo. As we drove through Kingston, I noticed some locals sitting outside on their verandas eating dinners of chicken, rice and peas. Most of the houses were run down, dilapidated, and the roofs were made of corrugated iron. There were shops galore, most of which advertised through hand-written signs that they sold soft drinks and local produce. In the middle of Kingston, we stopped in traffic and to my astonishment and delight I also saw a bookmaker's shop. I thought about wandering in there the next day to back Bo and trying to get my holiday money in.

My driver was called Renford, a larger-than-life character with dreadlocks, a broad grin and big white teeth. He spoke non-stop about how magnificent Jamaica was. Our drive to Ocho Rios took a couple of hours, over the most dreadful roads I had come across in the world: twisty, dusty and pot-holed. We hardly passed another car. Upon arriving at the Sans Souci, I was ravenous, but the restaurant was closed and the bar was deserted. It took an hour for my luggage to arrive in my room. There was no minibar. The phone rang three times – all wrong numbers. The cleaning lady barged in unannounced while I was in the bath. To say I was unimpressed with the Sans Souci Hotel was an understatement. I phoned Renford to take me back to Kingston for some nightlife, but he had clocked off for the day. I didn't like this place one bit and must have been barmy to have come here. I decided there and then to cut my trip short and return home in two days time. I phoned BA to change my flight and then turned in for an early night.

I was awoken on my first morning in Jamaica, on race day, by a phone call from hotel reception telling me that a fax had arrived for me from England. I had it brought up while I showered and shaved. It was from Havana Horse Ltd, corporate-speak for Andy Smith. It read: 'Weather fine today – light rain overnight – going good. All stations go. Good luck, Andy.'

There then followed a listing of the 17 runners and riders, together with pages of form from that morning's *Sporting Life*. We were quoted at 12–1. I stood to win twenty-four grand if the price held and we romped home.

I dressed and phoned down to book Renford to take me to Kingston. The bookmaker's shop was packed with chain-smoking locals, not all of whom were on cigarettes. They all ran up to the counter to have their couple of quid on some dog race which SIS were covering from Crayford. The minute the bell went and the hare was running there was a stampede to the counter. On the walls of the brightly lit but smoke-filled shop, race cards for all the English meetings were pasted up, and some early prices had been pencilled in. I wandered up to the counter to see if I could take some early odds about my race.

'What price Bo Knows Best in the three o'clock at Nottingham? He's quoted at twelves in the *Life*.'

The bookmaker eyed me up, not sure if I was some mug tourist or a shrewdie. 'You can have five hundred on him at eights, what you like SP.'

I had brought two grand with me to back the horse, so I had the monkey on at eights and gave him another grand to win at

SP, and a further monkey a place, just to be on the safe side. As I handed over my wedge, the whole of Jamaica decided that they wanted to back my horse, and there was another stampede to the counter, the 12.48 from Crayford running unnoticed. Although there were still a few hours to the race, I decided I had better go back to the hotel, just in case we got beaten. The clientele at the shop looked quite capable of lynching me if Bo didn't produce the goods. Now, here's some advice. Don't ever try dialling into 0898 race lines from Jamaican hotel rooms. They're expensive and unreliable. I did a dummy run for the 2.30 and got cut off twice during the race. By the time I eventually got through the third time, they were already announcing the runners and riders for my race. I stayed on the phone for the off. God only knew how much it was costing me. Mercifully, this time, I stayed connected.

There was just over a furlong to go, when I heard the words every owner dreams of: ' . . . and here comes Bo Knows Best slicing through the pack like butter, going one, two, three lengths clear . . .' Then the phone went dead. I had been cut off again.

I desperately tried to ring back, to confirm we'd won, hoping to God some other horse hadn't sprouted wings in the last furlong and gone past us, but frustratingly got the engaged tone. I felt sure we had won, but my mind started to play tricks with me as I tried to recall exactly what the commentator had said. Then the phone rang. It was Andy.

'Do you want the good news, or the bad news?'

I hate it when people say that to me.

'Go on, Andy, give me the good news first.'

'The good news is the win. The bad news is the price. He ended up at 9–4.'

My heart sank. My first coup had been thwarted by the bookies wising up to a hot horse, but at least it was my first win as an owner.

The following morning, Renford drove via the bookie's on the way to the airport so I could collect my winnings. I couldn't wait to get back home and meet up with John Sutcliffe to celebrate the win and make plans for Bo's next race. Unbeknown to me, John had already entered the horse for another race a few days later at Goodwood, before Bo went up in the weights, to keep us ahead of the handicapper.

At Kingston Airport, I was upgraded to first class and shown to BA's lounge on the first floor, which it shared with Air Jamaica. It consisted of a small office down a long corridor, with no bar or refreshments, just a couple of easy chairs. A Jamaican family with three noisy kids occupied the seating and shared a carton of orange juice between them, which the kids noisily slurped through straws. I had been in Jamaica for just over 48 hours and couldn't wait to get out of the place.

I was gently woken from my virtually horizontal slumber by a tactile hostess, trolley in tow. I had first class almost to myself. I peered out of the window as we made our approach to London, watching through the misty clouds, the acres of fields, the roads with cars the size of ants marching to their destinations. Then the outskirts of London itself – as regimented as an army.

At Heathrow, I took a cab to the Carlton Towers and booked myself into the Tower Suite.

An hour later, I was sipping a glass of champagne in the lounge of the Clermont Club in Berkeley Square, where just before lunch John Sutcliffe had handed me a beige envelope with my name typed on it.

'Two thousand pounds, tax paid, at 9–4. There's a cheque in there for you for £4,500.'

Some considerable time later, over lunch in the Rib Room of the hotel, Mike Dillon of Ladbrokes let slip that John had backed the horse with him the night before the race at generous odds. I never did get round to asking him just how much he had made on that little wheeze.

The £14 Million Windfall

42

John Sutcliffe and I ran up our profits a week later as Bo Knows Best romped home again at Goodwood, beating a grey called Crackling, trained by Dougie Marks. We were going for the three timer a fortnight later at Salisbury. Again, we won – although this was a much closer run thing, as the handicapper started to get to grips with us.

We were relieving the bookies of substantial wedges. On 16 September, we were entered to run again at Sandown, in a stakes race. This was a fashionable meeting at the Esher track, and Al and Tom asked if they could join me. This was to turn out to be a very special day for me in more ways than one.

My position on the LIFFE was creeping up again. There were rumours in the City that the Chancellor Norman Lamont would be forced to put up interest rates to keep the pound stable. Many shrewd speculators were now positioning themselves not only on the interest rate front, but also taking substantial bets on sterling itself. My contracts were already showing me substantial profits of tens of thousands of pounds, and I decided to hold on for a few more days to see if the Chancellor's hand would be forced.

By a strange twist of fate, I still had my position live on 16

September, the day of the Sandown race. The rumours were getting even stronger now, the Chancellor looking as if he would act at any minute.

I set off in my Ferrari for Sandown at about three o'clock. Bo Knows Best's race was at ten past five. We had arranged to meet up with Tom and John Sutcliffe in the owners' and trainers' champagne bar in the grandstand. The bar was run by Beryl and Rene, two middle-aged women who were real characters. 'Hello, dear, lovely to see you again. Nice bottle of cold Krug for you, Nigel. Mr Sutcliffe has been in, he'll be back in a moment. Fancy yours tonight, Nigel? Shall I have a couple of quid on the Tote with you?'

We chatted until John arrived and I filled his glass. 'How do you think we'll go today?' I enquired of John.

'I think the horse will run very well.' John, in his typical shy way, was keeping his cards very close to his chest, but his manner told me that I could expect a good run again. My horse probably represented even money in the race, in true terms, so when he opened up at sevens, I decided to venture out into the fresh air to have a bet or three.

'Don't go mad,' he advised.

I sauntered down to the rails as the horses cantered up to the start. I wore the expression of a professional gambler on my face. People think gamblers are wild and reckless; I was as wild and reckless as a brain surgeon. That day, anyway. I wanted one touch, though. It is like launching a skier off the snowline onto the Cresta run – the only way is down. The bookies were all in line at their rails pitches, waiting like murderers for their victims. Executioners, stranglers, snipers, hangmen. Killers, the lot of them. Down the rails I went – betting with Hector McDonald, William Hill, Ladbrokes, Heathorns (much obliged), Victor Chandler, Sunderlands and Robin Grossmith. I flirted with them all, a monkey or a grand at a time, all around the 5–1 or 6–1 mark. Then I made my way into the ring and pressed my bets up in cash with the boards, until my pockets were emptied of the five

The £14 Million Windfall

grand I had brought along with me for that purpose. I then retired to the stands just as the horses were loading to watch the race with Sutcliffe and his daughter Nichola. We won, and comfortably too. Jockey Nickey Adams as delighted as the connections, punching the air with his whip as Bo went past the winning post, he too celebrating his own victory, breaking his bok after a long fallow period without a win.

Back at the books, I was a solitary figure being paid out. This death-row inmate had been reprieved. Losers hovered around the pitches like addicts, waiting for the odds for the next race to be chalked up, shaking their heads at the ease with which we had just won the last race. 'Seven to fucking one,' I heard a punter mutter as he shrugged his shoulders and ripped up his losing ticket.

These pitches are really for laying on a bet only; the trip to the payout window is a rare thing. I made a visit that day, though, in style. I wish to Christ I'd had more on, but those were early days, before I heard the news. Before I was really on the case.

I had no idea what was happening in the City, of course. No idea? Well, an inkling, maybe. Over the years I keep on coming back to it, to relive the moment. I have since thought about it many times, checking and rechecking the times and figures over and over. It was while Bo was running that something very significant took place in the City, once regular trading had closed at five o'clock. An announcement that would shift billions in equity like magic amongst the players. Norman Lamont increased the base rate. Not by a fraction, but by a whopping 4 per cent. You probably remember the day clearly; I can never forget it. And then, in what seemed to be a moment of madness, he did it again – in total, an 8 per cent increase. While it was happening, I was upstairs in the private box of the race sponsors, Headway Property. I was totally oblivious to it all, soaking up the champagne and ether of Bo's performance and the not-inconsiderable touch I had just landed, courtesy of the bookies. That touch was to pale into insignificance compared to what had just occurred though.

High Stakes

My first realisation that something had happened was when the man from Headway mentioned the rates had just gone up twice. At first, I thought that he must be talking about two little hikes in base, maybe an eighth each time. It soon became apparent, however, that he was talking about something much more substantial. Then I heard – a massive 8 per cent hike! I nearly broke a leg running to the pay phone, having left my mobile in the car ringing off the hook (phones weren't allowed on the course in those days). I immediately phoned my broker's office.

'We've been trying to reach you every five minutes for the last hour, Nigel. You won't believe this, Lamont's put base up eight. Your position in the market is unreal, amazing. Your contracts have soared in value, you're still making fortunes as we speak.'

I took a deep breath. 'How much am I making?' I could barely get the words out. 'Thirteen point eight, as you stand right now.'

'Liquidate them,' I yelled down the phone. 'Liquidate them all. Now.'

I stayed on the line just long enough to make sure they understood my instructions. On the LIFFE, I could imagine the pit, swarming with traders. My broker executed my trade in 20 seconds and retired to his booth. Like a huge game of electronic poker, a fortune changed hands and zoomed home in my direction.

On that autumnal afternoon, I made nearly £14 million out of the futures markets.

I copped a nice few grand out of Bo Knows Best, too.

My Ferrari screamed home to Marlow like an express train.

43

It's weird, but to this day I still cannot fathom out where it all went. There might still be some left lying in a remote offshore account somewhere that I've forgotten about, who knows? Who cares any more? My £14 million, which I got wired to me the very next day, melted like some hideous, monstrous glacier, as though it had never existed in the first place. Sure, some of it went on keeping my beloved RCI afloat for a few more months, but in the end even that made no difference. How the fuck did I get through the whole lot, though? I'm still trying to work that out, years later. I've gone through more A4 lined pads than I care to remember trying to add it all up again and again in neat columns. I recall some dangerous 'swap' deals (high-risk trades involving government debt) on the markets that went pear-shaped for about five (or was it seven?) million. And the loan to a famous pop star's accountant (£800,000). Oh, yes, and the dabble in platinum (that was £600,000 in five days). Thirty grand here, forty grand there, giant games of roulette, more margin calls than I care to remember, rugby handicap betting, cricket spreads, racing certainties, greyhound dabbles, sponsorship, AIM share deals, OTC share deals (I swear one of the salesmen sounded just like Al). One-hundred-grand days at Ascot. Thirty-thousand days at Newmarket. Fifty at Windsor. Twenty at Salisbury. First-class flights around the world. Cars, girls, drinks. It all evaporated into thin air. After a while, I decided it was time to get back to normality before it was too late. Even Zena, my latest flame, probably one of the smartest and most intelligent girls I have ever dated, kept asking me why I couldn't be *normal*. I think she understood how desperate I was to be loved, and how much I really did have to offer, but it was from solitude that I really needed protection. I mention this en passant to show that I was still wide awake. Wide awake all right, and in need of protection from the black-lacquered nightmares I had of millions of pounds shooting like arrows into a black hole of oblivion on bum trades I should never have even considered. Wide awake in the realisation that, yet again, despite this gift from the gods, I was in serious trouble. Wide awake after the recurring dreams of freakish trades in the futures markets, backing bogies at the races, once my ally, but no longer so kind or forgiving. The frequently changing price screens were winking green rates in my head deep into the middle of the night as I tried to sleep; course bookmakers were screaming odds at me, which I took up like a sucker.

Money smiled on me that summer evening in 1992, and I should have had the sense to make it last, to respect it and to take care of myself. Maybe I should have settled down, bought a house, started a family. But, instead, I set in motion a nightmare that hung over me for the ensuing six years. I kept saying to myself that I should really make an effort to go back to normality before it was too late. Before it was too late.

44

RCI had just made it, coughing and spluttering, to June 1993, by which time it was so deep in the mire that even I couldn't handle it any more. Not even with all my front, my talent for juggling and the unlimited (or so I thought) resources up my sleeve. RCI had been consumed by my old friend the hungry tiger. Consumed for breakfast, digested and regurgitated right in front of me. I sat in my office one Thursday evening in early June and gingerly opened the left drawer of my desk. It was crammed full of unpaid bills, County Court summonses and High Court writs that I had hidden from my bookkeeper and accountant. I pulled them out, scratched my head and starting adding them up. Then I got to work on the right-hand drawer. The large middle drawer of my desk was locked, and that was where the really juicy unpaids lived. I never did get round to unlocking that drawer – I had already got to over a million added up in the other two piles. I stared at a fly-sheet I had received in the mail the previous week, addressed to the chairman, marked 'Strictly Private and Confidential – To be Opened by Addressee Only'.

The £14 Million Windfall

It spelt it out nice and clear:

COMPANY IN TROUBLE? CONTACT SPECTRUM
SERVICES.

ALL COMPANIES TAKEN OVER – WE SPECIALISE IN
INSOLVENT CASES, ALL CREDITORS HANDLED, WE
FIELD THE PHONE CALLS.

DIRECTORS IN TROUBLE? WALK AWAY FROM YOUR
PROBLEMS.
 LEAVE EVERYTHING TO US.

JOHN ROBERTS, SPECTRUM SERVICES

Spectrum's fee structure was listed. You paid them a fee, on a
sliding scale, depending on the number of creditors you had. I
started shredding from my two piles and picked up the phone to
call Spectrum's proprietor, John Roberts. He was a little difficult
to understand at first, but I was impressed by his knowledge of
the Companies Act. Within two hours, he was seated in Old
Bridge House and I immediately knew what caused his speech
impediment – he had a three-inch scar on the right-hand corner
of his mouth.

I signed the forms he had brought with him, which effectively
appointed him as secretary of RCI and one of his colleagues as
managing director. I handed over his fee: six grand, in cash. I had
walked away from a nightmare, my only remaining task to divert
the office phones to his number in Farnham. There were no flies
on John Roberts, and he seemed quite happy to field the flack for
his fee. The following morning, I went to my office, dismissed all
the staff, diverted the phones and handed over the keys to
Spectrum. I used RCI's corporate Visa card to book myself into
Champneys Health Resort for a fortnight to lie low while the shit
hit the fan.

High Stakes

Zena popped by to stay for a few days courtesy of RCI (in liquidation) and after a fortnight's rest, I decided it was safe to venture back into the big wide world. I had shed a much-needed stone and a half, but, like so many times before, I was destined to put it all back on again, and more, within a few weeks. Stress, you understand. Comfort eating, social drinking, late-night curries after marathon booze-ups. I had retained the Ferrari and had a large quantity of the company's gold sovereigns in my possession. Now desperate for funds, I arranged to meet a fellow coin dealer at the Art and Antiques Fair at Olympia, where I was to knock out about 400 of my sovereigns for £19,000 in cash. This was pocket money for me, to try and keep things going for a few months.

This part of the deal went well enough, the parcel of bullion being exchanged for a carrier bag of cash in the restaurant at Olympia, but once I ventured outside, there was a reception party of my creditors waiting for me, together with a private detective. I had been set up, the creditors were all in on the deal and were keen to relieve me of my nineteen grand, to go towards their losses at RCI. The fact that I didn't have anything more to do with RCI didn't hold water with this gang. A kerfuffle ensued, with me jumping into a cab, and the creditors forcing their way in to join me. The cabbie didn't want to know, refused to budge and the police were called. We were all arrested, and I was led off to be interviewed at Hammersmith Police Station. Just as I was being led off by the police, my mobile rang. It was Zena. Her timing was incredible. Sadly, I was forced to cancel our dinner that evening. And that was how I first met Detective Sergeant Alan Fitzgerald of the Hammersmith Crime Squad. I was to spend the next 48 hours as his guest, and the next 3 years as his number one pending case awaiting trial.

Charged with Deception

45

In late June 1993, Detective Sergeant Alan Fitzgerald knew all too well the charts and diagrams of fraud – the pie segments, the audit trails, the bank reconciliations, their arrows, their pointers. He could quickly recognise the snakes and ladders of fraud, the telltale entries and the telltale omissions; the colour codes, the criteria.

I looked up from the interview tape. Something was troubling Fitzgerald, I could see it in his face. He observed me, watched me like a vulture. He was contemplating assessing me. Working out his plan, my future. I was no longer simply his interviewee, I was his captive, his prisoner. Nigel Goldman, a reckless, scheming fraudster. A clever fraudster, too clever by half, too big for his own boots. I needed pulling down a peg or two, and Fitz was the man to pull me down, oh yes, brother, you'd better believe it. Fitz had available a vast armoury of weapons specifically designed for torturing and pulling down the likes of me. He must have been glad, in a way, that my fraud was just under the million mark, that way he wouldn't have to hand my case over to the cronies at the Serious Fraud Office (SFO).

46

I suppose the most uncomfortable part of all that followed (apart from my two nights in the police cells at Hammersmith Police Station) was the search of Old Bridge House. I felt degraded, used and violated. Although I had had property searched before by Customs and Excise, this search was more thorough and took on a far more serious air than previously. For some reason it left a terrible feeling in my stomach. Everyone has their secrets, their hiding places.

I decided to let them get on with it and retired to my living room to have a drink while they carried on with the search. They were making their way towards my bedroom, but seemed to be spending an extraordinary amount of time going through all the paperwork in my study. One of the officers was drawing a floor plan of the apartment, carefully marking where the evidence had been found.

Fitzgerald was in my lounge, crouched down in a squatting position by a bottom cupboard, rummaging through my selection of pornographic videos from Amsterdam – *Rubber Maid, Sub Sluts, House of Dom, Bizarre Latex.* I disturbed him as I walked into the room carrying a magnum of chilled Louis Roederer Cristal champagne in a silver ice bucket.

He declined my offer of a glass. 'It's vintage,' I said, pouring him one anyway.

The rest of his crew had given up on my study, and Fitz's right-hand man, DC Brown, had gathered up a huge clear-plastic bag of evidence marked 'Metropolitan Police', which he tagged and sealed, and left for the time being in my study. At the time, I couldn't bear to think what incriminating evidence was in that bag, but there was likely to be a pile of juicy exhibits for them to get their teeth into once they got the bag back to the police station.

'By the way,' he said as he lugged the bag nearer to my study door, 'who on earth is Lydia Shourne? You've written her a huge number of cheques.' I couldn't fathom out what on earth he was talking about, and then it struck me. Lydia Shourne was the limited company that ran Maxim's casino. He had seen all the cheques I had gambled with, and thought they were payments to some girlie. Now, who said never overestimate the police?

Three hours later, they had amassed several bags of evidence to take back to the station and sift through. As we were about to leave, each officer grabbed two or three of the bulging plastic bags from my hallway, and we made our way down the staircase. I looked out of the window at the tranquil setting in the gardens, the trees rustling slightly in the early evening breeze. The sky was angry, looking down and mocking me like a jester. I had polished off the magnum nearly all to myself and felt a little unsteady on my feet. It did occur to me to wonder how long it would be before I might be back. I had visions of spending the next few months in custody. On the huge driveway, I plucked up the courage to ask Fitz. 'You're not going to do anything silly like objecting to bail are you?'

'It looks like a lot of money, Nigel. We'll have to see.'

Back at Hammersmith, I phoned Martin Murray, my solicitor, and he arranged for representation for me at the police station. I said nothing to the police during any of the interviews. The phone lines burnt late into the night as Martin did his best to get me released early on bail.

It felt strange when it eventually happened, some 23 hours after I was first hauled in, and I was grateful to get back home to have a bath and change my clothes. The first thing I did was to go into my study to see what had been taken. I couldn't believe my luck when I opened my study door and saw a large plastic bag of evidence staring me right in the face. In the commotion, this potentially damning and incriminating evidence had quite simply been left behind.

This was the first of two enormous boobs Fitz was about to make in my case; the second one was to keep Al Rubin out of the dock. My steaming-hot Versace bubble bath had to wait a half hour or so while I got to work on the shredder.

47

I was to spend three long years on police bail, awaiting trial. Anybody will tell you that the feeling of helplessness when you have a Crown Court case hanging over you is unbearable. You think about it every waking moment of your life: from the minute you get up in the morning to the minute you put your head on the pillow at night. There's always the possibility of losing your liberty, your possessions and home – your life.

Of course, I could have opted to spend those three years on remand in custody, but the option of bail seemed too attractive to turn down. I managed to maintain some sort of decorum for several months, helped by £650,000 which I had extracted from RCI. This was liquid money, readies. Well, almost. It was certainly liquid – krugerrands, sovereigns, gold bullion bars, foreign currency, travellers cheques. But soon the word got out and spread quickly. I was required to report to Hammersmith Police Station at increasingly regular intervals, and the press got hold of the story.

Sutcliffe summoned me for a meeting and lunch at Maxim's casino. 'I've been having a few phone calls, enquiries from punters and the press. Wanting to know if your company had any interest in your horses. Is everything going to be all right?'

He knew I was in some sort of trouble and was keen to have an in-depth chat to see if it was viable for me to carry on my expensive hobby of racehorse ownership; whether I was in a position to maintain payment of my monthly training fees, which were now rolling in at around three grand a month – 'Quite steamy,' Sutcliffe called them.

I put on an air of defiance and assured John that everything would turn out all right, and that I could pay the training fees, even without the back-up of the mighty RCI behind me. To this day, I am sure that John believed I was some kind of eccentric millionaire at that time. I certainly behaved like one. I can remember telling him at Sandown, on my big pay day, that of course one had to take into account the cost of the time off work when calculating the viability of racing.

'What you fail to realise,' Sutty replied, 'is that none of my other owners work at all.' I had now joined these hallowed ranks – if you ignored the pending prosecution, which I found hard to, although I did put on a brave face.

'This case is a crock of shit, John. I'm sure I'll get out of it.' We drank to my delicate future and over brandies and kümmel I enquired when Bo Knows Best would next run.

'There's a little race down the road for him on August Bank Holiday Monday. There's appearance money of a monkey. The horse is well. I think we should have a crack at it.'

48

Zena and I awoke that late-summer morning in 1993 at my Marlow apartment and went into the sitting room to listen to *The Archers* while I squeezed some oranges and brewed a pot of tea. I tried desperately not to think about my arrest some two and a half months earlier, hoping against hope that what was hanging over me wouldn't intrude and spoil what could turn out to be a memorable and exciting day.

High Stakes

It was a glorious summer's morning, and the sun streamed through the windows, causing the pink patterns of the drapes to sprinkle pretty designs over the bright room. Radio Four's horse of the day was Bo Knows Best in the 3.10 at Epsom.

The BBC weren't the only people in England to fancy my chances that day. I had already made up my mind to have a substantial wager myself and was certain that we would win. I was amazed to see that we were quoted at 10–1 on teletext and decided to take a short stroll up Marlow High Street to have an early-morning bet. I raided the safe for the first time that day. Zena clipped open her purse. 'Put a tenner each way on for me, too,' she called after me.

At Ladbrokes, I wrote out two betting slips: one for Zena with her score of sovereigns, and one for me with £1,500 to win, £500 to place. On both tickets, I filled in the 10–1 early price and paid the tax. One of the Ladbrokes girls got straight on the phone to head office to check if they could accept the large wager and, to my delight, they did. The two tickets went through the tills, and my bundle of readies were counted out. This was the start of my attempt to have a big touch. I then walked up to Coral's and Hill's, and did the same again. At Hill's, I noticed one of the girls from Ladbrokes pop in and have her own few quid on. I started to ask myself what would happen in a bizarre world where everyone backed winners with everyone else. By the time I got back home, half an hour later, I had pink, blue and yellow betting slips in my pockets and had backed Bo Knows Best to win some £50,000.

Zena and I had been invited to the Sutcliffe's for late-morning champagne and canapés before the race, and by the time we set off to Epsom in the Ferrari, Bo Knows Best was the buzz horse of the day and down to 13–2.

The question on everybody's lips as we stepped into Sutcliffe's living room that Bank Holiday Monday was 'Can we win?' Liz Sutcliffe laid out plates of smoked salmon sandwiches, and John thrust large glasses of chilled bubbly into his guests' hands the minute we arrived.

Charged with Deception

After our nosh, we walked Bo up to the racecourse paddock. The first race had just been run, and I stood there for a moment and took in the beauty of the clear blue sky perched high above the emerald green track.

The sun scorched down on us, and I could smell the cut of the grass, and the scent of the money in the ring. I noticed on the programme that the 3.10 race was the feature race of the day – the Moët and Chandon Silver Magnum, otherwise known as the Gentlemen's Derby, where all the riders are amateur jockeys. Moët were celebrating their 250th anniversary and had pushed the boat out with bunting and placards everywhere. A picture of the famous Silver Magnum featured on the programme cover. I saw that their name even appeared on the green diamond-shaped owners' badges we were wearing. It was immediately apparent that Sutcliffe, in his usual shy way and with his dry sense of humour, had gone out of his way to play down the importance of the race. I decided there and then to press up my action.

We went to the stables to saddle up Bo. He looked at me with those mad eyes and defiantly kicked at his box. He was on his toes. The lad sponged his mouth and then led him round the pre-parade ring, while our entourage made its way to the parade ring to meet up with our jockey. We had employed the services of Señor Louis Urbano from Spain on account of the fact that he had ridden a winner for the Queen the previous Saturday at Goodwood. I saw him approach us with my red-and-beige striped silks, twirling his whip. He immediately struck me as rather tall for a jockey, but as soon as he arrived in the ring the more pressing problem was that he hardly spoke a word of English. His father, who had won this race twice in the '70s, barged through the crowd of owners and trainers, binoculars swinging about his ample frame and quickly introduced himself to the connections. His role, it seemed, was to translate the race instructions from Sutcliffe to Urbano Jnr. It appeared both father and son were taking the event extremely seriously. I was quickly informed that they had walked the track that morning already.

217

High Stakes

John's instructions were relayed in crisp Spanish tones to Louis, and then it was time to leg him up and make our way via the bookmakers to our vantage point on the roof of the owners' and trainers' champagne bar.

The horses were making their way down to the start, being announced to the crowds as they did so. Men queued at the bars beside the course, laughing amongst themselves as the horses cantered past them down to the start (they could always watch the proceedings on the telly). Crowd and horses were both doing what mattered to them, neither being affected by the indifference of the other.

The sun had risen into a hot and sultry sky, and Epsom was sweltering. The crowd was drawn to this Bank Holiday meeting by English notions of class and tradition, of sport and good times; an attempt to affirm their connection with their past and their country by wearing it, parading it and displaying it to the crowd. And betting, too. In the ring, our price now hovered around 5–1, half the odds that were available early that morning, and the crowd were backing my horse with their Bank Holiday weekend cash. On the rails, with the bigger layers, Bo was still available at sixes. I hesitated, instinct telling me that at any second we might soften just a touch further. The horses were loading into the starting stalls, and the time to bet was evaporating. Then, quite suddenly, the Ladbrokes man offered 13–2 about Bo. I swivelled round and struck like a floor trader executing a large order for an important client. 'I'll have £10,000 on my horse, Bo Knows Best, and I'll take the 13–2.'

'Sixty-five thousand pounds to ten, Bo Knows Best, down to Mr Goldman. Much obliged, sir, and good luck.'

I joined up with Zena, John, Bernard Bates and the rest of the gang on the roof and focused my binoculars on the start, a mile and a half or so away. There were just a couple more to load, then the gates flew open and the stampede was on. Urbano settled my horse in mid-division and let the other less-experienced jockeys do the donkey work up-front. As the horses approached

218

Charged with Deception

Tattenham Corner, I counted seven in front of us, and we were eight to ten lengths off the pace. I gripped my binoculars tightly with white knuckles. Up on the stand, John thought we had gone, and for a brief second I thought it was all over too. We didn't dare look at each other; the tension was electric.

My hands were shaking as I waited for Urbano to make what might amount to a hundred grand move, and I could see him ease Bo to the outside.

The race for the Silver Magnum was erupting with excitement, and the crowd was already on its feet as the commentator shouted: 'At the two pole here comes Bo Knows Best in the striped jacket on the wide outside.' Sure enough, there he was, in third place, wide, racing down the centre of the track like a bat out of hell. Louis Urbano had Bo perfectly balanced, running down the outside of the field in his glorious powerful stride, my gelding firing along perfectly. He was flying over the ground, slicing into the lead of Shadows of Silver on the rail, but the finish line was looming ahead and, 100 yards out, Shadows of Silver was still ahead. Urbano, crouching low, kicked on, stylishly driving Bo through the dying yards of the race to snatch victory just before the line, winning by a snug length and a quarter. We rushed down to welcome the horse into the winners' enclosure, and the reception was rapturous. I gave Bo a friendly pat on the shoulder and his eye twinkled back at me. Channel 4 interviewed Urbano Snr, who recalled with pride his two winning rides in the race all those years ago, and then I was presented to Lady Marchwood to receive the Silver Magnum trophy, a magnificent prize. We retired upstairs for a celebratory drink, guests of Moët.

My father was also following the progress of my horse with quiet amusement and had put a tenner on the nose. He had watched the race on TV. 'Well done, Nigel,' he said softly to the empty room. 'Well done, my son. I thought he ran very nicely indeed.'

49

I was soon having to spend ever-increasing amounts of uncomfortable time with my legal team, which consisted of solicitor Martin Murray, his clerk Luc Salmon and Michael Egan and Edmund Lawson, QC from chambers. I was in capable hands: Lawson was about to (successfully) defend Kevin Maxwell, and he had been appointed head of chambers. I got busy answering their questions, as they delicately probed my business affairs of the previous few years. The police meanwhile were slowly gathering their evidence together. The prospect of going to court loomed.

All this started to dampen my enthusiasm for life and cast a shadow over even memorable wins with Bo Knows Best. In an attempt to make me feel better and more secure, John persuaded me to invest in five more racehorses: Go With Bo, Bo Knows Nigel, Let's Go Bo, Here Comes Bo and Mighty Kingdom.

Bo Knows Nigel in many respects was my most memorable purchase. He was a lovely looking horse and I sent him to Geoff Lewis's yard, who primed him to racing fitness. On the way to the race in which we were hoping to recoup our investment and cover costs, Bo began to cough. He was duly withdrawn from the competition, but with a large amount of money riding on him, the racing authorites suspected foul play. When an initial dope test proved positive, the media had a field day. An independent test followed, in which Bo Knows Nigel was found not to have been under the influence of illegal chemicals, but in terms of controversy, this horse was my best investment.

I would usually be jolted back into reality, like getting an electric shock, and remember my delicate predicament at the time when I should have been relaxing and soaking up the atmosphere of a joyous occasion. I started to suffer from terrible mood swings and began to put on weight at an alarming rate. I was drinking heavily and was seriously depressed. I would pace around my apartment, angrily kicking the furniture and raging furiously against everything and everyone – the home, my lack of friends and family, the boredom and frustration of waiting for the inevitable to happen. The police were painstakingly paying visits to everyone I knew, from every walk of life, to gather evidence and take statements. Every day, I would receive phone calls from ex-colleagues, ex-friends and ex-clients informing me of what was going on, and how it was probably best that we weren't in contact for a while. The police even went to the trouble of visiting all the London clubs and casinos of which I was a member, asking for a computer printout of my gambling activities, and freebie meals and drinks, so that when I arrived at the clubs I found that I had been blackballed. Next, they visited all my bookmakers, then stockbrokers and futures brokers. Finally, they got to work on my Filofax and rang up every phone number they could find. When they went to interview Zena for the third time, at her offices, she had had enough and called the whole thing off. I couldn't really blame her, although I was terribly sad to lose her. I would not see her again until she appeared as a prosecution witness in court. I was being sent to Coventry, *persona non grata*. I had gone through all this once before and knew how bad it was – how bad it was going to be: a moment of fear that could be anticipated.

I started to retreat into my shell and spent long hours at home drinking. Then, in a moment of madness, I would take five grand from my safe and go to London for an expensive night out to cheer myself up. My self-esteem and confidence were at rock bottom. I would return the next day knackered, feeling even worse. This went on for months. My cash pile was starting to get seriously eroded.

By mid-1994, I had been charged with conspiracy to obtain

property by deception along with three separate charges of theft. My co-conspirators were Al Rubin, who was still in Toronto, but who the police assured everyone would be in the dock to answer the charges, Sidney Longman, 'Simon Jacks' and 'Michael Williams'.

Despite what was going on, I was still paying the rent on the apartment in Marlow and still had six horses in training at Woodruffe. I decided that I needed a change, a rest. I despatched all my possessions to Sotheby's in Billingshurst for sale by auction, told Michael Davis that I was leaving and moved down to Brighton and rented a furnished flat in Brighton Marina.

In Brighton, I immediately fell in with a new crowd – professional punters of long-standing, who respected me as a racehorse owner and were keen to stand right behind me for the touch – knocker boys, punters, tipsters, antiques rogues. Knocker boys – the name says it all. The two most colourful ones were 'Paul Hackett' and 'Richard Mitchell', and we would often spend entire afternoons together drinking in Sinatra's wine bar on Second Avenue, which was owned by a terrific chap called Ray Williams. The knocker boys were brilliant at what they did, which was the opposite of my modus operandi. While I had spent my entire business life charging my victims ten times what something was worth, they spent their time buying things for a tenth of what they were worth. And there was Robin Morris, the colourful racing tipster, who I shared voluminous quantities of alcohol with. I met them all in the watering holes and bookmakers of Hove and Brighton, and got on well in my new-found cobwebbed environment. In Hove, my standing was higher than ever; nobody seemed to care two hoots that I had a major fraud trial coming up.

In Gary Newton's betting shop, where I whiled away most afternoons glued to SIS, I met Ray Miller, a man who I had heard of over the years as one of the shrewdest punters around. I was fascinated with the perms and spreads that he got involved in, bets that most bookmakers didn't understand, and I was keen to spend my time emulating his formulas and taking shares in his action. I wish to Christ I had met him in my early days, when I was going for all those touches. And I met Sidney Harris, too, an eccentric millionaire punter-come-tipster who longed to write sitcoms. You still see his distinctive adverts in the *Racing Post*. And Ashley Carr, Danny Blour and his brother Jeff. All racing faces.

And then I bumped into 'Gary Self'. What a character he turned out to be. One dark evening, he sold me a VHS video recorder for a hundred quid. When I got home and took it out of its box, I discovered it was an ancient top-loading Betamax. Unused, but probably 20 years old. When I challenged him the following day, he took a deep breath, put his hand on his chest and told me, 'It came from Victor Chandler; he never used it. He only wears his clothes once, too.'

Gary was a loser, you could tell that immediately. Financially, this was not a good time for him; few times were. It was apparent that the prospect of a refund for the video was extremely remote indeed. Even during his best periods – his purple patches of kiting, dealing, fiddling and diddling, when he had money coming in from all directions – Gary never had a good time. Financially. Always at some point in the day a bitter destiny awaited him at Ladbrokes. He always lost everything, without fail. Well, sometimes he won, but he always persevered until he had lost everything. His wife, who didn't know a tenth of it, used to ask him where all the money went, those rolls of tenners, those envelopes bursting with twenties, the odd folded fifty, the sixty quid from Victor's video. Gary's day usually began and ended with him upending her handbag on the lounge table. Where did it all go? His missus asked the question regularly, patiently, democratically, a million times. It made him mad, all the questioning. How could he make progress, get anywhere, with a wife who thought with such limited horizons. 'For God's sake, investments, like,' he would tell her, 'motor trading, currency speculation, stock clearances, futures, like.' He'd learnt all about what he thought were futures from Ladbrokes and his fellow cronies standing around all day trying to predict the future with nothing around to help them except the *Sporting Life*.

One day I bumped into him at Ladbrokes, just before racing started. 'It's the pits,' he was saying, 'I can't get a handle on this punting.' He took one of his familiar, pensive deep breaths, 'I mean, I ain't losing. I'm even.'

'Sure you are,' I told him. 'You start with nothing and you end with nothing.'

'Take a share with me for luck.' Of course, I couldn't help but take the odd share in the place pot with him on occasions. That day, almost uniquely, Gary had got through to the last race. All he had to do was to get one of his two selections placed in this last race – the crescendo of a day's trading. But another thing stood in his path as we headed towards the final race and our bitter destiny – it had at last dawned on me that Gary wasn't very good at picking winners.

Sid Harris was far better, though, and so was Ray Miller. One Sunday, I got seven out of eight with their help, and it paid handsomely. It also put me in good stead and on guard as a bookmaker in the years to come. With all this new-found local enthusiasm, though, I put all my energies back into racing, started spending an increasing amount of time with John and Liz Sutcliffe, often going down to Woodruffe to escape for long, boozy weekends. They knew about the pending trial, but it was a subject that was rarely brought up. At Woodruffe, I felt safe; protected by the memories and potential still to be eked out of my bloodstock. I even went through a period of coming right back out of my shell and being all high-profile again, and relatively happy. I purchased a spacious flat on Hove seafront at a knockdown price, got a golden retriever, which I named Oscar, and really started to convince myself that the case would never get to court.

I was soon brought back down to earth with a bump when I had my first conference with my junior trial barrister, Michael

Egan, in chambers. 'You're looking at six years if this goes wrong, Mr Goldman. This is a serious conspiracy allegation. The prosecution are going to make a big issue of your Ferrari, your lifestyle, the gambling, the first-class trips all over the world, the holidays.' Now I was being told what I would be doing two, three, maybe even five years ahead. Gradually, the truth began to dawn and, from that moment, I began to feel increasingly apprehensive.

Asking a criminal defence barrister if you have a good defence to a complicated fraud allegation is a bit like asking a barber if you need a haircut, and chambers were keen to point out to me that they saw no mileage (and little fee revenue) in a guilty plea.

With the surprising permission of Hammersmith police and a windfall profit on my horse accumulator, I flew off to Cape Town for a three-week holiday at Christmas to mull things over.

I immediately fell in love with South Africa: the climate, the country, the people, the accent, the racing. On my first evening, propping up the bar at the Peninsular Hotel, I was recognised. Recognised, thousands of miles from home. I was glad that I had the surprising permission of Hammersmith police; one never knew who one would bump into in far-off shores. It was harmless enough, though. I had been recognised by a South African racing enthusiast who had seen me on the telly in England collecting a trophy. He invited me to the races that Saturday at Kenilworth, offering to pick me up at 10.30. I graciously accepted. I could hardly believe my luck. I had been in South Africa a few hours, and I was already on my way to the track, as a guest, no less, of a steward of the local Jockey Club. Now what price is that?

The thing about South Africa is the terrific value. The exchange rate was six to one then, but it's ten or eleven now. At Kenilworth races we got our car park members' badge, a splendid lunch and wine in the VIP box all thrown in for 100 rand. That's seventeen quid in English money – about the cost of a badge and hot dog mid-week at rainy Plumpton.

I backed some winners, too, getting introduced to an owner

who had a filly in the fifth called Bella Louise that obliged. As I went to the bookies to collect, I saw a quite smartly dressed man whom I thought I recognised from somewhere in my past, loitering at the back of my mind. But I couldn't lock into who he was, no matter how hard I tried. I saw him again, after the next race, and again I got the jolt of familiarity, the recognition. But again, nothing. It was at the bar, up close, that I got the clue. In South Africa, the name badges in the members' enclosure reveal your identity. I peered closer. In one of life's amazing coincidences, I had bumped into my old VAT man on a busman's holiday in South Africa.

What a small, wonderful world this fabulous South Africa place was turning out to be. In hindsight, my mistake was coming back home.

50

My legal problems took a temporary, short-lived turn for the better when I returned from South Africa at the beginning of 1995. Sidney Longman had decided to exercise his legal right to go for an old-style committal at the Magistrates' Court. This is a procedure where a defendant claims that he has no case to answer and that the matter should go no further. The danger with this tactic, which is rarely used nowadays and not encouraged, is that both sides are forced to show their hands and, while weaknesses in the defence case are hard to put right after an unsuccessful old-style committal, the prosecution get a dress rehearsal free of charge and can tidy up their act in time for Crown Court should the application fail. To my counsel's astonishment, all the other defendants also opted to go the same route, and we all gathered in the spring for the hearing at the Stipendiary Magistrates' Court in the City.

Charged with Deception

The prosecution called one or two of my investors to give evidence of how they had been sold coins over the phone that they had then lost money on, and even Tom McLoughlan was called to talk about what he had seen in terms of goings-on at the office. I realised that Tom was angry with me for not putting him in on the touch with Bo at Epsom, but he did wink at me in the foyer which was comforting.

To Sidney Longman's delight, and everyone else's surprise, his application succeeded, and it was ruled that there was indeed insufficient evidence for the case to proceed against him. However, the magistrate ruled that all the others had a case to answer, including Rubin, who was still (we were assured) awaiting extradition from Canada.

The police were horrified that Longman had slid out of the frame and immediately informed everyone that they were going to a judge to ask for a voluntary bill of indictment. This is a little-used instrument whereby the prosecution can challenge a magistrate's decision, but it is normally reserved for only very serious offences. This immediately showed us how seriously the case was being taken at the highest levels, and Sidney would have to wait for a few weeks for the judge's decision. At the end of the summer, to everyone's astonishment, instead of rubber stamping the application as most judges do, this particular judge decided that the matter needed further probing and took his time going through the case papers. He found that, for Longman, the prosecution case against him just wasn't strong enough. The ruling put the prosecution in a rather difficult and delicate situation. If the judge found that Longman had no case to answer, and he was number three in the pecking order, after myself and Rubin, what hope did they have of securing convictions against Jacks and Williams, who were right down at the bottom of the table? They went away for a re-think and after an agonising few months, just before Christmas 1995, we returned to court to find out if charges were being dropped against the others. Because of a technicality involving extradition papers, Al Rubin was off the hook.

Surprisingly, Jacks didn't turn up to court and had to wait a further 48 hours for his good news. Egan and Lawson were delighted – they thought that it was particularly good news for me too. They hadn't particularly fancied a cut-throat defence on a conspiracy charge. They indicated that the prosecution would have to come up with new charges against me, and the one that was being bandied around as favourite was a charge of 'fraudulent trading under the Companies Act of 1948', which, at the time, carried a maximum sentence of two years' imprisonment. I went home to Brighton that evening with my spirits uplifted. It had been a long year, but I felt as though, at last, things were going my way. My stars were shining kindly on me, Lady Luck was in vogue.

And then, cruelly, the pendulum swung noisily the other way. In my mind, I heard it, like the noisy crash of 1,000 bottles. The Home Secretary, Michael Howard, rushed through the Criminal Justice Bill and, almost unnoticed, increased the maximum sentence for fraudulent trading from two to seven years to 'reflect the Government's concern at the prevalence of this crime, and to maintain faith in the City of London'.

The next time I attended for conference, chambers had taken on an eerie glow of seriousness. Even the receptionist, normally cheerful and smiling, looked very serious today. Martin Murray did his best to take the sting out of the situation during those long meetings in the boardrooms of Bell Yard. He shopped for expensive bottles of claret, which he generously plied us with at lunchtime, and decent rounds of sandwiches which were at hand. I even had a lunch with my QC at El Vino, where I desperately tried not to talk about the trial. But deep down, by that stage, I knew that I was in trouble – the case was looking more serious than ever. Again, I was persuaded that there was no value in a guilty plea, but was told in no uncertain terms that the tariff was back in the original ballpark. I was looking at four to six years if I got convicted. I had a fight on my hands, and I was due in Snaresbrook Crown Court in April, just over four months away.

I started to have panic attacks about the close proximity of the trial. After nearly three years on police bail, I suppose I had put the actual prospect of going to court out of my mind, hoping against hope that the nightmare would go away. But I knew it wouldn't and as doomsday loomed, the clock had started ticking.

I started to rehearse what I was going to say in the box as I walked Oscar on the long winter mornings leading up to the trial. I started to rehearse what I would say, the excuses I would make, the sincerity of my passionate belief in coins as a safe and wise investment. The pie charts, the graphs, the criteria. I started to imagine the questions I would be asked in cross-examination. I went about practising long, loud rehearsals of speeches delivered in a clear and steady voice to the 12 people who would decide my fate. Not just in the mornings, but soon late into the night, too. Over and over again, as I walked in the cold late-winter mornings along Hove esplanade, while Oscar went about his doggy things. Over and over again, late into the night, when sleep eluded me. Over and over again, as I took the train in and out of London, almost on a daily basis, in the early months of 1996, for last-minute conferences with barristers. I should have saved my breath. In the end, I wasn't even going in the box.

51

At Snaresbrook Crown Court near Epping, His Honour Judge John Martineau, in his wig and purple gown, walked the 20 or so strides from his chambers into the courtroom. Three brisk knocks from his usher announced his imminent arrival and the court rose. As he entered the courtroom that April morning in 1996, he carried an air of enormous self-importance about him and I thought he turned up his nose at everyone as though there was a perpetual bad smell under it.

High Stakes

The courtroom was modern, well lit and air conditioned. In front of the dock were several rows of benches and desks for the prosecution and defence solicitors and barristers. In front of the judge sat the clerk to the court and the stenographer and, behind them, raised on a dais, facing the dock, was the Bench where His Honour Judge Martineau presided. To his right, and on our left, were the seats for the press and members of the public, which included a number of Snaresbrook regulars, as I called them: old-age pensioners mainly, who lived locally and who came to court on a daily basis for entertainment. To the right of the dock were the jurors' seats and, just behind the dock, was a door with a spy hole that led to the cells below via a labyrinth of concrete corridors. I imagined a prison officer looking at me through the spy hole, examining his potential prey like a lion crouched in the savannah.

I spent my first day in Crown Court wearing a mask of riveted horror. Even my clothes were stained with unhappiness and apprehension. I had always pleaded not guilty before and had a good result. Why should I change? Of course, I should have known that past performance, as they say, is no guarantee of future success. And that years in prison can go up, as well as down.

I had been assured, though, that Snaresbrook had a higher rate of acquittal than any other Crown Court in the London area because the jurors from its catchment area tended to mistrust the police. As a result, they tended to side with defendants. This jury, though, were an unusual assortment. By the way they carried themselves, I was convinced they were long-term unemployed, mainly. Dole-signers, the lot of them. No doubt about it, I could tell for sure. You're supposed to be tried by your peers, but let's face it, how many businessmen can really afford to take an indefinite time off work?

The jury shuffled in, each person taking a seat. It consisted of seven men and five women. One of the younger men at the back wore shorts and another had a William Hill betting-shop pen

230

stuck behind his ear – I could just make it out. On the front row, a woman juror seemed to have brought a couple of carrier bags of shopping with her into court, and I noticed that she wore knee-high hold-ups when her skirt rode up her ample legs as she sat down at the end of the front row. She was panting, maybe at the exertion of carrying her bags into the box. At the other end of the front row, one of the girls had arrived in motorbike leathers and, as she peeled off her jacket, I saw that her arms were tattooed.

Eventually, all 12 were seated and the proceedings commenced. Edmund Lawson, QC, immediately stood up and requested that the judge allow me to leave the dock and be seated right behind him on the Bench next to my solicitor's clerk. 'In a case of this nature, your honour, with the voluminous quantity of paperwork involved, it would be of great assistance if my client could be seated next to the bundles.'

'Yes, very well, then.' The judge indicated with a slight gesture of his hand that the request be allowed, and I walked swiftly from the dock to the relative safety of the Bench.

1–0, Goldman.

The Crown had a strong cast assembled to support their case and after the legal niceties were disposed of, Michael Austin-Smith, QC, laid out his wares for the jury, immediately getting into soft ground when Ed Lawson got up and interrupted his opening speech.

'Your Honour, we understood, and I put it no higher than that, that the gist of this case revolved around the valuations of the expert witnesses of the merchandise sold by the defendant. The Crown seem to be introducing material in their opening speech which is of a surprising nature to us, and I feel that it is my duty to interrupt to put my friend on notice that we do not appreciate his attempt at hijacking our defence.'

'Yes, quite right, Mr Lawson. Thank you. Mr Austin-Smith, would you please keep to the flavour of the opening speech as disclosed to the other side?'

2–0, Goldman.

I couldn't believe to what depths the Crown would stoop in order to pick up crumbs. Throughout the few days that followed, Lawson and Austin-Smith would periodically get up to interrupt each other: as one rose, the other sat, like a see-saw. This was their opening gambit to make the other ill at ease, like a boxer dancing around his opponent in the early rounds of a bout. Lawson got the better of Austin-Smith most times. Even my junior, Michael Egan, noticed that Austin-Smith was starting to tread more carefully, choosing his words precisely and was, as Egan put it, 'a little ginger of Lawson'.

These were two of London's leading silks, pitching battle. They didn't care what I had done – they probably didn't care if I had even done *anything* – each of their jobs was to outsmart their opponent, to win the case. I was heartened to see that my team were wasting no time in setting the ground rules and getting me off to a good start. Austin-Smith continued with his opening speech. It was to last all day.

'Members of the jury, the Crown alleges in this case that the defendant, through his company Rare Coin Investments plc, systematically and deliberately defrauded investors of massive sums of money. In some cases, their entire life savings. The Crown will show you how the defendant marked up his merchandise by up to 1,000 per cent at times, employed a team of ruthless salesmen, who operated over the phone under aliases, no doubt because everything they said was untrue, and while these hapless investors, some of whom were elderly or infirm, were being defrauded of huge sums of money, the defendant continued to live the life of Riley. He enjoyed money, an expensive apartment, a Ferrari, first-class trips abroad, casinos, handmade clothes and racehorses. It is the Crown's case, members of the jury, that this was a highly intelligent man who knew exactly what he was doing, an expert in his field, who was motivated entirely by greed. A pioneer of the rare-coin market in slabbed coins, a subject which I will pursue with you at a later stage. A pioneer who passionately believed in the value of coins as an investment, but who used his knowledge and

232

the gullibility of his victims to exploit the marketplace. In short, members of the jury, a greedy man who didn't care tuppence, if you'll excuse the pun, for the well-being of his clients.

'His company traded from 1988 until 1993, when it went into administrative receivership. Most of the clients didn't even know anything was wrong until the police went to visit them. Some had entrusted their coins to be held in the company vaults for safekeeping, but when the receivers opened the safes they were empty.

'All in all, members of the jury, we will show you during the trial ample evidence that this defendant knew that he was going about a dishonest enterprise from start to finish. We will show you corporate brochures he had printed which contain lies. He talks of client funds being held in a segregated bank account; there was no such account. He talks of graphs showing the increases in value on a rare-coin portfolio – we will show you that all the figures in those graphs are bogus. He talks of money-back guarantees; most clients who asked for their money back were fobbed off with excuses.

'We will bring in a client who invested over £200,000 with this firm and lost the lot, his entire life savings. We are certain, once you have heard all the evidence in this case, that you will want to convict Mr Goldman on the charges of the indictment.'

Well, he certainly timed it well, old Austin-Smith. It was almost four o'clock when he sat down, just in time for the judge to adjourn until the following morning.

I knew it would sound bad the first day, and it sure did. The only consolation was that we hadn't had a look in yet. I didn't dare try and figure out where we stood, scorewise. But 2–0 up was an aberration, a temporary flash in the pan, of that I was certain. On my way out of court after that first gruelling session, even DS Fitzgerald noticed I looked particularly gloomy. My get up and go had got up and gone. He shared in my plight.

'Don't worry,' he assured me, 'it always sounds bad on the first day.'

For him though, he must have secretly hoped to God it continued to look this bad for me, or worse, as the trial progressed over the coming weeks.

52

The Crown had carefully chosen their cast of witnesses. They did, after all, have plenty of choice to start with, many hundreds of clients – most of them substantial losers. So they went about their task thoroughly and conclusively, until they had selected the six most jury-friendly victims they could find. And they certainly found them. I always knew they would. The cases they wheeled into court would haunt me in their attempt to secure their precious conviction. The losers they would produce would generate the maximum jury sympathy: the elderly man, the naive man, the greedy man, the working man, the shrewd man and the gullible woman. Their witnesses were chosen with great care and thought, and fully briefed by the Crown as to the vitally important role that they were about to play. The role that they were about to play in condemning me to jail.

By far their most important witness was Patrick Watson, an elderly man in his 80s who had invested with us substantially. A member of the Royal Mint Coin Club, he was easily persuaded by Al to part with over a quarter of a million pounds in overpriced slabs.

When things had got really tight, Al and I had even gone to his home to prise a further sixty grand from him. I knew it was wrong, but we just really needed the money at the time. He took us to his bank for the draft – the same branch that had cocked up in the Bearwater share certificate fiasco with me years earlier. As I was handed the draft, I had to smile; they would have gone ballistic if they had known who I was. The same bloody branch where all those extra shares had come from, free of charge, in the late 1980s. If only they had known. They could never imagine what worms lay in that unopened can.

So, Patrick Watson was definitely their star witness, but first, on day two, they chose to bring in 'the naive man'. I looked on in horror. Here he was in real life, somebody who I had never met before, but who I had sold to over the phone in those early days, in the late 1980s, when I had first started.

'Mr Hutchins, you first replied to an advert from Rare Coin Investments that you saw in *Moneywise*, is that correct?'

'Yes, your Honour.'

'And you were impressed by the huge predictions in that advert, so impressed that you decided to fill in the coupon and reply to the advert. If it may help your Honour, the copy advert appears in the jury bundle as exhibit A118.

'And then you received the colour glossy brochure from the company – jury bundle C216 – and you liked what you read in that about the appreciation of coins. What was it on the inside back cover of this glossy brochure that impressed you? Was it the fact that all client funds were held in a client bank account, until the coins were despatched to you, perhaps, Mr Hutchins?'

'Yes, your Honour.'

'Did you receive your coins, Mr Hutchins?'

'Yes, your Honour.'

'But had you known that they were being sold to you at five times what they were worth, you wouldn't have bought them, would you, Mr Hutchins?'

'No, your Honour.'

'Stay there, Mr Hutchins. My friend may have some questions for you.'

The see-saw got back into action as Lawson stood up and Austin-Smith sat down.

'No questions, your Honour.'

'The Crown calls Mr Simpson.'

Now, Simpson had invested heavily, and he was a client of

long-standing. He started off as a punter at the Scottish Money Show, and Al had loaded him over the phone on many occasions. Loaded him in Scotland right up to the eyeballs. 'Now, Mr Simpson, what is it that the defendant said to you about the capital appreciation of the coins he was selling you?'

'He told me that the coins were going up at a rate of 15 per cent per annum. I even entered the new prices in my home computer, which I had bought for this very purpose. It was because of this spectacular growth that I invested more and more. I now know, of course, that I had been led up the garden path. Completely taken in by Mr Goldman, more fool me.'

'And if you had known that the coins you had been sold were worth less than a fifth of the price you had been charged for them, would you still have purchased them?'

'Oh, no, your Honour. Most certainly not.'

And then the working man. The working miner, to be precise. From down the pits. 'And Mr Strickland, if you had known that all the coins you were being supplied by this company were being sold to you at ten times the price they were worth, would you have bought them?'

'No, your Honour.'

'Your Honour, our next witness is Patrick Watson, an elderly man in his 80s. The police are going to travel to Leigh-on-Sea to collect him, and he would like very much to be back home the same day. Would now be an appropriate time to adjourn, so that I can deal with Mr Watson tomorrow?'

'Yes, very well, Mr Austin-Smith.'

'Court rise.'

Another losing session.

The following day, they walked Watson in. Literally. DS Fitzgerald and DC Brown held him on either side as they walked him into the courtroom and led him into the witness box. They were getting maximum jury sympathy by this stage. 'Are you comfortable there, Mr Watson? We can get a chair brought into the witness box, if you prefer, Mr Watson.'

236

'I'll stand,' he croaked.

'Mr Watson, you are 83 years old, is that correct?'

'Pardon?'

'You're 83, is that right?'

'Oh, yes, 83.'

'And you invested over £200,000 with this company?'

'I just want to know what has happened to all my money. What's happened to all my money? *Where has all my money gone?*' I didn't dare glance over at the jury, the silence in the courtroom spoke volumes. You could hear a pin drop. That sentence was the pinnacle of the prosecution case, that was for sure.

After a few more investors, they brought in their expert witnesses, one of whom was Michael Sharpe, who had spent weeks going through every single coin that I had invoiced, lowballing them into obscurity. He was the best witness for us too, working as he did for AH Baldwins, a respected firm of numismatists on Adelphi Terrace in London. I always thought he looked a lot like Charles I, the way he trimmed his beard. He was in the witness box for days, valuing pages and pages of coins I had sold over the years. I encouraged Lawson to cross-examine him in the afternoons, after he had had a few drinks at lunchtime.

'Eh hem, Mr Sharpe. You value this MS64 gold sovereign at only £150. That's unrealistic, isn't it? We have our own valuations here from other experts in the United States. What do you have to say about Mr Byers's valuation of $1,000?'

'Outrageous!'

'What about Oak Tree's valuation of $2,000?'

'Bloody unbelievable!'

'And $5,000?'

'On another planet.'

I looked over to the jury. We were gaining valuable Brownie points here. They looked as though they were listening to something in Swahili, with Moroccan subtitles. The young man on the back row was picking some dirt from under his nails, while another was flicking through the jury bundles, bored to death.

'And how about $1,500 for an 1817 George III half crown in MS65?' Lawson enquired.

'High enough to scare the cat,' Sharpe blurted out.

Next up, another customer. A young man in the computer business. This time one who had actually come to the office in person to buy. He had been well rehearsed. 'What did you see when you arrived at the office premises of Rare Coin Investments?'

'I saw Mr Goldman's bright-red Ferrari parked outside.'

'A Ferrari, eh? I see. A Ferrari,' Austin-Smith whispered loudly to the jury.

Then the commercial witnesses. To give flavour to the case, to illustrate the strokes I had pulled in commercial life while running the company, as well as the rip-off scams that they could prove through the investors. These characters were the Crown's icing on the cake.

'Mrs Carmichael, you are the financial controller for *Reader's Digest* magazine, that is correct?'

'Yes, your Honour.'

'And among the publications that come under your group are the magazines *Moneywise* and *What Investment?*, is that correct?'

'Yes, your Honour.'

'And the defendant, Mr Nigel Goldman, advertised his company Rare Coin Investments plc in your magazines, is that correct?'

'Yes, your Honour.'

'What sort of adverts were these?'

'Full-page colour advertisements, your Honour.'

'And roughly speaking, how much did these adverts cost?'

'Between £8,000 and £12,000 each, your Honour.'

Austin-Smith swivelled to face the jury. 'Eight to twelve-thousand pounds apiece, members of the jury.'

'And at what stage did you have cause to telephone the defendant, Mr Nigel Goldman?'

'When his advertising account got up to over £100,000.'

Austin-Smith swivelled again. 'A hundred thousand pounds. And what did he say to you, when you phoned him? What did Mr Goldman tell you when you phoned him up and asked him for his cheque for over £100,000 to clear your firm's outstanding account?'

'He told me that at the end of every month, he put all his unpaid bills into a hat, shuffled them up and then pulled a few out and paid them, and that if I kept on phoning him he wouldn't even put my invoice into the hat.'

The jury erupted.

'Thank you, Mrs Carmichael.'

If the trial had finished there and then, the jury would have gone out and convicted me in five minutes flat. No doubt about it. But the prosecution still had a large number of people to call, and they had over-egged their pudding. We were to gain valuable ground over the days which followed, as their next stack of witnesses were unreliable and came across poorly for the Crown in cross-examination. We had a few good days in a row and all of a sudden my prospects brightened. Especially when the receivers were called to give evidence. They were a firm called Levy Gee and had been appointed by my bank. They pulled strokes in the liquidation by knocking out my personal property from the office building without my permission, but the real horror story unfolded when their witness, Sarah Rayment, was cross-examined about how she had handled the large quantity of coins that were left behind in the office, some of which clearly belonged to clients.

Lawson quickly got to work on her, attacking her Achilles heel. She was very attractive and married to a partner in the firm, but was clearly out of her depth in court.

'Eh hem, Mrs Rayment. Help me with this. What did your firm actually do with all the coins that were situated at the office premises of Rare Coin Investments?'

'We sold them.'

'You sold them, after presumably removing any coins that

belonged to clients of the firm and after having them professionally valued?'

'No, we stuck 'em in a van and sold 'em to a dealer we knew in London.'

'In a van? There were that many coins?'

'There were actually so many coins that they didn't fit into one van, we had to hire two vans.'

The jury mumbled.

'So, these two van loads of rare coins – which you had no idea what they were worth – were knocked out to this dealer. For how much please?'

'Seven thousand pounds, plus VAT.'

'I see. For £7,000, plus VAT. Didn't it occur to you that that may have been a bargain-basement price?'

'We were trying to liquidate the company assets as quickly as possible to service our fees and to repay the bank overdraft as quickly as possible.'

Later, we cross-examined the buyer of the coins, a small-time dealer, who I didn't recognise. He made out that he had paid market price for the coins, but it was obvious to me that he was lying and that the stock had been knocked out to him very much on the cheap.

We had gained some very valuable points and also thrown doubt on the evidence of the clients who had complained that their coins had been stored by my company for safekeeping and had disappeared after the liquidation.

Wigged, gowned and bespectacled, Edmund Lawson, QC, drew on his cigarette in the barristers' conference room by Court 1. 'You've had a good few days,' he told me, as we left court for the weekend.

53

The trial had been going on for just over a month, and I was exhausted. I was travelling to Snaresbrook Crown Court every morning from Hove and back again in the evenings. I would get up at 4.45 in the morning, after a fitful night's sleep, take Oscar for a long walk, get back by quarter to six, and shower and get dressed in time to catch the 6.38 into London. I would get to London at around 8.15, take a Tube through the crowded city in the rush hour, then grab the Central Line out to Snaresbrook. I would get to court by about a quarter to ten, in time for a couple of coffees and a quick chat with counsel. Poor little Oscar, I'm sure he thought I had become deranged, getting him up for his walks that early in the morning. During the day, the girl from the Lion d'Or wine bar would come round to the flat to look after him and take him for more walkies. I would stop at the Lion d'Or on the way home, down a few glasses of wine and mull over the day's proceedings, before making my weary way home.

So, when the mother of one of the jurors died suddenly, and we were given a few days off from court, I was grateful for the break. It came at a time when things were going our way, and I would say that, to be entirely fair and accurate, honours were level. We hadn't heard from DS Fitzgerald yet, though. He was to swing things back round in favour of the Crown once more. Which was unfortunate for me.

After our few days' rest, Fitzgerald strode into the witness box. I noticed that he had put on a new suit and had had a haircut.

He lifted the Bible in his right hand and spoke in a clear and steady voice to the jury. 'Detective Sergeant Alan Fitzgerald.

Hammersmith Crime Squad.' Austin-Smith was quick to get to work on him.

'DS Fitzgerald, you have been investigating this defendant for about three years now. You have visited his home, his business premises and more than 20 countries all over the world where he has conducted business. Help me with this. His home. What is Old Bridge House?'

'Old Bridge House is a Victorian house set in grounds by the River Thames at Marlow, and it is divided into two apartments. Mr Goldman occupied the middle floor of the building. In all my years as an investigating police officer, involved in major fraud and drug investigations, I have never come across a home so lavishly and expensively appointed, decorated to such a high standard, so beautifully furnished, with so many bedrooms and reception rooms, with views . . .'

'I think we get the picture DS Fitzgerald. And the business trips abroad, help us with those.'

'Always first class, always the best hotels, restaurants and bars. Very extravagant. At the investors' expense, of course.'

'And the state of the company while all this was going on?'

'Insolvent. Unable to meet its liabilities as and when they became due.'

'Thank you, DS Fitzgerald, you've been most helpful.'

Lawson got up to cross-examine.

'Is it not true that Mr Goldman pumped nearly £14 million into his company in September 1992 – £14 million of his own money – in order to stave the company up?'

'You can imagine what state things would have been if he hadn't. It beggars belief.'

They then called Gary Charman, of the Format Coin Company in Birmingham. A formidable witness, I had warned Edmund Lawson. He had, in fact, been a business rival at one stage. His evidence clearly wouldn't help me. However, fortunately I had some good documentary evidence and a great legal team, which together helped lessen the blow.

Charged with Deception

They then called Zena. I had taken her to Singapore for a coin show, and we had stayed at Raffles Hotel, Singapore's finest. Austin-Smith thought he could bully her in the box, but he quickly found out he was mistaken.

'When you travelled to Singapore, how did you get there?'

'By plane.'

'Yes, of course, but what I meant was, did you travel coach?'

'Sorry.'

'Coach.'

'Oh no, we travelled first class.'

Austin-Smith turned to face the jury, smiling. 'First class, I see.'

'Yes, first class. My boyfriend, Nigel Goldman, got an upgrade on Singapore Airlines. I couldn't believe it. He told them he normally flew BA and was trying Singapore Airlines for the first time, and they upgraded us. To try to win him over as a client, I suppose.'

Nice one, Zena.

Lawson, too, had been doing a brilliant job in cross-examination. Throwing reasonable doubt on all the witnesses. Throwing doubt on the valuations and the expert testimonies. It was clear that the jury were confused, swaying one way, then the other. Siding with me, and then with the prosecution. It almost depended on who had been in the box last.

They were obviously having difficulty with the case and would be relying, no doubt, on how they were to be directed by the judge when he summed up.

After 12 weeks, the prosecution case drew to a close, and it was time for us to decide if we were to call any witnesses, and whether I would go into the box to give evidence myself. This was a major decision. There had been changes to the law regarding defendants who didn't give evidence, while I had been on bail. The new rules allowed the trial judge to direct a jury that they could find adverse inference in a defendant who decided not to go into the witness box and tell his version of events. This struck me as odd for two reasons. First, I had been within my rights at

243

the time to make a 'no comment' interview at the police station, so if I went into the box to explain things now it could be argued by the prosecution that I had had three years to think about what I was going to say and had made it all up. And if I didn't go in the box, the jury could think ill of me. As I went away that evening to make up my mind on probably one of the most important decisions in my life, I realised that the law really is an ass.

In the end, in a monumentally dreadful error of judgement, I didn't go into the box. I didn't say a word. I wish to Christ I had. Things certainly couldn't have turned out any worse. We didn't call any witnesses, either. We gambled with my future on the jury having taken on board sufficient reasonable doubt to acquit me. I should have gone in the box, I really should. I would have been good, too.

But now it was time for both sides to sum up, followed by the judge. Then the jury would be sent out to deliberate and decide my fate.

But with no defence having been made, I felt uncomfortable almost immediately. I knew this was a mistake. Only guilty people decline to be cross-examined and rely on prosecution incompetence to gain their freedom.

As soon as I got home that evening, I phoned the kennels: 'You'd better take him in. Just in case,' I said, a little defeated.

54

Austin-Smith had moved himself and his papers to the edge of the barristers' long table and was now facing the jury full on.

'This is a case that is all about whether you consider that the defendant was running an honest, decent and legal business. We say fraud. We say that it was fraudulent from the outset – riddled with dishonesty. You have heard over the past few weeks how the defendant, Nigel Goldman, published glossy brochures and adverts that were purposely designed to deceive – how the graphs showing profits were uplifted from an advert from a firm called MicroPal without their permission. You have heard how he employed teams of ruthless salesmen, many of whom had worked under aliases, who bullied and cajoled the clients into parting with huge sums of money, in some cases their life savings, for nearly worthless investment portfolios in coins. We have heard how he didn't pay his business's advertising bills. While all this was going on, he continued to live the life of Riley – the apartment, casinos, first-class trips abroad, the Ferrari, the racehorses. Is that what honest, normal, people would call legal? We say fraud, members of the jury, and we invite you to convict.'

Lawson rose. 'Members of the jury, this was a case that was bound to happen sooner or later, if you believe everything you have just heard. But the defendant's business wasn't fraudulent from the outset, as it has been put to you. He had a genuine, passionate belief that the coins that he was supplying were likely to go up in value. We have heard him described as an expert in his field – a pioneer. It would be entirely speculative to convict him on whether he had overcharged his clients, because we just don't know what he had supplied was going to be worth in three, five years time. How would you feel if you convicted him, and then the coin market shot up in value and all the customers made a whopping profit while he is condemned to prison? That would hardly be fair, would it? And that is what I am asking of you, members of the jury. To be fair. We have heard a lot over the past few weeks about the defendant's lifestyle. There's nothing wrong in driving a Ferrari, or owning a string of racehorses that run with funny names, as long as it is paid for from legitimate means. Mr Goldman never stole from RCI, on the contrary, we have heard how he pumped nearly £14 million of his own money into the company when it got into difficulties. Is this the behaviour of a dishonest man?

'Now, let's deal with the actual accusation, what Mr Goldman is precisely accused of in the indictment: fraudulent trading, under the Companies Act of 1948. The Crown have done a splendid job of wheeling in half a dozen witnesses who have complained to the police that their investments were overpriced. But that is only the tip of the iceberg, members of the jury. You have seen the evidence provided to you by Mr Egan, in your jury bundles. This company sold over £60 million worth of coins over its trading period, and these complaints, if you like, only amount to £700,000 worth. About 1 per cent of the total turnover. The Crown could only find 1 per cent of the total sales of this company that were questionable. And even then, their expert witnesses differed wildly on their valuations. Remember Mr Sharpe? And then the experts from the United States? They all differed wildly in their valuations, sometimes by as much as 500 per cent. All in all, members of the jury, I beg you, implore you, not to convict this man, not to condemn him on this flimsy evidence. You should weigh up all the points you have heard and come to the only sensible and just conclusion. Acquit.'

His Honour Judge Martineau addressed the court. It was approaching three o'clock on the afternoon of Wednesday, 26 June 1996.

'I do not propose to start my summing up today. I will sum up tomorrow and then send you out to deliberate on Friday morning.'

'All rise.'

55

The judge commenced his summing up. 'Members of the jury. This has been a long and complicated case. You may have various emotions and feelings. Maybe emotions of sympathy for the victims, especially the elderly ones we have seen. You may have emotions of jealousy against the defendant because of the millionaire lifestyle he has led. I want you to put all those feelings entirely to one side and deal with the evidence you have heard in this case. You must decide if the defendant knowingly went about his business with a fraudulent purpose in mind. You must decide if he knowingly published his brochures and adverts with the intent to mislead, and you must decide if he encouraged his teams of salesmen to tell lies over the telephone. If you accept that he passionately believed, as we have heard, that the value of the coins that he was marketing were at market price, and they were likely to increase in value, and that is what he thought, then you should acquit him. Of course, you should also look at the motivation of the defendant and consider this – was it greed that motivated him? Greed is a very powerful emotion and is hard to control. Or maybe the defendant was reckless in the promises he made to his clients. If you believe that, then you should also convict him.'

The trial judge, in his wisdom, had just left the door wide open for us if we should be convicted, because this was the first time that recklessness had arisen in this case, and there were strong legal grounds for him not to have confused the jury with it. It was not the charge, had not been explored in the evidence and had not been dealt with by either side in their summing up. I noticed Egan busy scribbling away in his notebook.

'As I said yesterday, members of the jury, I do not propose to send you out to deliberate today. We will adjourn until tomorrow morning, when you will go out and reach your verdict.'

I went home that evening with very mixed emotions. We had done all we could to win the case, and the judge's summing up had been quite fair. Egan had made a big issue about the recklessness matter, and we decided that, should I be convicted, we would definitely use it as grounds for appeal.

I popped into the Lion d'Or and got drunk. The next morning, I met up with Colin Miller, a drinking buddy, who had decided to come with me to see how things were going. At the railway station, he jokingly asked if we were going right to

London, or left to the ferry. After all I had gone though, I was determined to see this out.

At court, no one on the team could shed any light on the jury's probable outcome. They simply didn't know. When lunchtime arrived and they hadn't reached a verdict, Colin went and got some wine, and we sat outside in the garden around Snaresbrook Crown Court by the lake, and I slowly started drinking myself into blissful oblivion. My rude awakening came at around quarter to four. Martin's clerk came running out. The jury were coming back in – with a verdict.

We rushed back into the court. Michael Egan told me that I had to stand in the dock, the safe sanctuary of the Bench now out of bounds. I knew that if the jury looked at me, made eye contact as they walked into the courtroom, that would indicate an acquittal. Only juries who have found the defendant guilty fail to look at the person they have condemned.

The jury shuffled in to return their verdict. I glanced over at them. For an instant, I thought that they were looking at me encouragingly. But the eye is a fickle harlot, and when I looked back, all 12 pairs of eyes avoided my stare. I stood to attention in the dock, hands firmly behind my back, trying not to sway. The door to the labyrinth opened and a black, muscly security guard walked in and stood behind me in the dock, ready to take me down if the jury convicted me.

The clerk read out the charge on the indictment to the jury foreperson, the young girl at the far end of the first row, who was originally in motorbike leathers with tattoos. Ominously, still no one glanced over at me.

'And how do you find the defendant, guilty or not guilty?'
'Guilty.'

In my mind, I heard the cell door slam and shut my world away like the melancholy thud of the guillotine. Once proud and walking the tightrope, I had fallen. Lawson rose and glanced over his shoulder to make sure I was still with him. 'Your Honour, I can't persuade you to release him on bail, pending sentence?' The judge was already shaking his head. He expressed his decision in fluent legalese, which was muttered rapidly to the court. I was being remanded in custody to Pentonville Prison for two weeks for the preparation of pre-sentence reports by the probation service.

I was led through the door at the side of the dock into the labyrinth. There were a number of guards standing around in their green shirts and trousers. They were intimidating – I felt them staring and whispering comments under their breath. The atmosphere was unhealthily confrontational. Some were chewing gum with what seemed to me an air of casual aggression.

On the wall there was a whiteboard with the names of prisoners and the length of their sentences written up in felt-tip pen and, by the cells, small blackboards were fastened to the wall with the names of prisoners chalked up. My name was scribbled with the nonchalance of a six year old practising joined-up writing.

It felt odd to be immersed into a prisoner's world, when less than half an hour earlier I had been free as a bird, sipping wine on the grass in the sunshine. It felt strange to have to ask to have a door opened, or make a request for permission to use the toilet. It was disturbing to be reduced to such a state of dependency normally only associated with young children or the elderly. But I had half expected it, really. And I had been here before, as practice, preparation for this – the big one.

I was locked in a cell with a young man who was pacing up and down furiously. His eyes were streaming – he had just been handed a life sentence. I noticed an alarm button at head height on the wall, but I took little comfort in it – what if this maniac I was banged up with took his vengeance out on me?

The wicket – that hatch at eye level on the cell door – flew open. The guard was careful to keep his head well away from the opening – he'd heard the horror stories about jailers leaning too far though the wicket hole and having their noses bitten off or faeces stuffed in their mouths.

'Goldman – legal.'

High Stakes

The door unlocked, and I was led to the interview room down the corridor. One of the guards pushed himself off the wall he was leaning against, like a schoolboy being told to stop hanging around. He unlocked the door to the interview room where Lawson, Egan and Martin Murray were seated on a bench. I couldn't help notice it was bolted to the floor.

As I entered the interview room they all stood up to greet me. 'Well, gentlemen,' I announced, putting on a brave face, 'we always knew we had a fight on our hands, I would just like to thank you all for doing such a good job on my behalf, for trying so hard.'

Egan seemed grateful and Murray was obviously disappointed at the result. I shook their hands and was then led back to the cells to await my transportation to Pentonville Prison.

As the three members of my legal team walked past my cell on their way out of the building, I heard Martin say, 'I hope to hell he did it, for his sake.'

Egan replied, 'Who the hell knows? What's it got to do with anything, anyway?'

An hour later, I was walked to the waiting white convoy of heavy prison vans – sweat boxes to the cons. Each van was partitioned into fourteen separate cubicles, seven each side, with a central walkway. As the doors slammed shut, and the engine signalled the start of my journey to hell, I peered out of the tiny window aperture at the shops and houses that we were passing and promised myself that today would be the start of the rest of my life.

The Big One

56

The sweat box pulled up to the huge Victorian iron doors at the gate lodge of Pentonville Prison and waited, engine idling. We had done the rounds of all the inner-London nicks, dropping off prisoners at Brixton, Belmarsh, Wormwood Scrubbs and Wandsworth. As it was approaching nine o'clock in the evening, I was the last prisoner to be delivered to jail. I had been in the confines of the sweat box for three and half hours and was baking in the tiny, restrictive cubicle. I thought how, just a few days earlier, I had seen scores of women at Shoreham protesting about the shipment of live *animals* in better conditions than this.

The iron doors opened, and the driver engaged first gear, chugging into the prison courtyard. Out of the tiny window aperture, I could see some prison officers unstrapping their radio trans receivers as they clocked off for the evening. Others were removing the ten-inch wooden batons from their trouser pockets to hand in before they knocked off for the evening.

We reversed up to the prison door, and I felt the first wave of fresh air as the sweat box was opened up and I was led out into the prison yard in handcuffs, a sealed and tagged bag containing my briefcase and possessions accompanying me. I was walked straight into the prison reception area where a number of officers awaited my arrival, as well as a couple of trusty cons – orderlies. They had heard about my conviction on the radio and were keen to inspect the fraudster in real life. Most of the officers stood around in shirtsleeves, although a couple wore thick, ribbed regulation dark-blue sweaters, with HM Prison Service embroidered on the cloth epaulettes.

The senior officer on duty that evening was a friendly one. He stood propping up the reception desk. He obviously relished his position, eyeballing all the new inmates who arrived. The two orderlies hovered around, one seemed to be winking at me non-stop. The other, who I found out later was a lifer, enquired how long I was looking at. When I replied four years or so, he laughed my sentence off as risible – 'a walk in the park'.

Prison staff are not by their nature, or inclination, pleasant people, but the senior officer on duty was an exception. He allowed me whatever I wanted out of my briefcase, including a cigar, which someone in Hove had given me the previous evening for luck. My Filofax, stamps, Mont Blanc pen and own shoes accompanied me to my cell for the evening. I was taken up the metal staircase to the fourth-floor landing and banged up with my new cellmate, who was serving 12 months for driving while disqualified. A self-confessed drug addict, he was a friendly face and spent most of the evening grinning at me with his toothless smile, trying to probe me about my crime.

Nothing much had changed since my brief incarceration a decade earlier, although I was glad to see that the slop buckets had been replaced with flush sanitation. And some of the prison screws were female, sort of.

I was allowed a quick shower. The shower felt good. I thought of the power showers at the Hyatt in Jo'burg. Things change.

I spent the next fortnight waiting for someone from the East Sussex probation department to come and interview me about my pre-sentence reports. They never turned up. It soon emerged that once I had been sentenced, I would be moved to a long-term prison. I had got on well with the reception senior officer, and he had already pencilled me in as a D-category prisoner, the lowest risk, and had promised me a good job in the prison once I was sentenced. He then assured me that I would be shipped out to an open prison after a few weeks. About a week into my stay at Pentonville, I got a job in the workshop, counting out plastic spoons and popping them into cellophane packaging for the princely wage of £7.50 a week.

My first contact with the outside world was when Debbie Rogers, a friend from Hove, sent me a letter. She had gone to the trouble of going to the kennels to see how Oscar was and had found him a home with a family on a farm. I will never forget her kindness. Enclosed in the envelope was a £50 note so that I could do some shopping in the prison shop, and she promised to send me in £20 every week I would be in prison. I went back to my cell feeling on top of the world, under the circumstances,. Her generosity and kindness was overwhelming, and I immediately called her up to thank her from the bottom of my heart. The following day, Richard Williams wrote and also sent me some money and promised to visit. Harry Conway wrote a long letter and sent me a cheque for £100. Even Michael Williams obliged with £200 worth of postal orders. My spirits lifted even higher.

Exactly two weeks after being convicted, I was back in a sweat box on my way to court for sentencing. I had no idea what to expect. The trial judge had moved courts from Snaresbrook and was now sitting at Southwark Crown Court, so that was where we were heading. In the holding cells below the court, which I shared with about another dozen cons waiting to be weighed off, I was allowed a quick conference with my legal team. I looked, and felt, like shit. My suit was crumpled from its two-week stay in a HM Prisons cardboard box, and I had my hair cut short by another con for the cost of a phonecard. I had also probably dropped over a stone in weight, so much so in fact that Lawson was shocked to see me. He told me to expect four to six years. That's quite a big spread, unless it's a quote by a spread betting firm on the second favourite in a twelve-race handicap. Four to six. I converted it into traditional odds. Odds-on four years; 5–2, four and a half; fives for five; ten for five and a half; and 33–1 the six-year outsider. In my naivety, I had assumed that Lawson had purposely painted a black picture, so that when I got less than four years I would congratulate him. A bit like the tricks auction houses play with their estimates. Two black female guards came to take me up for sentencing. On the way up they asked me what I was expecting. 'Oh, my barrister tells me that I'm going home. The two weeks in Pentonville was given as a shock, to teach me a lesson. He'll suspend the sentence and give me community service,' I said. I couldn't wait to see the look on their faces when they took me back down to the cells ten minutes later.

Ping. The lift had reached the court and out we stepped. I saw DS Fitzgerald and DC Brown sitting there gloating, although they avoided my stare. Martin Murray, his clerk, Egan and Lawson were all in place. And in the public rows were two female members of the jury, to witness the end of the charade; the final act.

We all rose as the judge walked in, and then sat again as the prosecution got to work. 'This was a deliberate, massive fraud and we feel a sentence approaching the maximum is justified.'

Lawson got up. 'Your Honour. If I may start from the top. Seven years is reserved for the most serious of frauds, those involving millions of pounds, carried out over long periods of time, usually by people working in positions of trust for institutions in the City. This was no such case. Mr Goldman's company slowly got itself into difficulties, and he did all he could to prevent it from going under. I would urge you to consider a sentence on the low end of the tariff.'

'Stand up, Mr Goldman. Where are the pre-sentence reports I ordered into this defendant?'

Lawson got up. 'I'm afraid that the probation department don't appear to have visited the defendant in prison, your Honour.'

The Big One

The judge proceeded, regardless. 'Nigel Goldman, you would have received a very substantial discount if you had pleaded guilty for three important reasons. First, it would have shown remorse. Second, it would have saved an enormous amount of court time and expense, although there would still have been the enormous cost of the police investigation, which in my opinion was carried out very efficiently by DS Fitzgerald and DC Clark [this was actually DC Brown], who are to be commended. Third, and most importantly, a guilty plea would have avoided the necessity of witnesses attending court to relive their painful financial experiences at your hands. All in all, you misappropriated *over seven hundred thousand pounds* [it sounded like a fortune in Crown Court], while, to use the words of the prosecution, you lived the life of Riley. You enjoyed money, first-class trips abroad, a Ferrari, racehorses and a lavish lifestyle, while your investors lost their savings. You must go to prison for six years.'

Six years, holy shit. The 33–1 fucking outsider.

The guard to my left let out a sigh; she had seen and heard it all before. The court emptied save for barristers hovering around for the next case and the jury women sitting at the back of the public rows. They were in tears. I was taken back down to the holding cell where I was allowed a quick word or two with the team. 'I'm sure we'll get it reduced on appeal,' Lawson assured me. 'And don't forget, Egan has already drafted out grounds for appeal against conviction on the judge's summing up. We'll definitely appeal both sentence and conviction, whatever the single judge says. Meanwhile, you had better just get on with it and sit tight until you hear from us.'

I urged Martin Murray to enquire from the probation service why they hadn't come to interview me for the pre-sentence report, as I felt a report into my circumstances could only have been helpful.

To my horror, I discovered that I wouldn't be going back to Pentonville. Southwark sent all their sentenced prisoners to Brixton. My dreams of an easy job and imminent transfer to an open prison at the hands of my friendly senior officer quickly evaporated as I made yet another journey in a sweat box, this time to HMP Brixton.

57

After just a week in Brixton, I was told that I was going to be transferred to a long-term prison on an overcrowding draft. I tried desperately to reinstate my D-category status, but the allocation officer was having none of it. 'They don't like us sending prisoners doing over five years to open prisons.' So, he marked me as C-category, which meant that I would have to go to a closed prison until I had 'got some bird behind me', as he put it. He sent me to The Mount, a newish prison in Bovingdon, near Hemel Hempstead in Hertfordshire. The Home Office's definition of a C-category prisoner is one for whom 'escape must be made very difficult'.

At The Mount, all around me were drug addicts, homosexuals and social misfits, injecting drugs with filthy needles and playing loud music late into the night, making sleep impossible. The cell blocks were laid out in spur arrangements – 20 or so cells to each spur. Every cell had its own sink and lavatory and, mercifully, they were all single occupancy. The welcome pack contained one blue plastic mug, one blue plastic bowl (for shaving and eating breakfast cereal), one blue plastic plate and a set of white plastic cutlery. Inmates progressed through the regime and moved from house block to house block, every one an improvement on the previous one. When you got to enhanced status, which meant that you had behaved well (not been nicked for breaking any of the prison rules for six months) and passed the newly introduced mandatory drug tests disgracefully introduced by Ann Widdecombe, you were moved on to Brister, the enhanced house, where you were allowed a television in your cell as a reward for your good behaviour. It was quickly pointed out to everyone, though, that any breaking of the prison rules would get you shipped back to the poorer wings. In short, the screws had you by the bollocks. The new drug tests, I was soon to discover, were directly responsible for a huge increase in heroin addiction inside British prisons. While cannabis would stay in the system for over three weeks, resulting in a positive drug test, and added weeks or months to an inmate's sentence, heroin passed through the body within a day or two. Most inmates who used smack passed the drug tests with flying colours and served the minimum term. It was enough to make my blood boil. I saw inmates injecting themselves between the toes, even in their eyeballs, to get a hit. You probably wonder where the gear and the syringes came from. Well, a civvy working in the prison at that time had been convicted of smuggling gear in – while the main section of his rucksack was searched, the handles were not, and grams of valuable drugs got into circulation within the prison. How did he get paid? Simple – someone on the out, a friend or relative of the inmate, sent money to his house, or paid it into one of his accounts. The drug culture in British prisons is one of the disgraces of modern society and, until it is stamped out, the inmates have no hope, no chance on release.

I stood out above the riff-raff at The Mount and was determined to get myself enhanced as quickly as possible. The prospect of being banged up for years didn't appeal to me in the slightest, so I was keen to relieve the boredom of the place by at least having a television in my cell.

I enrolled with the education department and was quickly asked if I would like to be their orderly, one of the most trusted jobs in the prison. I eagerly agreed and was given a room to work in where I brewed coffee all day and did the rounds at break time, in between classes, serving up beverages. The crowd of civvies who ran education were a great bunch, led by Rosemary Pettman, who did her best to make her orderly's job as pleasant as possible. After getting to know her over a few months, I started telling her some of my tales of woe, which tickled her pink.

In prison, I was walking tall, respected by the officers and inmates, and the time started to pass quickly as I got into the routine of things. My first few months were spent looking forward to my appeal, where on continuous bullish reports from Martin Murray I was getting my hopes up for a substantial reduction in sentence, and the possibility of a walk out. Every week my twenty quid arrived from Debbie, and I shopped for food in the prison shop. Good food like fruit and vegetables, and tins of tuna and pasta, which I cooked in the evenings in the wing kitchens and took back to my cell.

Prison seemed to have solved my weight problem, too. What a couple of decades of health farms and dieting never quite achieved, prison had done handsomely. I enjoyed healthy lunches, and prison offered its own keep-fit programme.

Soon the winter arrived – I had been inside for nearly six months. The appeal had been granted by the single judge, both against conviction and sentence, and I was due to appear in the Court of Appeal at Easter. During my first Christmas in prison, I received over 100 cards from well-wishers and friends, and even got one from Edmund Lawson, QC.

Suzy Watson came to visit with her new fiancé, Grahame Penny, and I really appreciated the visit. I could tell immediately that they felt uncomfortable in the prison visits hall, which was revolting, but they made a big effort to cheer me up for which I was extremely grateful. I was so pleased to get so much support from true friends I could rely on. Richard Williams visited every month. 'Paul Saidelbaum' sent in cash and stamps, and a friend called Dick Parker wrote to me regularly from Florida, enclosing stamps and cash. Harry Conway kept sending me in books and his coin catalogues to relieve the boredom. At this time, I was laying the foundations for lifelong friendships. However, I knew deep down that if I didn't change my ways upon release, I would let them all down once again.

The Big One

My father's health was deteriorating, though, and it was decided to move him into a home in Scotland, where some of his family still lived. Not one of them got in touch with me during all the time I was inside – a reflection of their cold attitude to me throughout the previous 25 years. Something that happened in my childhood had caused a terrible family rift, and I never found out what it was, but I do remember one bar mitzvah card being sent back with a black border around it. They all despised me, and then, in my most vulnerable state, when they could have offered comfort, they couldn't give a tinker's cuss or a two-penny damn about me. Sod the lot of them, I thought.

58

Wearing a smartly pressed Byblos suit, crisp white shirt (two phonecards, laundry orderly) and my Armani silk tie, I permitted myself a soft, indulgent smile as the officer unlocked the gates leading to reception. That could have been my last day of imprisonment, if my legal team were spot on. I had been assured by Martin Murray that the judge's summing up had been so flawed that the Court of Appeal would order a retrial. If that failed, I was definitely looking at a substantial reduction in the sentence which was 'manifestly excessive', according to Egan.

Two orderlies were mopping the floor. They eased deferentially aside as I passed by. One of them managed a hushed, 'Morning, Nigel. Good luck at court.'

I slowed. 'Your mother's better now, is she, Clement?' I enquired, condescending to show a half interest in those mortals less fortunate than myself.

'Keep walking, Goldman,' the screw barked, and I gave a pained sigh and raised my eyebrows as I walked on. Alan Wells, the other trusty, clutching his mop, dropped his head in a nod that was almost a bow. Passing on, I favoured him with a quick, surreptitious wink. 'Good luck,' Wells mouthed back.

Two officers were waiting at the gate to reception. Both were over 6-foot tall and, together with the guard accompanying me, had a combined weight of over 50 stone.

Every prisoner coming in or going out was dealt with in reception. It was there that new inmates were received and processed, given a prison number, allocated a cell, and where the belongings and valuables they had brought with them were stored. In my case, this was where they were collected to be transported to the Court of Appeal. Full discharge procedures had been undertaken in my case, so that if I walked out of court, all my property was with me. The previous day all my possessions had been bagged up from my cell in a transparent plastic bin liner with HM Prison stamped on it, and were waiting to go in the sweat box with me to the Strand. I was really hoping that I wouldn't be unpacking them again that evening back in my cell.

A sealed plastic bag was brought from the valuables storage and placed on the counter. The duty officer checked each item on a file as it was taken out. Louis Vuitton wallet. Credit cards. Business cards. A thick wedge of currency – he estimated it was about a monkey. He was close – the counterfoil I signed stated £565, the proceeds of careful scrimping and saving from the money I had been sent, and my prison wages of £7.50 a week. Enough, surely, for a decent night out in London, if I was to gain my freedom. Securicor had the privilege of taking me to court in a new-style mini-sweatbox: I was their only prisoner that day, and the female driver was reasonable, allowing me to hang my jacket in her cab. We were on our way to London before eight o'clock that morning, before the rest of the prison had even been unlocked. As we approached London, I glanced out of the window of my cubicle. This was my first glimpse of civilisation for nearly a year. Glamorous and smiling women, the likes of whom had existed only as photos on prison-cell walls, strode purposefully down the pavement of the capital. I was in love with life and longed to be set free.

The Big One

The Court of Appeal is a huge intimidating building, even for the initiated. Inside, at a quick conference with Michael Egan, I was informed that the single judge had allowed my appeal through gritted teeth. 'Don't expect too much today, Mr Goldman,' Egan advised.

'It has all been decided already, hasn't it?' I said, disconsolately.

'Well, I wouldn't tell most clients this, but yes, of course it has. What happens in court today is mere play-acting. Cosmetic. Your fate was decided days, if not weeks, ago. Today, though, it will be delivered to open court for the first time, that's all.'

'But, what if . . .?'

'Mr Goldman, let's not speculate. I'll do my best for you.' I was taken back to the holding cell and a few minutes later walked up a spiral stone staircase to the top of the court building.

The three judges – Rose, Keene and Hyam – were already seated. I was right at the top of the court building, high up, adjacent to the three judges in a mini prisoner-dock with one prison officer and his clipboard next to me on my left. If I had leant over, I could have touched the end judge. Much lower, deep in the well of the court, was Egan, ready to deliver the speech which could set me free. In the visitors' rows, I saw Paul Saidelbaum and Richard Williams, as well as Bernard Bates who had travelled down from Ascot to hear the result.

Egan got to his feet. He submitted that the Crown's case had been based on deliberate false representations that had persisted throughout the trial. He acknowledged that a possible verdict based on reckless dishonesty is something recognised by the Theft Act of 1968, but he went on to argue that that was a possibility not canvassed by the learned judge with counsel before speeches, or indeed at any time prior to the summing up.

He then went on in fluent legalese to point out a passage in the transcript at the end of the first day of summing up, where junior counsel for the Crown suggested that recklessness may have been an extension upon the prosecution case, and junior counsel indicated that he wished to discuss that with his leader who was not at that moment present. In fact, on the resumption of the trial, Mr Austin-Smith, who was leading for the prosecution, said that the case had been put essentially on the basis of deliberate false representation, but that reckless misrepresentation would fall 'within the ambit of the prosecution which has been brought'. Defence counsel had said nothing on this topic at the end of the first day's summing up, but now indicated that he was not wholly in agreement with what Mr Austin-Smith had said. The matter was left at that, and the judge did not run to that topic in the remainder of his summing up. Mr Egan then referred to a number of authorities which dealt with situations where the trial judge introduces in summing up a possible basis for conviction which has not been canvassed hitherto. One of the precedents was a case involving a client called Gascoigne and he submitted that my case fell into that same category. In Gascoigne's case, he was set free. Mr Egan then went on to pose the question of whether, given the way in which this matter was summed up, the jury could have confused recklessness and dishonesty. He then went on to rely on the decision of *Regina* v. *Feeny*, where again the Court of Appeal found in the appellant's favour.

In particular, in the more recent case of *R* v. *Japes*, it was ruled that the trial judge was not bound by the way in which the prosecution opened its case. They ruled that the trial judge's direction to the jury would have to reflect the evidence which had been given during trial, and that may indicate a somewhat different basis for the offence than that which was originally opened.

'We are against you on conviction, Mr Egan, for reasons we will give shortly. What have you to say about sentence?'

Egan told them that the sentence was far too high. The three judges huddled around, then delivered their bombshell.

'The amounts involved in this offence were very large indeed. It was an immense fraud upon investors. There was no credit to be given for a guilty plea because there was no such plea. While the jury may have convicted on a basis of reckless deception, they must have been satisfied as to the appellant's dishonesty. As for the argument that there was a gradual fall into dishonesty, that was not the view formed by the trial judge, who had to deal with this matter over a long trial. He concluded that the business had been fraudulent from the outset and we, for our part, can see no basis upon which that conclusion should be criticised.

'For a deliberate massive fraud of this kind, a sentence approaching the maximum was, in our judgment, entirely appropriate, and the appeal against sentence will therefore be dismissed.'

The journey back to prison felt twice as long as the one into court.

I immediately wrote to everyone to tell them the news, then immersed myself in writing and attending the gym to get fit.

On the bright side, with parole, I could be out in 25 months. On the dark side, my father's health was deteriorating rapidly, my flat in Hove was about to be repossessed and I still had at least 25 months' imprisonment to serve. It felt like a lifetime.

59

My father became seriously ill towards the end of the summer of 1997. At first, it was a chest infection, but, as so often happens with the frail and elderly, it quickly turned into pneumonia. He was rushed to hospital, where things rapidly became worse. Within a few days, he was on a ventilator and a couple of days after that, he went into a coma. I felt so utterly helpless and hopeless banged up in prison while my dear father was dying. There was nothing I could do but hope and pray that he would pull through. He didn't and, when he died, I had to beg to be allowed to attend the funeral. At first, they wanted to send me there in handcuffs, escorted by two officers in uniform, but after a lot of persuasion, I finally got them to come round to my way of thinking and allow me to travel on licence with an officer out of uniform and no handcuffs. They pushed out all the rules to grant me this privilege, and I was promised that if I didn't fuck up, they would move me to an open prison.

There is no doubt that in the days leading up to the funeral the hostility some members of the family felt towards their imprisoned relative came to the surface. I had created nothing but trouble and embarrassment over the years, and here, on the occasion of my father's death, they managed to make the experience as uncomfortable as possible for me. At the funeral, I felt ignored.

Nothing will ever describe how I felt that night back in my cell, banged up. A few days later, letters of comfort arrived from friends, along with a letter from the rabbi, who had responded to my relatives' behaviour.

The following June, the prison authorities kept their promise, and I got my dream ticket move to Ford Open Prison in Arundel, West Sussex.

60

I was driven to Ford by an officer in an ordinary van, together with my plastic bag of possessions and my sealed confidential inmate's prison file, the van doors unlocked. I was greeted in HMP Ford reception by Officer Michael Kemp. 'Where the fucking hell have you been, Goldman? We've been waiting nearly two fucking years for you.' If you read a similar version of events in Jeffrey Archer's prison diaries, let me assure you that this version of events is also true, but happened first. For the previous couple of years, I had been having difficulty making up my mind whether or not to go and live in Brighton again after my release, but this gesture made me feel at home in Sussex. After two years of virtual solitude, any gesture of welcome was obviously very well received. All I had to do was my easy time at Ford, get parole in a year's time, then get back to work on the outside and make up for lost time.

Ford was so different to what I had just experienced that it took a few days to adjust. I was allowed to eat with metal cutlery for the first time in two years, and food was served on proper crockery. There were no more long, lonely nights locked up in a cold cell and there was plenty of fresh country air. I was shown round the vast estate, which covered over 100 acres of Sussex countryside, with a main road through the middle of the grounds, by the induction orderly.

The prison is divided into two sections, 'A' block and 'B' block. 'A' block is a large concrete building, the size of about 30 semi-detached houses, in which are located the dining room, library and the single-dormitory accommodation. 'B' block is on the other side of the cricket pitch and consists of several old billet huts (Ford is an old air force base from the Second World War). On the other side of the main road is the industrial estate where inmates work in factories, making crash dummies (the dummy shop – no reflection on the quality of inmate, surely), shirts and prison gates, and where they run the laundry and do painting and decorating courses. The orderly kindly showed me round, pointing out places of interest: '. . . this is where you get your hair cut, that's stores, where you get your clothing and kit changed, this is the cricket pitch (hallowed turf – don't ever get caught walking across it), there's the 'A' wing office, where you make applications or report to the screws, there's the 'B' wing office, the church, there's the synagogue [all of a sudden I was proud to be Jewish], there's the cinema, the mail room, the education department and gym. Dinner is at six after the bell, make sure you are in your billet for roll call at 5.30 and nine o'clock. As you are the only inmate who has arrived here today, you can spend your induction fortnight in my billet in 'B' block.'

High Stakes

The billets housed 24 inmates in single-bed, dormitory-style accommodation, a bit like boarding school. The orderly had his own room at the end of the billet with a key to the door, his own television and video, pay phone, kitchen and fridge with padlock. We shared the billet on our own that night, drank coffee and ate sandwiches while watching television; I immediately got on with him and got to work to find out all the wheezes and moves of the nick. He was very helpful, explaining: 'The best job is mine, next best is hospital orderly, and then there is the job of education orderly. I'm sure you'll land a good one, you seem OK. Avoid the gardens like the plague, you'll be out there in the winter digging.' The following day, I went through the induction talks and went for various job interviews. I met a charming lady from the East Sussex probation service. I didn't mention the lack of reports for my trial and, to my relief, neither did she. I ventured over to the education department and was met by a character who wore a trilby like Dick Tracy. They were looking for a new orderly and I immediately landed the job, one of the best in the nick. I was responsible for the processing and induction of inmates wanting to do courses in such things as crafts, computer courses and art. It was all so different to what I had been used to over the past couple of years.

At the synagogue later that day, I was greeted by a famous fraudster, who was compulsive on the gee-gees and had been sent down for eight years for a public company fraud. I also spent time with a really nice chap from Johannesburg, who had been done for smuggling drugs into Heathrow. Ford housed a different class of inmate to The Mount – generally fraudsters, struck-off solicitors and accountants, although there were a number of lifers finishing off long sentences for murder, spending their last couple of years under Home Office rules in open conditions before being released on life licence into the community. There was also the possibility of 'comserve' – community service – which usually meant charity work in the local villages. All in all, life in Ford was very tolerable, although, unless you kept yourself busy, very boring. Very healthy, though. I used the gym regularly, walked miles a day around the perimeter of the nick in my free time and must have watched over 300 movies. As a Jewish prisoner, I had unlimited access to the synagogue and really good-quality Kosher food was sent in by the Jewish Prisoner Association. We used to cook this in the synagogue kitchen and have a small service and dinner every evening. The Jewish boys had a good rapport together, and the time started to pass quickly. There was a healthy interest in horseracing, too, and I soon became the nick's bookie, taking wagers (in prison phonecards) on all the big races. After a couple of weeks at Ford, I was moved to my own room in 'A' block.

Around a month later, the induction orderly got a week's home leave as he was due to be released in a short time, and I was asked if I would like to do his job while he was away. It was made clear to me by the screws that if I did this job well, I could land it when he was released. Six weeks later, I landed the best job in the nick, together with my own room and key, and got busy showing all the new arrivals around. I did my bit for charity, too, going out at weekends to erect signposts for an event organised by a local volunteer group held across the road from the nick. Then I was asked by one of the senior officers to help raise funds for a kid dying of leukaemia. As it was nearly Christmas, I got permission for various goodies, normally prohibited items, to be sent in so that I could auction them to the inmates. The response was phenomenal – we had a box of Havana cigars sent in from Aspinal's casino, Christmas cakes (laced with alcohol), tickets for nights out in London (check your release date), music, sets of glasses and cutlery. We printed catalogues in the education department and I had a clerk (a struck-off accountant) and a showman to display the lots on the night. I held the auction in the chapel and nearly all the inmates turned up. The lads were allowed to use their private funds, held in their prison account, to bid and right away I knew we were going to exceed all expectations. I climbed up on my temporary rostrum, with my clerk seated in front of me and my showman standing alongside. 'Lot one: a box of Havana cigars (showing here, sir) £50, £60, £80, £100, £120, £150, £180, £200 against you at the back, £220, £250, £280, £300, one more?' I glanced over at another inmate, he nodded and I sold the first lot amid huge cheers and clapping for £320! Soon, the officers who were patrolling the deserted nick and wondering where everyone was turned up to watch the show. We raised over £1,500 in total to send the poor kid to Disney World. Soon, I was venturing out at weekends into Brighton for lunch and getting a serious number of visitors. John Sutcliffe and another friend, Tony Ingham, came to visit and I was promised help with lists of names if I decided to go into the horse-tipping business when I was released. I knew then that I was on the home straight. Life looked up, and I even started attending the synagogue regularly to say prayers, at first for my father, and then, sod it, even for myself.

On Monday, 20 June 1999, I was released on parole to a room in a friend's flat on the Esplanade in Hove. Tony kept his promise, provided me with massive lists of names of punters to cold call and I started hitting the names in style. Within days, I was copping some big bucks and started promoting the horseracing business in my own name. Of course, I was still bankrupt, so had to be careful what I did with the readies.

Being a crook while on parole was one of the most exciting times in my life.

EPILOGUE

Life on the Costa del Crime

For three long years while in the nick (most nights after release, in vividly coloured dreams, I thought I was still there), I kept thinking how I must try and go back to normality. I even had a folder of certificates to ease my return to normal civilian life: an offending behaviour certificate, a drug-free certificate, a writers' certificate and a basic computer skills certificate. But I quickly realised the difficulties I would encounter: the prejudice, the loss of opportunities. I kept thinking about how I must try and go back, back into civilization, to normality. Of course, now I never will. So far away. So long ago. If I permit myself to shut my eyes and concentrate, I can still visualise the clear blue sky perched high above the emerald green track. I can still see the paddocks, the trees, the grandstands, the bars, the bonhomie, the action. If I close my eyes and hold my breath, I can still smell the dew in the air and the cut of the summer grass during early-morning gallops, the scent of money in the rings of the racetracks and the exchanges. I played there once, in that great playground of the rich, but it was so long ago now it feels like a dream, like another lifetime. So long ago now, I sometimes can't believe it ever really happened.

But then it happened again, in real life, with my reignited enthusiasm for money, sex and the high life. And I managed to make it last for a couple of years, too, until business went a little quirky on me – again. I ended up owing all the lads and blew the credit on my so-easily acquired charge and store cards within an instant. And I fucked the bank. Again.

I decided to nip over to Spain to relieve the strain and when the shit hit the fan in my absence, I decided to stay there, on the Costa del Sol.

'You all end up here, you know.'

He was Scottish, rather drunk, badly dressed and could have done with losing some weight. He was on the first day of a two-week break on the Costa del Sol, having popped in for a drink and a bet on the way to his rented apartment. He had just arrived in Spain with £800 in Scottish banknotes, 750 euros in large denomination notes and £500 in travellers cheques. I took the lot. I smiled as I rubbed out 11–8 on my odds board and changed it, like magic, to 5–4 to keep in line with the betting show *At the Races*, which was blasting out on a television in the corner of the bar. There were about 20 in that day, quite busy for a Friday, and the results were going my way. I'd just had the second well-backed favourite of the day ironed out.

I was *in situ* in a small bar in southern Spain run by a couple called Jean and Stuart (I never found out their surnames). I ran the book there. I loved it, I really did. I think being a bookmaker is the most exciting job of my varied business career. At the time, I thought I'd found my niche in life. I paid them a commission from my takings and they paid the bills. It worked quite well, but there were a few shrewdies around, so I had to keep my wits about me. A few doors down the road was a bar owned by Mark and run by Dessie and Mark's girlfriend, Beckie. Mark used to work in a bookie's and was always trying to tuck me up, running in with complicated multiples for me. He should have become a bookie himself. And then there were the Irish lads, Craig and Brian – couldn't understand a word they said. And Big Pete, too, with his help from the stables back home. And Gordon (who used to own the bar) with his occasional shrewd punts that normally obliged.

'You all end up here, you lot.' He was back in front of me, leaning on the desk to see how strong it was, his breath stinking of whisky. 'Think you are clever and can make it big in the City and all that. They all end up here, doing something spivvy like timeshare or bookmaking. And that's just the girls. Tell you what, I'm going to the cash point to get another £300, and then I'm coming back here to fleece you on a big-priced winner!' He staggered out, narrowly missing the step. I never saw him again.

There is a saying on the Costa that 90 per cent of the English are here because they have to be, not because they want to be. I definitely fall into that category. After things went pear-shaped in Rottingdean, where I was renting a house from an old prison buddy for some exorbitant price, I suppose I ended up a couple of hundred thousand behind (I again took the opportunity to calculate my dues on the plane over here) and another quick escape was essential. I really thought about going to South Africa and had a one-way first-class ticket on me at Heathrow. But someone told me you could only stay there for three months so I ripped it up, took a cab to Gatwick and here I am.

'Thirteen to eight the field, five bar,' I shout and they keep coming for more. They keep coming for more from all directions on the Costa and I keep copping. Well, sometimes I lose, but most weeks I cop. I gave up on Jean and Stuart's bar fairly rapidly, or rather they gave up on me. Paul Dunn, my old clerk, took over with his wife Les. Sometimes I pop in for a drink in the evenings with his brother. I now move from bar to bar, take bets on the phone from approved clients and other bookmakers on sports and racing, and generally have a decent time. On busy days, I juggle three phones and take calls from all over the coast. An old associate from my horse days calls from Marbella (even though he is really in Estepona, but the locals think Marbella just sounds *so* much better) and plays. So do all the lads. Even Tony from

271

Brighton has joined me over here with his girlfriend, and also runs a book. I have found a smashing new girlfriend, met some good friends and owe no money and take no credit for the very first time in my life. My Spanish has even improved.

Of course, I often think back, but I try not to. The £14 million (that's about 20 million euros over here) would have come in *so* handy. I've got to be philosophical, though. And the cars. Phew, how I miss them! I spent my first year here in an 80-euro-a-week hire car. Then there's the girls. Shame. And the horses. I heard one went to Singapore and won quite a few races for his new owner. Well done! Now most of my ex-girlfriends are happily settled. The one thing I have in my favour, though, is my experience, education and knowledge. Now, no one's going to take that away from me, are they?

Regrets? None. Aspirations? Plenty. Temptations? Who knows?

Of course, I won't be returning to the UK. Not now. Not ever again. So long ago, so far away. So long ago that I can't believe it all ever really happened.